# CHARLES READE

By ELTON E. SMITH
*University of South Florida*

**TWAYNE PUBLISHERS**
A Division of G. K. Hall & Co.
Boston, Massachusetts, U. S. A.

1976

**Library of Congress Cataloging in Publication Data**

Smith, Elton Edward, 1915-
  Charles Reade.

  (Twayne's English authors series ; TEAS 186)
  Bibliography: p. 165 - 73.
  Includes index.
  1. Reade, Charles, 1814-1884 — Criticism and interpretation.
PR5217.S57      828'.8'08.      76-2546
ISBN 0-8057-6660-X

*Twayne's English Authors Series*

Sylvia E. Bowman, *Editor*

INDIANA UNIVERSITY

*Charles Reade*

TEAS 186

Charles Reade

To friends

103, 104

# Contents

# About the Author

Elton Edward Smith is Professor of English at the University of South Florida in Tampa. He received the Bachelor of Science degree from New York University, with honors in philosophy; the Bachelor of Divinity degree from Andover Newton Theological School and the Master of Sacred Theology degree from Harvard Divinity School. He received an honorary degree of Doctor of Divinity from Linfield College, Oregon and the Master of Arts and the Doctor of Philosophy degrees from Syracuse University. Ordained to the ministry, Dr. Smith has served college churches in Massachusetts, Oregon, New York, and Florida.

His first book was *"The Two Voices": A Tennyson Study* (1964). In collaboration with his wife, Dr. Esther Greenwell Smith, he is co-author of the volume on *William Godwin* in Twayne's English Authors Series, 1965. In 1970 his study, *Louis MacNeice*, was published by Twayne, and in 1975, arising out of the research for the volume on Louis MacNeice, he has published a group study entitled *"The Angry Young Men of the Thirties:" Day Lewis, Spender, MacNeice, Auden*. As senior Fulbright-Hays lecturer, he spent 1970-71 at L'Université d'Alger, Algeria, and 1974-75 at L'Université Mohammed V., Marocco.

# *Preface*

A certain sadness is inherent in dealing with the relicts of a writer like Charles Reade who enjoyed great popular acclaim in his own lifetime but has since fallen upon the thorns of adverse criticism. With the sadness goes a threefold temptation: to sentimentalize about the whirligig of time and popular taste; to defend the discredited author against all posthumous critical attack; and to rejoice sneeringly at the fall of the once mighty.

Charles Reade loved melodrama and placed it ahead of the novel as his chief claim to fame. The Victorian era responded enthusiastically to melodrama, and encouraged the dramatic extravagance that later exposed popular authors to withering criticism in a more realistic period. Both the favor of the moment and the long verdict of literary criticism are recognized and justified in this study. In regard to the temptations to sentimentalize, to grow defensive, or to sit in the scoffer's seat, this study occupies a more modest position: if Charles Reade is not Charles Dickens's greater successor, neither is he entirely unimportant and irrelevant. Instead, he occupies a worthy but lesser position among those who are not quite first rank and yet are better than second because they were innovators and initiators of important literary movements.

The realism of Charles Reade, as William Dean Howells indicated, served mechanical melodramatic plots and exploited sentimental reactions. But an examination of both the dramas and the novels of Charles Reade shows that the stylistic conformist was at the same time a topical rebel. His discussion of place and situation was realistic — a solid fiction based on journalistic face; of persons, it was naturalistic — animal instincts pulsed beneath human skin. Yet his plots hinge on the old melodramatic formulae of black-white delineation, the hairbreadth escape, and the sentimental solution.

The writing of Honoré de Balzac might be described in strikingly similar ways: a technique of meticulously observed details to serve the most theatrical and even lurid plots. Conspicuous in this twentieth-century televised age is the scrupulous devotion to realistic detail of setting, dialogue, characterization — but all done to serve plot conventions of the most banal and preconceived sort. The violent techniques of the sensational dramatist or novelist are not only in use today but enjoy a marked ascendancy. Although the hero may be neither so handsome nor so good as Victorian heroes, the intrinsic interest still focuses upon the thundering odds against which he operates, the hairbreadth narrowness of his escapes, and the sure comfort of knowing that he always wins in the end. In black comedy, in the antiheroic novel, or in the pornographic revelation, the stuff of the writer is sensation, necessarily served in increasingly enormous gobs. If any era can be expected to understand and appreciate Victorian stages and pages, this present one should do so.

Although most of Charles Reade's plays are discussed in this book, his incessant journalistic contributions and his readiness to leap irritably into legal fray are largely omitted. Since this study is primarily concerned with Reade's reputation as a novelist, the section on drama simply illuminates Reade's custom of writing novels based on his own plays. In terms of secondary sources, it was considered more important to annotate a few major sources than to list all the wealth of critical comment available.

My thanks to Professor William Scheuerle, who read and criticized every chapter of the first rough draft of this manuscript (his comments are often maintained as a sort of professorial dialogue in the Notes); to Elizabeth Ernst, who provided two useful bibliographies; to Jill Lones, who typed the manuscript; and to librarians at Princeton University, the New York Public Library, the Pierpont Morgan Library, and the University of South Florida Library, who managed a steady and invaluable flow of documents into the hands of the working critic. I am grateful to the University of South Florida for released time under the Faculty Development Program and Sponsored Research Grants to give the manuscript that final heave over the top.

ELTON SMITH

*Lakeland, Florida*

# *Chronology*

1814    Charles Reade born June 8, Ipsden House, Oxford.

1831    Matriculates at Oxford University; wins demyship at Magdalen College, July 26.

1835    Graduates with third in Greats, June 18. July 22, becomes probationary fellow at Oxford. Entered at Lincoln's Inn, November 20.

1838    Receives Master of Arts degree, April 26.

1851    Publishes dramatic version of Tobias Smollett's *Peregrine Pickle* at his own expense. Becomes vice-president of Magdalen College. In April, begins *Masks and Faces* in collaboration with Tom Taylor. Produces *The Ladies' Battle* at Olympic Theatre, May 7. *Angelo* presented at Olympic Theatre, August 11.

1852    *A Village Tale (Rachel the Reaper)*, Strand Theatre, April 12. *The Lost Husband* presented at the Strand, April 26. Finishes *Peg Woffington* at Durham, August 3; begins *Gold*. *Masks and Faces* presented at Haymarket Theatre, November 20. *Peg Woffington* published December 17; *Christie Johnstone* begun.

1853    *Gold* produced at Drury Lane, January 10.

1854    Presents *Two Loves and a Life* (in collaboration with Tom Taylor) at the Adelphi Theatre, March 20. *Art* at St. James's Theatre on April 17. *The Courier of Lyons* at the Princess's Theatre, June 26 (revived 1870; renamed *The Lyons Mail*). Opens season at St. James's Theatre in joint management with Mrs. Seymour, presenting *The King's Rival* (written in collaboration with Tom Taylor), October 2. *Honour before Titles: or Nobs and Snobs*, presented at St. James's, October 3.

1855     Hard at work on *It Is Never Too Late to Mend*. Reade becomes lodger of Mrs. Seymour in the fall. Adapts *Les Pauvres de Paris*, by Edouard Brisebarre and Eugène Nus, retitled *Poverty and Pride*.

1856     *The First Printer* (collaboration with Tom Taylor) presented at Princess's Theatre, March 3.

1857     *White Lies* appears as serial in *London Journal*, July 11 to December 5 (published, 3 volumes, December).

1858     Writes *Love Me Little, Love Me Long* (published, 2 volumes, April, 1859). Begins *The Eighth Commandment* (published July, 1860). *The Hypochondriac* taken on tour by Mrs. Seymour.

1859     Writes *A Good Fight* (serial in *Once a Week*, July to October). Visits Edward Bulwer-Lytton at Knebworth in November.

1861     *The Cloister and the Hearth* published, October.

1863     *Hard Cash* appears in Charles Dickens's magazine *All the Year Round*, March to December (published in 3 volumes, December 15).

1865     *It Is Never Too Late to Mend* first presented at the Princess's Theatre, October 4.

1866     *Griffith Gaunt* appears as serial in the *Argosy*, January to November (published, 3 volumes, October).

1867     *Dora* presented at the Adelphi Theatre, June 1. *The Double Marriage* presented at the Queen's Theatre, October 24. Produces *Griffith Gaunt* at Newcastle in the fall.

1868     Finishes *Foul Play* (in collaboration with Dion Boucicault), which appears serially in *Once a Week*, January to June (published June). *Foul Play* (Boucicault and Reade dramatic version) presented at Holborn, May 28. Leaves Bolton Row, lodging temporarily at St. George's Road, Pimlico.

1869     *Put Yourself in His Place* appears serially in *Cornhill*, March, 1869 to July, 1870 (published in June). Moves to 2 Albert Terrace, Knightsbridge.

1870     Makes dramatic version *(Free Labor)* of novel *Put Yourself in His Place*. The drama, which later reverted to the novel title, plays at the Adelphi, May 28. *The Robust Invalid* presented at the Adelphi, June 15.

1871     *A Terrible Temptation* appears serially in *Cassell's Magazine*, beginning in the April issue (published August). *An Actress of Daylight* presented at St. James's Theatre, April 8. Begins *A Simpleton* at Oxford.

1872    Produces *Shilly-Shally* (dramatic version of Anthony Trol-
        lope's *Ralph the Heir*) at the Gaiety Theatre, April 1. *A
        Simpleton* appears serially in *London Society*, August, 1872,
        to August, 1873 (published August, 1873). *The Wandering
        Heir* published in the *Graphic* at Christmas. Takes libel
        action against the *Morning Advertiser* and other news-
        papers.
1873    Produces dramatic version of *The Wandering Heir* at the
        Queen's Theatre, November 15.
1874    Brings Ellen Terry out of retirement to play in London and
        take *Our Seamen* on tour. *Rachel the Reaper* presented at
        the Queen's Theatre, March 9. *A Hero and a Martyr* ap-
        pears in the *Pall Mall Gazette*.
1875    Writes *The Rights and Wrongs of Authors*.
1876    *Good Stories of Man and Other Animals* appears in *Bel-
        gravia* from June, 1876, to June, 1877. *A Woman-Hater*
        appears serially in *Blackwood's* from June, 1876, through
        June, 1877 (published, 3 volumes, June, 1877).
1877    *The Scuttled Ship* presented at the Olympic, April 2. Writes
        *Hang in Haste, Repent at Leisure* and wins the reprieve of
        the alleged Penge murderers. *The Jilt: A Novel* appears
        March to June in *Belgravia*. *The Lyons Mail* presented at
        the Lyceum, May 19.
1878    Writes *Private Bills and Public Wrongs* and *The History of
        an Acre* in agitation against demolition of Albert Terrace.
        Publishes pamphlet defending his dramatic adaptation of
        Alfred Tennyson's poem *Dora*. *Jealousy* presented at the
        Olympic, April 22. *Joan* (dramatic version of Mrs. Hodgson
        Burnett's *That Lass o' Lowrie's*) produced at Liverpool in
        September and then taken on tour.
1879    *Drink* at the Princess's Theatre. Disputes with E. Romaine
        Callender over production rights. Mrs. Seymour dies Sep-
        tember 27. In December meets the Reverend Charles Gra-
        ham, clergyman influential in Reade's last days.
1881    Moves to 3 Blomfield Villas, Uxbridge Road. Writes *Single-
        heart and Doubleface* and some short stories.
1882    *Singleheart and Doubleface* produced at the Royal Prin-
        cess's Theatre, Edinburgh, June 1. *Love and Money*, his
        last venture in theatrical management (in collaboration with
        Henry Pettitt), presented at the Adelphi, November 18.
1883    *Nance Oldfield* presented at the Olympic, February 24.
        Almost fatally ill in March; spends summer on the Con-

tinent. Last visit to a theater on August 4. Finishes *A Perilous Secret;* writes *Bible Characters.* Goes to Cannes in early December.

1884    Returns to London in late February. Dies on Good Friday, April 11, at 3 Blomfield Villas. *Singleheart and Doubleface* published.

CHAPTER 1

# The Stage

" THE morning had been cold and grey, but the moment we left the church the sun shone forth bright and glorious on the masses of flowers which were heaped upon the coffin, on the lid of which was the following inscription:
CHARLES READE,
Dramatist, Novelist, and Journalist.
Born June 8, 1814.
Died April 11, 1884
'Dramatist' first — always first! At his own request the words were thus placed. The ruling passion was strong in death, and to the very last he remained faithful to his first and early love — the Drama.''[1]

This love did not add greatly to either Charles Reade's literary reputation or his financial success. When the Reverend Compton Reade, nephew and principal author of Reade's *Memoir*, was considering whether a Presbyterian divine ought to accept a bequest from a man whose money had been derived in part from the stage, the clergyman wryly commented that, whereas the novelist made handsome sums of money from his novels, he was singularly unfortunate in nearly all his theatrical ventures. Rather than being swelled by theatrical income, the bequest was probably considerably diminished.[2]

By the time Charles Reade was nearly forty years of age, he had written only two novels: *Peg Woffington* (a narrative version of his comedy *Masks and Faces*, written with the expert theatrical assistance of Tom Taylor) in 1852, and *Christie Johnstone* in 1853. Essentially novels about women, one-volume in a three-volume age, both were characterized by fresh, vigorous youthfulness, dramatic intensity, and stylistic eccentricities. Although Reade declared, "I studied the great art of Fiction closely for fifteen years before I wrote a line,"[3] he had already written at least fifteen plays; and he continued to write more plays and to revise and present the old ones as long as he lived. Both his novels and his plays met contemporary standards of taste with great exactitude: the novels were sensational, and the dramas all melodramas. Reade exemplified in his creative works what Mark Rutherford described as the era: "If it is true that the Victorian time was ugly and vulgar, the excitement of those years between 1848 and 1890 was something like that of a religious revival."[4] It was vulgar without question, and it certainly had the special quality of excitement of a "religious revival," or what Jerome Hamilton Buckley later described as "the conversion-pattern of Victorian literature."[5]

Perhaps the central reason that Reade's novels succeeded and that the plays often failed lies in the distinction James Joyce made among the lyric, the epic, and the dramatic form. In Reade's *Christie Johnstone*, the lyric form that arose from his personal frustration as a result of the celibate requirements of his university fellowship is full of the artist's life, shaped into novelistic form by the artist's imagination. Later novels in the epic form are replete with much of the vital, masculine forcefulness of Charles Reade; but the personality of the artist tends to pass "into the narration itself, flowing round and round the persons and action like a vital sea." The dramatic form is objective; the playwright, standing in the wings, is entirely outside his play, indifferently watching the actors on stage.[6] In the novels, the authorial personality is sometimes as irritating as the patter of a peevish showman; yet it always expresses the emotional reactions of a man who is unlimited in his enthusiasms and passionate in his hatred of injustice.

The standard English drama of the mid-Victorian era was largely based on the elegant and contrived French plays of Augustine Eugène Scribe, Ernest Legouvé, Victorien Sardou, and other popular playwrights; but such dramas were always reshaped by a British emphasis upon morality and violence. The Gallic tradition contributed lost letters, disguised women, deliberate impostures, complications of *l'amour*, and the rhetorical diction of Jean Racine and Pierre Corneille. But it was Queen Victoria who set the moral tone that Coventry Patmore expressed as "angels in the house."[7] In Victorian England righteousness had to triumph; nonetheless, in drama or novel, the struggle with evil had to engross the audience. In addition, there was the British fondness for hunting and country humor; for bulldogs in pit battles; for dancing bears; for the blunt, bluff speech of yeomen; and for the Cockney clamor of the city rabble —

elements that reshaped the well-contrived and elegant plays of France into complicated series of violent, melodramatic episodes.

In a large folio notebook called "Red Digest," Reade wrote quite frankly about the usefulness of French drama: "The French are so excellent in form (drama) that I am convinced much might be done by studying very largely and closely the scaffolding of their most successful plays. . . . This might be done in a large book with spaces for interstitial scenes. Old Bailey and other reports, Police, might enable me to graft English characters on French form. Surely this might be done in a narrative as well as in drama."[8] Some of these "English characters" came from Reade's own confused vocational interests. At the age of seventeen, thanks to a prize essay, he won a demyship at Magdalen College, Oxford; and four years later, on July 22, 1835, he was elected a Fellow of the college. He suffered the fiscal problem of a living of six hundred pounds a year paid by his college, but only to celibate dons. He accepted the money, but he cared little for his colleagues of the high table, "some of the thickest skulls I have ever encountered,"[9] or for the life of a Fellow, although in 1851, under pressure, he did consent to remain in residence as vice-president of Magdalen.

Thereafter, Reade's chief use of Oxford was as a set of quiet rooms where he might literally hide for the production of a book, or as the obvious place to find a donnish hack who could ransack Bodleian Library for those facts for which he had so enormous an appetite and with which he proudly overloaded his novels. Although Reade was called to the bar, he never practiced law professionally: he tried medicine at Edinburgh, but he fainted in the dissecting room; his mother's piety impelled him at least to make a pretense of considering a church calling. These false starts, abortive vocationally, bore rich fruit in the novels, most of which include both an adept and a hidebound barrister, a bloodletting doctor of the old school, a modern enlightened physician who feeds his patients well and allows their illnesses to subside in their own rhythm, and an ecclesiastic with a passion for social reform.

## I   *Translations and Adaptations*

Reade began his career as a playwright after a trip to Paris to purchase antique violins.[10] When he saw a play by Scribe and Legouvé, called *La Bataille des Dames,* he translated it and adapted it, quite without permission, to the British stage, and it was produced as *The Ladies' Battle* at the Royal Olympic Theatre in 1851. Reade commented that he was condensing the French comedy and making only trifling changes, but he considered the vigorous acting of Mrs. Stirling in the part of the Countess in his own version to be far superior to the refined vagaries of the French actress. When Reade describes Mrs. Stirling's playing of the soliloquy in Act I — the longest assigned to an actress in an English comedy — one wonders if Messrs. Scribe and Legouvé would have been so pleased: "The irresolute inspection of the mirror, the ejaculation, and, still more, the look that precedes it, are fine strokes of Art. It is more than a change of expression; a new face, radiant with beauty, and hope, glides into the place of one clouded with misgivings."[11] The description sounds like the exaggerated mimicry, the hammy histrionics, that make Victorian drama almost impossible to produce today without its seeming to parody itself. Indeed, what Reade considered to be British strengthening of French drama were those broad, farcical touches so delightful to his London audience — touches that would, however, have constituted serious breaches of decorum to the French playwrights. For example, the French version of *La Bataille des Dames* ends delicately with a typical double entendre:

LA COMTESSE: Que voulez-vous, baron? pour gagner, il ne suffit pas de bien jouer!
MONTRICHARD: Il faut avoir pour soi les as et les rois.
LA COMTESSE: (à part, régardant Henri). Le roi surtout! . . . dans les batailles des dames.[12]

But Reade's heavy-handed English version reads:

COUNTESS:   Did I play ill? and yet I lose the game.
            More just your hearts, or are you all the same?
            Sore wounded here, what from despair can save us?
            Fresh duties — change of scene, and — come — Gustavus!
            (making a step as to go — returns and advances)
            But stop — what! leave so old and tried a friend,
            And live in Languedoc, at the world's end?
            I will not go for one, if you invite
            Us five to meet you here to-morrow night!

With this commercial invitation for the audience to return the following night, the Countess, quasi - ticket seller, sweeps regally away. Unfortunately, this same ending is repeated in many Reade plays in order to assure an audience "to-morrow night," whether or not art be served.

That same year Reade translated and adapted Victor Hugo's prose play *Angelo, Tyran de Padoue,* and saw it produced at the Olympic Theatre on August 11, 1851. When he visited Paris in March of the next year, he saw a performance of Annicet Bourgeois's four-act drama *La Dame de la Halle,* which he adapted and called *The Lost Husband.* On April 12, 1852, he produced at the Strand Theatre his translation and adaptation of George Sand's *Claudie* under the title *The Village Tale* (later renamed *Rachel the Reaper,* the basis of the short novel *Clouds and Sunshine*). Then, after the failure of the play to attract an audience, he rented the same theater to produce *The Lost Husband* on April 26, 1852; but it too was a failure.

Another import, *The Courier of Lyons: or The Attack Upon the Mail,* a drama in four acts, was translated by Reade from the French of collaborators Eugène Moreau, Paul Siraudin, and Alfred Delacour. On the opening night, June 26, 1854, the Queen and the Prince Consort honored the drama with their presence; and the play was a success! So dazed and delighted was Reade that he seemed to feel some explanation was necessary: "As *The Courier of Lyons* is successful the causes of its success ought not to be misunderstood." Reade then gave a very handsome acknowledgment to the manager of the Princess's Theatre, who had not only suggested the subject but had also provided a condensed outline to assure its unity: "The stage artifice, by which Dubosc's 'double' takes Dubosc's place in the last act . . . is Mr. Kean's idea, and is my property solely by that gentleman's liberality." With unerring bad taste, Reade indicated with a special compliment the contrived and overworked gag of the "double" who takes the place of another at the climactic moment. In addition, Reade felt that a playwright had good fortune to have his works produced at the Princess's Theatre, where "the play is dressed, and put on the stage, and acted *to perfection.*" He begged any provincial managers who wished to present *The Courier of Lyons* to visit the theater in Oxford Street in order to study the performance and the arrangements of staging so as "not to prepare for themselves disappointment by hoping everything from the bare text of this play."[13]

Of interest in the study of Victorian drama is the extraordinary importance of costume, acting style, and handling of stage business. Such was the emphasis upon intricate contrivance of stagecraft that the mere words of a drama were not expected to carry the piece to a successful conclusion. Reade's naive confession that invaluable condensation was done by the stage manner during "my absence from the country" is in marked contrast to the incredible difficulties that

Tom Taylor faced in attempting to abbreviate *Masks and Faces* —
one of Reade's plays with interminable and complicated plots.

The French original of *The Courier of Lyons* had been based upon
a remarkable court trial at the conclusion of the eighteenth century
in which a M. Lesurques was a victim of his extraordinary resemblance to an assassin and died at the guillotine in a dramatic mis-
carriage of justice. When the French playwrights produced the
drama, they faithfully adhered to the actual occurrence — the hero
is executed at the very moment that the villains are making belated
confessions and that friends of the victim are appealing to posterity
to right the perpetrated wrongs of the law. But Charles Reade's very
free translation complies with the British demand for the final
triumph of right: the real culprit is discovered just in time to allow
dramatic justice to be dealt to the innocent as well as to the guilty.

*Poverty and Pride*, a drama in five acts presented in 1857, was the
authorized English version of *Les Pauvres de Paris* by Edouard
Brisebarre and Eugène Nus. *The Hypochondriac*, an adaptation of
Molière's *L'Invalid Imaginaire*, was published in the late 1850s,
probably at Reade's own expense. The play was later revised and
produced in 1870 at the Adelphi Theatre but it was not well
received. On May 28, 1870, Reade presented a dramatic version of
his novel *Put Yourself in His Place*, entitled *Free Labour*, which
started at seven-thirty in the evening, and played past midnight.
Since the audience response to so long an evening was tepid, Reade
decided to bolster the theatrical fare by making it even longer! On
June 15, he added as an afterpiece his adaptation of *L'Invalid
Imaginaire*, now under the title *The Robust Invalid*. The stratagem
of two dramatic failures for the price of one did not save the show;
consequently, the losses of the dramas *Free Labour* and *The
Hypochondriac* probably absorbed most of the profits of the novel
*Put Yourself in His Place*.

Reade adapted British as well as French works to the English
stage. Concerning one such adaptation, Malcolm Elwin records that
Charles Reade "laid violent hands upon Tennyson's *The Promise of
May* and wrote a dramatic version under the title of *Dora*."[14] Actually, Reade simply took the 173 lines of Tennyson's poem "Dora"
and amplified them into what may be his finest play. In Tennyson's
poem, the son, William Allan, sets his will against his father's: "And
half in love, half spite, he woo'd and wed / a labourer's daughter,
Mary Morrison." Reade adds to the drama a very adequate motivation for William's rebellion: he had already secretly married Mary

when he was commanded by his father to marry Dora. Both Tennyson and Reade, however, have William confess on his deathbed that he should not have crossed his father and married a girl of his own choice.

Reade found Tennyson's speech good enough dialogue to use it almost verbatim, but this use creates both the strength and the problem of the play. The celebrated Tennyson melancholia lies heavy upon the poem; when Reade uses it, he eschews his customary theatrical vivacity and ends with a richer play. But the dialogue is not Reade's style; it is a drama organized enthusiastically by Reade, but the tone is the Tennyson of "after many a summer dies the swan." Nevertheless, Reade could not resist both his own and his audience's penchant for the happy ending; and, although Tennyson was characteristically willing to condemn Dora to perpetual maidenhood, Reade marries her at the conclusion to Luke Blomfield.

After all values and ambiguities have been duly recorded, Reade's drama still leaves the reader with three basic questions: Would crusty Farmer Allan really have been transformed so immediately and conveniently by the mere sight of William's child? How does it happen that the novelistic crusader never challenges the laureate's motto for Farmer Allan: "my will is law"? And, finally, is a man to be cheered and revered who has driven out his son, and thus killed him, and who has let his own brother die unreconciled after an argument over a hayrick? Although the reviewer for the *Athenaeum* called *Dora* "a stage portrait of distinctive elegance,"[15] the play was nevertheless a decisive failure in terms of audience response.

An amusing aftermath of the unsuccessful adaptation of Tennyson's poetry is provided by Reade's pamphlet *Dora: or The History of a Play* (1877). The playwright rejoices in his cast; which included such veterans as H. Neville, Miss Kate Terry, and Miss Hughes. "I felt so strong in my actors that I was not much alarmed when I found the scene-painter was disorderly. Alas! I underrated the *destructive* powers of a drunkard and a fool!" In the drama, as in the poem, the cornfield plays a principal part because it is on the old farmer's joy and pride in his crop that Dora relies to soften him toward his stepdaughter and his grandchild, as well as to lessen her own hazard in working upon his feelings. On the stage, the setting demanded a "flowery mound and two wheat sheaves"; but the painter's stagecloth represented "a turnpike road, with three rows of cut stubble (property), and his cornfield a shapeless mass streaked with fiery red and yellow ochre." The audience evidently looked at the setting with indifference, for there was yet "no distinct ground for offence, since not a soul in front, except the poor author, could possibly divine what the monstrous thing was intended to libel." But when Farmer Allan entered and interpreted the daub, " 'Dora, my girl, come to have a look at the wheat,' every cockney who had voyaged into the the bowels of the land as far as Richmond began to snigger." Of course each time "the old farmer persisted in an illusion he had all to himself the merriment swelled." John Coleman referred to the pamphlet as "a curiosity on the gentle art of Vituperation."[16]

By special correspondence and mutual commercial arrangement, Reade translated August Maquet's drama *Le Château Grantier*. He hawked it rather extensively about London but found the managers entirely cold to any arrangement for its performance. This rejection especially aggrieved the translator because, for once, an English playwright had done "the right thing" by the author of a French play: he had purchased the rights as his exclusive property in England. While managers of London playhouses snapped up thefts of far less merit as translations from the French stage, Reade's legitimate and entirely acceptable adaptation went unwanted; but what he could not sell as a translated play, he could use as the basis of a novel *(White Lies)* for which he already had a contract. At least ten years later, Alfred Wigan directed the play as *The Double Marriage*, a drama in five acts, in October 24, 1867, in Henry Labouchere's new Queen's Theatre in Long Acre. But the translation of a play that did well enough for the basis of a novel ironically failed utterly on the stage.

Two more French plays complete the roster of Reade's translations and adaptations. Reade worked over Sardou's play *Andrée* and had it produced as *Jealousy* on April 22, 1878. On June 2 of the following year, he produced a far more significant work, the English dramatic version of Emile Zola's novel *L'Assomoir* (dramatized by the author in collaboration with Messrs. William Bertrand Busnach and Octave Gastineau) under the title *Drink*. John Hollingshead, in both his autobiography and his *Gaiety Chronicles*, was eager to claim that he first suggested to Reade the idea of adapting *L'Assomoir*. But Hollingshead was also insistent in his claim that the adaptation was the great dramatic success of Reade's career and that Reade himself was a "double-handed" writer who surpassed both Dickens and Thackeray by being equally successful as dramatist and novelist.

When *Drink* was produced on Whit Monday, June 2, 1879, the critics who had some notion of French realism and Zola's place as the great naturalist were delighted; but the more conservative critics were shocked and dismayed. Charles Reade, with his intense devotion to realistic detail and his technique of composing plays and novels from a montage of newspaper clippings, was the right translator to present Zola's work to the British theater. But one of the stranger aspects of the translation is the avoidance of Reade's usual technique of Anglicizing any foreign drama by broad touches of rural youth, local color, and farcical and violent action. In the Zola drama, he had the problem of transplanting a play full of the realistic presentation of low life in Paris to an audience that knew little about Paris and cared less. What a temptation to remove the action to the English scene. Instead, Reade evidently decided that so long as the heroine spoke in the tones of a suffering, struggling wife and mother, and her accents were genuine and her grief sincere, it made little difference whether she was called Gervaise Coupeau or Nancy Taylor. The central theme — a faithful picture of the ravages of what many earnest Victorians considered to be the great vice of their age — was quite as much, if not more, at home in the Princess's Theatre as in the Parisian *ambigu*. Whether absinthe or gin, the demon operated the same way in both England and France.

William Archer, a drama critic who was usually prejudiced against Reade for both his bombastic egoism and the inordinate length of his sensational spectacles, had a quite different reaction to *Drink:* "I am no great believer in the direct and immediate moral effect of stage representations, but if there ever was a drama which would cause instant conversions from evil ways, 'Drink' was that drama. Mr. Reade and Mr. Charles Warner between them made a terrible 'call to the unconverted.'" Archer was more impressed by the "gradual decline of a working man from sober domestic happiness to a degraded and ghastly death, set forth with such striking and concentrated reality" than by all the homilies of the total abstainers. He even risked an accusation of Zolaism when he claimed that the play "rose above the conventional melodrama" because it was a more or less "truthful illustration of life."[17]

In these translations and adaptations, there seems to have been a certain naiveté about the precise limits of *meum* and *teum*. "5g," the quaint title of a plot book compiled by the playwright during 1876, contains the newly invented term "bilogy." Obviously referring to a translated literary product, Reade chose as his prime example "Conscience a drama by Dumas is in 6 acts. 3 admirable. 3 bosh. Cut away the 3 bosh, and invent or steal 3 quite different." With all his pamphleteering and his many lawsuits concerning not only the rights of authors but also the wrongs of plagiarism and libel, Reade obviously passed through a period in which borrowing wholesale the plots of successful French plays seems to have been entirely legal and natural. Perhaps because so many of his own plots were lifted in the first place from newspaper reports or records of sensational court cases, the manuscripts of other authors seemed like so much more raw material for him to masticate in the voracious maw of his eclectic taste.

## II  *Collaborations*

Besides turning to works from the French stage to translate and to adapt, Reade occasionally sought the assistance of persons of proven theatrical competence to collaborate on the preparation of a play. On June 10, 1852, Reade finished his novel *Peg Woffington;* on November 3, it was published by Richard Bentley. *Masks and Faces: or Before and Behind the Curtain* was presented on November 20, 1852; a comedy in two acts and one of Reade's most successful plays, it was originally called *Peg Woffington.* Thus it would seem that the novel preceded the play, but the record of the collaboration of Tom Taylor and Charles Reade is both instructive and amusing. This is Reade's account:

What is the history of this play? I wrote a certain Scene in which Triplet, whose broad outlines I then and there drew, figured; and another personation scene containing Peg Woffington, Colley Cibber, and James Quin. I showed these to Taylor as scenes. He liked these characters, and we agreed to write a comedy.

I began. I wrote the greater part of Act I, and sketched situations of a second act — viz. the company assembled in Mr Vane's house, and Mrs Vane's sudden appearance; her kindness to Triplet, a mere sketch; Triplet's house, the first picture-scene almost as it stands now; and I wrote a little of a third act. Well, Taylor came down to me, added to my first act, filled up the chinks, got Vane into a better position, and made the first scene an act. . . . He . . . read it to Mrs Stirling, who said plump, "It won't do." . . . Then he wrote to me, and I took the bull by the horns. *Flung Act I. into the fire,* and wrote a new act, dashing at once into the main story . . . on the plan of the great French dramatists, I made the plot work by a constant close battle between a man and a woman. I then took in hand Act II., and slashed through Taylor's verbosity, losing none of his beauties. . . . Then I came to Act III., where I found my own picture-scene wanted a little alteration.

Then, with the help of a speech or two of Mabel's I softened Woffington, so that she cried in the frame, and Mabel found her out.

Then I offered the MS. to Taylor. He did not like the fence-and-rail prepared for him, and he said, "You reconcile the two women and I'll go on." . . . He did not like my *dénouement*. Hence he altered it and read his to Webster, who did not like it. Taylor has altered it again, and so the matter stands.

For comparison, here is the version of Tom Taylor's brother, Arnold Taylor:

In 1851 or 1852 Reade had the idea of a play founded on Peg Woffington, and I have the authority of my brother's assertion, often repeated in my own hearing and that of others . . . that when Charles Reade came to him on the subject, he had one character, and a bit of one scene, together with some vague, crude ideas how the play was to be worked into shape.

In August 1851 my mother, brother, and others of my family went to live at Chiswick. . . . Reade was our guest at Chiswick Lodge, and the method of writing the play was this, that during the day (my brother being in town at his office) Reade wrote long passages, which were as ruthlessly cut to pieces, or rejected, at night by my brother, when they sat down to put together and complete their work. . . .

In this way the writing of the play went on till its completion in three acts. Amongst my brother's MSS, I have found a fair copy, corrected subsequently in my brother's handwriting . . . there is a great deal wholly omitted from the play as acted, but a great deal which was subsequently introduced by Reade into his novel of "Peg Woffington." . . . Very much to Reade's vexation, and contrary to all his ideas and wishes, *the play was cut down by my brother to two acts*, and worked by him into the shape in which it was finally acted at the Haymarket. . . . "Masks and Faces" proving a great success, Reade then, without so much as naming his intention to my brother, produced the novel of "Peg Woffington."

This naturally set people asking whether the play of "Masks and Faces" or the novel of "Peg Woffington" was written first? If the latter, all the credit or originality rested with Reade, and Tom Taylor had merely been asked to use his experience as a playwright, and throw the story into dramatic form. My brother having remonstrated with Reade on the line he had taken, the latter then prefixed to the novel the dedication, dated 15th December 1852, "To Tom Taylor, my friend and coadjutor in the comedy of 'Masks and Faces,' to whom the reader owes much of the best matter of this tale."

I find the same dedication repeated in a new edition of "Peg Woffington," published in 1857.

I thought, and still think, and said so at the time to my brother, that the language of the dedication was not adequate to the circumstances and the facts.

His answer, as far as I can recall it, was, "Reade's a queer fellow, with odd notions about the rights and wrongs of things, and I'm quite willing to let the whole thing pass and be forgotten."

But the matter left, I think, a soreness on both sides. . . . Shortly after the production of "Masks and Faces," Reade produced a play, all his own, "Gold," which I well remember seeing at Drury Lane.

It is only necessary to recall that immature production to be convinced that the hand that wrote it was incapable of the terse, sparkling, and polished finish of "Masks and Faces."[18]

As to the respective dates of play and novel, the record is full of discrepancies. Malcolm Elwin's biography (based on Reade's letters, etc.) is the authority for the priority of the novel: finished June 10, 1852; published November 3, 1852. John Coleman's biography, rather unchronological and based on free recollection rather than documentary evidence, is the fairly untrustworthy authority for the priority of the play. Yet, curiously enough, when compared with the other play-novel patterns, quite good internal evidence shows the drama was written first and then expanded sufficiently to make a novel.

Whatever the order of origin, the play was a decided success, especially to Mr. Webster, the theater manager, although only a slender dividend of one hundred and fifty pounds was divided between the collaborators. The source of the play title was found in Peg's long speech to Mrs. Vane in the last scene. With extraordinary humility and magnanimity, an actress, a profession that was almost a Victorian synonym for "fallen woman" delivers a wandering husband back to his bucolic wife: "Dear sister, when hereafter in your home of peace you hear harsh sentence passed on us, whose lot is admiration, but rarely love, triumph but never tranquillity — think sometimes of poor Peg Woffington, and say, stage masks may cover honest faces, and hearts beat true beneath a tinselled robe." At the very close of the play, with Reade's fondness for final addresses to the audience, Peg declaims:

> Yes, sure those kind eyes and bright smiles one traces
> Are not deceptive *masks* — but honest *faces*.
> I'll swear it — but if your hands make it certain,
> Then all is right on both sides of the curtain.

The second collaboration between Reade and Taylor resulted in *Two Loves and a Life*, a drama in four acts, produced by Webster at the Adelphi, March 20, 1854. The drama is set in England in the year 1745 when the Young Pretender was marching south from Scotland with five thousand Highlanders. The rather good, although involved, historical plot concerns Ruth Ravenscar, a young woman of Spanish appearance, who had been cast on the shore as an infant. As a young woman, Ruth volunteers to lead the loyal troops through deep mist across the shifting Leven ford when Father Radcliffe, a recusant priest who entered the priesthood after the loss of a wife and child by shipwreck, and Sir Gervase Rokewood fight on James Stuart's side and hope to surprise the troops of William Guelph (Duke of Cumberland) on the treacherous Leven sands.

Braving great danger, Ruth succeeds and becomes the local heroine (she knows the sands so well because she crosses them at all hours and seasons as part of her duties as assistant postmistress!). But, alas, as a result of her courage, her beloved Sir Gervase (under the alias William Hyde) is captured. Then she and Anne (daughter of Mr. Musgrave, the village postmaster and successful corn merchant) vie in deeds of ingenuity and courage to rescue their stupid joint swain. Ruth finally saves Rokewood by extorting his pardon from Cumberland in appreciation for her courage in guiding his troops across the sands. Then, of course, she hands the man she has just rescued to her rival Anne and leaves with James Radcliffe, her newly discovered father, who will plot no more against King George since he has found his daughter!

Characteristics of this rather rousing historical drama developed into the patterns of later Reade plays: the semihistorical plot with many ingenious interweavings of subplots; the emphasis upon human relationships that begin or eventuate in violent and heroic actions; the dual heroines — one dark and Latin and the other light and British;[19] characters who appear in two different roles with aliases; women who are far more courageous and inventive in dealing with danger than their men;[20] the successful but worldly heroine who, with sublime magnanimity, gives the hero she has just rescued to her purer rival; the man of business who is more likely to be a villain than otherwise; and the man of violently strong convictions who changes them at the end with not the slightest suggestion of any difficulty.

The third collaboration with Tom Taylor produced *The King's Rival* in the same year, 1854. The main plot line concerns the Duke of Richmond, who loves Miss Stewart, whom the King wishes to take for his mistress. Historical characters abound: Charles the Second,

Catherine of Braganza, the Duke of Richmond, Lord Shaftesbury, Sir George Etheredge, Samuel Pepys, Major Wildman, Nell Gwynne, Mrs. Middleton, and Lady Denham. Reade even inserts sections from Samuel Pepys's famous *Diary* into the dialogue (Act II, Scene i). A lively, virile play, *The King's Rival* ends with that appeal to the audience so dear to the hearts of Ben Jonson, the Restoration wits — and Charles Reade.

NELL GWYNN: It is our desire, your majesty, while we amuse to improve the mind — our aim is —
    By nature's study, to portray most clear,
    From Beaumont, Fletcher, Jonson — immortal Shakespeare —
    How Kings and Princes, by our mimic art,
    Yield their sway, and applaud the actor's part.
    . . . . . . . . . . . . . . . . . . . . . . . . . . . . . . .
    To-night, King, Queen, Lords and Ladies act their Part,
    Each prompted by the workings of the heart;
    And Nelly hopes they will not lose their cause —
    Nor will they — if favored by your applause.

The fourth and final dramatic collaboration of Charles Reade and Tom Taylor produced *The First Printer*, presented at the Princess's Theatre, Monday, March 3, 1856, under the management and direction of Charles Keane. The play, neither a translation nor an adaptation of any French drama, was based on the life of one of the many legendary originators of the movable printing press, Laurence Costar of Haarlem, who was robbed of his first model of the press by a runaway apprentice. Reade and Taylor, who confidently and audaciously identified John Gutenberg as the thief, even dared to add the romantic interest of an attempt by Gutenberg to seduce Costar's wife. After this imaginative historical drama, Reade produced, for good or for ill, no other plays for nine years.

### III  *Dramas Related to Novels*

Of greatest interest to the modern student of Reade are his dramas that either provided the dialogue skeleton for amplified novels or were themselves dramatized from novelistic originals. Some plays that might well have been treated in this section seemed more suitably discussed in other subdivisions of this chapter: *The Double Marriage*, based on Maquet's *Le Château Grantier* and the origin of the novel *White Lies; Free Labour*, a dramatization of *Put Yourself in His Place; Masks and Faces*, a dramatic version of the same plot line and characterization as Reade's novel *Peg Woffington; The Village Tale (Rachel the Reaper)*, the basis of the novel *Clouds and Sunshine*.

The painfully restricted prose of the *Memoir* places *Christie Johnstone* as "very much the product of the bright years of [Reade's] young manhood, though actually penned nearly two decades later."[21] Elwin, in his more venturesome biography, notes a relevant passage in Reade's notebooks of 1876:

"In my mediaeval romance *The Cloister and the Hearth* I use this expression celibacy of the clergy, an invention truly devilish. A French critic is surprized at the violence in me since the rest of my work in general deals benevolently and benignly with Pope, Priests, Convents, and the unreformed Church in general. . . . The opinion I uttered in 1860 was even then twenty years old in me: it is now thirty-six." Apparently something occurred in or about the year 1840 which incited Reade to vehement resentment of the celibate condition imposed upon him by the statutes of his college, and the heroine of the affair may well have been the prototype of Christie Johnstone.[22]

The astonishing and verbose reminiscences of Coleman go so far as to couch their revelations in the first person:

It was during one of these vacations that I drifted down to Newhaven, and became acquainted with Christie Johnstone and her belongings.

Yes, sir! I was the Ipsden of the story, and Christie, dear Christie, was — but that concerns no one but my darling and myself. . . .

When Christie and I agreed to differ (alas! that it should be so), I shook the dust of Scotland from my feet, and it was many a long day ere I crossed the Tweed again.[23]

Coleman, still in the first person, tells about a later visit Reade made to Edinburgh:

Leith! Suppose I were to stroll on to Newhaven — there could be no harm in my seeing — seeing *Her* — certainly not. . . . At last I reached Newhaven. When I approached the house the door was wide open; and the old woman was "ben."

"Christie," said I, "how's Christie?"

"God's truth!" and she dropped her knitting. "Div ye na ken?"

I shook my head. "Where is she?" I repeated.

"There!" and she pointed to the old kirkyard beyond.

I made my way there — and then —! Yes, then — I crawled back to Edinburgh.

I didn't go to the play that night. Had I done so "She" would have been
by my side, as she had been many a time before![24]

Somewhere between the chaste prose of the *Memoir*, the blunt
factuality of the biography, and the lachrymose excesses of the
recollections may lie the truth about the autobiographical genesis of
*Christie Johnstone*. At least it is known that, although this play was
presumably never produced, it is the very one that was submitted
first to the actress Mrs. Stirling; she passed it on to the dramatist
Tom Taylor, who declared to his brother that, although it was "full
of strength," it was "unfitted for the stage." Cruelest cut of all,
Taylor, just as Mrs. Stirling had done, suggested that Reade should
"make a novel of it." Reade later took their advice, successfully but
not happily; for one roar of applause from a packed house seems to
have meant more to him than any solid financial success folded
within the unresponsive covers of a book.

Years after, at the time of the publication of *Christie Johnstone* as
a novel, Reade penned a *jeu d'esprit* entitled "*Christie Johnstone*, an
Auto-Criticism."[25] Writing in the manner of a critic of his own novel,
he sadly insisted that "the plot, which is of that arbitrary kind that
befits a play rather than a story, can be disposed of in few words."
Befitting a play nor not, it ended as a novel — and as one of the best
Reade ever produced.

In one of his many notebooks, Reade commented that a useful
method of devising short stories is that of "turning good plays into
stories by interstitial scenes."[26] He practiced his own prescription in
*Peg Woffington*, *Christie Johnstone*, and *Art*. The last-named play
was listed by Elwin among his unacted plays in 1852 and by
Coleman as having been presented at the Strand in May, 1852.
Elwin insists that *Art* was not presented on the stage until 1855,
when it was revised by Genevieve Ward and entitled *Nance Old-
field*. Elwin also claims that the drama derived from the French of
Louis Pierre Narcisse Fournier; but Coleman calls it an adaptation of
Fournier's play *Tiridaté: ou comédie et tragédie*.[27] The only un-
contested fact was the publication, in two installments, of *Art: a
Dramatic Tale* in the December and January (1853 - 1854) issues of
*Bentley's Miscellany*.

The basic tale is the old one in which an actress turns the head of
an impressionable young law student; then, by contract with his
father, she disenchants him. Reade added that, when the father
pleads with her to do so, she enchants the almost moribund youth

once again by playing his unpublished and unperformed tragedy to perfection in a private showing. Such a story would appeal to Reade because of his fondness for plots that turn upon false *dénouements* not once, as in Molière, but two or three times until an audience is thoroughly weary. Nevertheless, since the play was written with considerable zest, it most resembles *Masks and Faces* in style and animation; and it became both a successful novelette and one of what Walter Frewen Lord calls Reade's only two "good acting plays."[28]

By June 10, 1852, Charles Reade had finished the novel *Peg Woffington* and had sketched the plot of *Gold*, a play that provided the genesis for the novel *It Is Never Too Late to Mend*. The drama was produced by E. T. Smith at Drury Lane Theatre on January 10, 1853. Reade subsequently presented himself at the box office and, probably inadvertently, was denied free admission. Not the man to bear lightly such an affront, he wrote to Mr. Charles Mathews, then performing at the theater, whom he evidently supposed to have been the manager and responsible for all the theatrical arrangements:

> Garrick Club, Covent Garden, November 28
> Dear Sir: I was stopped the other night at the stage-door of Drury Lane Theatre by people whom I remember to have seen at the Lyceum under your reign.
> This is the first time such an affront was ever put upon me in any theatre where I had produced a play, and is without precedent unless when an affront was intended. As I never forgive an affront, I am not hasty to suppose one intended. It is very possible that this was done inadvertently; and the present stage-list may have been made out without the older claims being examined.
> Will you be so kind as to let me know at once whether this is so, and if the people who stopped me at the stage-door are yours, will you protect the author of 'Gold,' etc. from any repetition of such an annoyance?
> I am, dear sir, yours faithfully.
> Charles Reade

To this imperious request, Mathews made a genial but infuriating reply:

> Dear Sir: If ignorance is bliss on general occasions, on the present it certainly would be folly to be wise. I am therefore happy to be able to inform you that I am ignorant of your having produced a play at this theatre; ignorant that your name has been erased from the list at the stage-door; ignorant that it had ever been on it; ignorant that you had presented yourself for admit-

tance; ignorant that it had been refused; ignorant that such a refusal was without precedent; ignorant that in the man who stopped you you recognized one of the persons lately with me at the Lyceum; ignorant that the doorkeeper was ever in that theatre; ignorant that you never forgive an affront; ignorant that any had been offered; ignorant of when, how, or by whom the list was made out, and equally so by whom it was altered.

Allow me to add that I am quite incapable of offering any discourtesy to a gentleman I have barely the leisure of knowing, and moreover have no power whatever to interfere with Mr. Smith's arrangements or disarrangements; and with this wholesale admission of ignorance, incapacity, and impotence, believe me

Faithfully yours,
C. T. Mathews[29]

First produced at the Theatre Royal, Drury Lane, on Monday, January 10, 1853, *Gold* enjoyed a short run during a period when the goldfields of Australia, the setting for two acts, excited a good bit of general interest. Under the inspiration of the international success of Harriet Beecher Stowe's *Uncle Tom's Cabin* in 1852, Reade decided to convert his short play *Gold* into the *Uncle Tom's Cabin* of the British prisons and their solitary confinement system. Forswearing his flair for the brief novel, he threw all his intense energies and extensive reading into the construction of what he called, in the dedication of *It Is Never Too Late to Mend*, "a solid fiction."

The result was so solid that he decided to publish *The Autobiography of a Thief* separately because, as he states in the previously mentioned dedication, "the novel, without the autobiography, was five ordinary volumes by printer's calculation."

Thus the topical melodrama *Gold* was split in half with a literary cleaver to become the frame for an overwhelmingly factual and horrendously sensational picture of prison life in England. Claiming that the idea came to him, not from the muse, but from his more usual source of inspiration, the *Times* of September 7 or 8, 1853, Reade set himself to a discipline that became the pattern of his later compositon: "June 20. The plan I propose to myself in writing stories, will, I see, cost me undeniable labour. I propose never to guess where I can know. For instance, Tom Robinson is in gaol. I have therefore been to Oxford Gaol and visited every inch, and shall do the same at Reading. Having also collected material in Durham Gaol, whatever I write about Tom Robinson's gaol will therefore carry, I hope, a physical exterior of truth."[30]

In 1864, Reade revised *Gold* to produce a play with the longer title

*It Is Never Too Late to Mend*. The action of *Gold*, the earlier version, occurs in England (spring of 1847) in the first and second acts; in Australia (January, 1848), third and fourth acts; and back in England (autumn, 1848), fifth act. Briefly stated, the original play about the Australian goldfields traces the odyssey of George Sandford, impoverished farmer, as he leaves "The Grove," Berkshire, to find his fortune in Australia as bailiff to the Honourable Frank Winchester. He leaves his brother William behind to watch over his fiancée, Susanna Merton, who is secretly beloved by John Meadows, a rich and unscrupulous speculator. A hundred miles inland from Sydney, George is given a flock of five hundred sheep by Winchester after working for him for only five months. The "scab" wipes out his flock; and George is nursed through fever by Jacky, an aborigine he rescued from sharks, and by his faithful dog Carlo. Gold dust in a stream leads them to great lodes. George, triumphant, returns to England to claim his fiancée, who is just about to marry Meadows as a result of a fraudulent newspaper announcement of George's marriage in Sydney. The lovers are united, and virtue triumphs while vice is defeated.

*It Is Never Too Late to Mend* makes two minor characters, Tom Robinson, reformed thief, and Francis Eden, saintly prison chaplain, become the major figures in a new central situation — the deplorable state of British jails and their desperate need of reform. This play, first built about one theme and then shifted to another, exemplifies some of Reade's worst dramatic foibles. When Henry Winchester tries to convince George Sandford that he should emigrate with him to Australia, he says to George: "Then I must enlighten you. *(Aside)* I won't give it up" (Act I). And so, in full hearing of the protagonist on the stage, he voices his private intent in melodramatic high style. Indeed, this Renaissance device of the soliloquy used for exposition is quite run into the ground. Early in Act I, almost at the beginning of the play, Meadows, probably literally grinding his teeth in the most villainous tradition, hisses:

And I have escaped love all these years, to dote upon a woman now! What magic is in this Susanna Merton, that I, who live for money, would pave the ground she walks upon with my gold, if she would but walk towards me. When I think that she prefers that George Sandford, I could curse all the world! — a dull dog, that would be just as happy with any other girl, — an oaf that does not even see his rivals — does not dream that his own brother loves her and that I love her, and will take her from both of them! A few weeks and a few mugs of ale would wash her from what little mind either of them has.

Unfortunately for the playwright, every perceptive person in the audience has come to precisely the same estimation of the hero and his stupid brother and agrees entirely with the villain. A bit later in the same act, appears the Oxford don's idea of how farm boys fight:

GEORGE: If you call me false I'll knock your ugly head off, Sulky Bill!
WILL: You're false! and a fool into the bargain, Bragging George!

Still later in the same act, a pat illustration occurs of the Victorian syndrome that heroines should be silly angels and that heroes should be honest, proud — and unfortunate — : when Susanna remarks: "There was no coolness between us, dear; you only fancied so. You don't know what fools women are — how they delight to tease the man they love, and to torment themselves. I always loved you dearly; but never as I do this day — so honest! — so proud! — so unfortunate! I love you, I honour you. I adore you! *(she clasps him in her arms — kisses him — he kisses her)*" (Act I, p. 19). Then, in two of his inimitable stage directions, the playwright adjures the director: "Meadows must be pale in the course of this scene, by those stage means that are commonly reserved for sudden displays of terror — this is very important to the scene. — C. R." (Act I, p. 19).

When George leaves for Australia, Reade reminds the musicians: "*Air, 'Home, Sweet Home,' played very piano in orchestra.*" In a rather extended footnote to the opening scene of Act IV, the author directs the scene designer and stagehands:

The sun begins to rise, and displays the following scene (which ought to be a very remarkable one) — a high bank L. H. — A high bank or cliff R. C., with rocks running all round stage — Low ground, and rocks beyond, C. — The River McQuarrie winding in a valley, along the banks of which are seen countless tents of every colour, size, shape, &c. — The whole extent of stage, and also rocks occupied by the Diggers, &c. who at the beginning of this change gradually awake, take up tools and proceed to work in groups.

All the beautiful concomitants of that great event in Nature — Sunrise — must be attended to. Undistinguishable sounds in the distance — sparkles of dew here and there. Men seen to draw open tents and issue forth to work. . . .

The more gradually the light breaks, the better; all that is required is that the music and the light should be progressive and the pantomime varied by several entries. Do not let them begin to work too soon, — you will find the audience very patient, if the music is good and the business rational. — C. R. MUSIC, subdued, but rising with the opening prospect — at last breaks into "Hail, Smiling Morn!"

*Gold* also boasts the rather banal use of national characters, stereotypes still found in amateur farce. Mary McDoggherty is the stock Irish comic character; vulgar, earthy, but honest and courageous, she speaks, of course, with a thick brogue: "Platinum, ye're the boy — seein' you're the queen of the metals. Captain, ye're a jewil — may ye live till the skirts of your coats knock your brains out. Here's wishin' ye both all sorts of luck — good, bad, and hindifferent. Platinum for ever, and gould to the divil! *(accompanies these words with a kick. Exits jumping and laughing)*" (Act IV).

On the other hand, Susanna's speech to the elderly Jew Levi is a particularly good example of Evangelical Victorian rhetoric: " 'Tis but a woman's frail voice, father — but with it, I can speak you words more beautiful than Lebanon's cedars or Galilee's shore, words that made the stars brighter, and the sons of the morning rejoice. I will not tell you whence I had them, but you will say, surely they came from heaven, these words that drop on man's hot passions like the dew, and speak of trespasses forgiven, and peace and goodwill among men" (Act II). It is interesting to note that in that era, just as John Ruskin and William Morris considered ecclesiastical Gothic architecture appropriate for banks, public halls, and parliamentary buildings, the language of the Church and the rhetoric of the pulpit were quite at home behind the flickering footlights of the local theaters.

The drama closes in the best light-opera tradition with a tableau: "GEORGE: *(reads proclamation)* which ends with 'God save the Queen!' SOLDIERS present arms — The National Anthem is played with the whole power of the band — Every person waving caps, &c., and shouting — As the Act Drop begins to descend, ROBINSON and JEM touch spring in dog, and gold dust pours out into box — ROBINSON shakes his fist at BLACK WILL and THIEVES. — Tableau" (Act IV). And then Reade's fondness for the closing address to the audience is repeated in Levi's lines: " 'I have seen a lot of man from east to west: we all pass through trouble at one hour or another of life's short day, and they are the happiest whose sorrows come in the morning; — their noon-day is often the brightest, and their sun sets in peace. So may it be with you, my children! *(a pause — to* AUDIENCE) And with you, our friends!' CURTAIN."

When *It Is Never Too Late to Mend* was first produced in 1865, the ghastly cruelty of the prison scenes caused some of the most extraordinary theatrical rioting of Victorian times. When the drama was revived on Boxing Night, 1878, at the Princess's Theatre, the sensational reception of thirteen years before was not repeated. In *English Dramatists of Today*, William Archer describes the Princess's revival and a later revival at the Adelphi as something less than triumphs — unless as the triumph of supreme tedium:

I have dwelt thus at length upon "Masks and Faces," because I believe it is the only one of Mr. Reade's works, as far as they are known to me, which is likely to hold the stage. He, on the other hand, believes in the immortality of "It's Never Too Late to Mend," which, he says, has outlived a hundred French dramas, and will outlive a hundred more. This is in a sense unquestionable — my only wonder is that it does not outlive its audiences. It has outlived me twice, so that after mature deliberation I have come to the conclusion that there is an M too much in its name, and that "It's Never Too Late to End" was the title to which it was "specially written up."

From the Adelphi revival, Mr. Archer fled the theater at eleven o'clock while the "humours of Jacky" were still in full swing and seemingly inexhaustible. "When the irrepressible Jacky took the centre of the stage and set himself to solve the mysteries of a cotton umbrella, I reflected that art is long and life is fleeting, and went. The problems presented by that umbrella to the aboriginal intellect of Mr. Calhaem were no doubt of absorbing interest, but one cannot sacrifice everything to scientific curiosity. I went, 'not that I loved Jacky less, but that I loved home more.'"

Mr. Archer was depressed not only by the endlessness of the drama but also by the excessive realism of Reade's setting. The program described the opening scene as "the Grove Farm with all the details of agricultural life — the farmyard, wall and gate — the straw-yard — the duck-pond — the barn — the barley-mow — pigeons, ducks, poultry, animals, &c., &c." Thinking that only a real pump was required to make the realism perfect, Archer was delighted to discover its use in the third act to produce a thrilling effect under the disguise of a mountain lake and water fall. "As for the pigeons, ducks, poultry, and animals, they were all letter-perfect in their parts and played, on the whole, with excellent spirit and discretion . . . the pigeons, ducks, poultry, and animals did not o'erstep the modesty of nature, and thoroughly carried out Hamlet's instructions so far as in them lay."

Rather wickedly, Archer interpreted the program's " &c., &c." to designate the relatively unimportant human actors in the play and professed to find them "almost as good in their way" as the barnyard fowl. The plot struck Archer as an alternation, in Mr. Gilbert's jingle, of "Blessings and curses/And ever-filled purses" that was judiciously tempered by the humors of Jacky. Indeed, before the curtain has been up five minutes, "the gentle Jew," Isaac Levi, curses "the hard Christian," Meadows. Then George Fielding bestows blessings and cursings rather indiscriminately on his acquaintance, until his sweetheart asks him how he can use language like that "within a stone's throw of a Christian church." In the second act, most of the condemnatory eloquence falls to the prisoner Tom Robinson. In the Australian scene, when his hired shepherd Abner deserts him in his distress, George Fielding remarks, "Wherever you go may sorrow and sickness — ! No, I leave that to Heaven!" (This remark Archer calls a "piece of self-abnegation and effacement which cannot be sufficiently admired.")[31]

On December 18, 1872, *The Wandering Heir* was published by Reade as a play in accordance with what had become standard practice to prevent dramatic pirates from stealing the plot, the choicest dialogue, and the best characterization from a periodical story. As the sole feature in the Christmas issue of the *Graphic,* the story version won such widespread popularity that Reade was able to boast a sale in Europe of two hundred thousand copies; in the United States, Harper's sold one hundred fifty thousand copies in their *Weekly* and eighty thousand additional copies in book form; in Canada, Rose and Hunter of Toronto sold ten thousand copies in their *Journal* and five thousand in book form.

On the fourth of January, 1873, a letter appeared in the *Press and the St. James's Chronicle* above the signature "Coecilius," and another in the *Athenaeum,* signed "C. F." Both pseudonymous letters accused the author of *The Wandering Heir* of gross plagiarism from Jonathan Swift's *Journal of a Modern Lady.* By not adducing the exact extent of the borrowing, they implied that the entire work was plagiarized. Reade was acute enough to recognize in both letters essentially the same hand, although one derided him as an "illiterate scribbler" who might someday learn to write novels if he could develop imagination and learn to write English, whereas the other was simply scornful of a contemporary attempt to make money from the use of a dead man's work.

In an appendix to *The Wandering Heir*, Reade reprinted most of the journalistic debate. "Coecilius" and "C. F." were simply Mortimer Collins and his wife.

He is my rival in business and in nothing else. He is a novelist. He is prolific, but not popular. His surname has a great and merited reputation, but it has never been able to drag his Christian name after it up the steps of "the Temple of Fame". . . . "Coecilius" used to write for the *Graphic*, but toward the end of 1872 that market was closed to his prolific but not popular pen. The novelist, fertile in failures, to whom the *Graphic* was closed for a time, sees another novelist write a story in the said *Graphic*, and learns the *Graphic* has sold a vast number of copies. Thereupon he and his wife sit down and multiply Malice.

Reade had actually used the passage from Swift to pad the dialogue of a single scene, occupying no more than five hundred words of the first chapter of his story. Nothing else in the chapter or in the remainder of the novelette is even vaguely related to any writing of Swift. Just as Sir Walter Scott relied upon Thomas Shadwell's play *Squire of Alsatia* (1688) in his novel *The Fortunes of Nigel* (1822), and just as Harrison Ainsworth used Hogarth's prints in his historical novel *Jack Sheppard* (1839), so Reade borrowed from a dominant writer of the eighteenth century to add realistic atmosphere to a story set in that same era.

In the appendix to *The Wandering Heir*, Charles Reade referred to both of his detractors as "criticasters, anonymuncula, and skuncula"; and he included his chief defense, an essay entitled "The Sham-Sample Swindle." The essence of the swindle is very tersely stated by Reade: "the detractor takes an exceptional passage from a meritorious work, cites it in full, and then slyly suggests that the whole work is of that character." This statement is precisely appropriate to the libel of "C. F.," who, after exposing the borrowings from Swift, confesses, "I have read little of Mr. Reade's story beyond what I have quoted. There may be more stuff of the same sort in it, as Mr. Reade makes a slight reference to 'Swift's Polite Conversation.' If this is how novels are made, surely novel-writing must be an easy art! Vulgar rumor says that Mr. Reade was paid for this at the rate of a penny a word! Who is to receive the pence for that part of the work which clearly belongs to Dean Swift? Was that great writer ever paid so well?"

So far as theme and plot structure are concerned, *The Wandering*

*Heir* much more closely resembles Mark Twain's *The Prince and the Pauper* and Daniel Defoe's documentary tales[32] than anything by Swift. In the spring of 1726, James Annesley, whose tuition has not been paid for fourteen months, starts walking from Matthew Hoolaghan's school for boys in Ireland to find his father, Lord Altham, in Dublin. Thus he becomes an earlier version of the aristocrat mistaken for a pauper. En route to Dublin, he experiences various picaresque adventures in the manner of Defoe's characters. Charles Reade loved the picaresque journey, the narrative of quest, quite as well as any eighteenth-century practitioner of the novel, and so James and his friend Philip (who, of course, turns out to be a girl named Philippa) travel all over the world as beggars, indentured servants, slaves, lord and lady, and criminals before the bar before the novel ends.

The third chapter begins wth a highly characteristic Reade pattern: "The James Annesley river is set flowing; so now for Joanna Philippa Chester, and old England." Reade likes to establish the flow of one life; to tuck it away for later reference; to reveal the springs of another destiny; and finally to bring them both together for a union that proves precipitate since more difficulties remain to be overcome before the united channel is reached.

When the ship *Bellona* is bearing home the true Lord Anglesey, Reade refers to an actual newspaper article: "*The Daily Post* announced it, and the *Gentleman's Magazine* copied, as indeed may be seen in the *Gentleman's Magazine* for February, 1741" (Chapter VII). An author is usually not so explicit about his source, but it was entirely characteristic of Charles Reade to find the germ of a novel and a play in the pages of an old magazine.

Along with many another author of the ancient, Renaissance, Restoration, or Victorian eras, Charles Reade was titillated by the idea of a heroine masquerading in men's clothing. Thus, in Chapter III of *The Wandering Heir,* Philippa becomes Philip and sails to Boston as a merchant's son; serves as indentured clerk on a Wilmington, Delaware, farm; and becomes James's devoted friend before he dreams that their love is erotic rather than filial. This transvestism intrigued Reade so much that he wrote a longish article entitled "Androgynism; or Woman Playing at Man."[33] He had just about decided that such an imposture would work neither on the stage nor in a novel when he read about Kate Tozer in the local newspaper.

Kate Tozer of Cheltenham, halfway through her teens, married her first cousin Tom Coombe, more than ten years her senior. They traveled about a bit looking for painting jobs in order to separate Kate from her possessive mother. At Woburn, Kate bought men's clothing with a ten-pound legacy from her Aunt Mary and became her husband's son at home and his apprentice at work. When they removed to Bedford, the transformation was so convincing that Nelly Smith fell in love with Kate (or Fred, as she now called herself); and the love was even reciprocated! When Fred met the Smith family, they thoroughly approved of their daughter's well-bred suitor. Some embarrassment ensued, since the Smith family consented enthusiastically to marriage, whereas Fred's feminine gender required an elopement. Since Fred naturally had insisted that, after the elopement, Nelly not write to her family, her father, alarmed, got the police on her trail; and all three were captured at the residence of Mrs. Whiting, in Moulton, where they were described by neighbors as being perfectly happy and well-behaved. Fred was accused of abduction and vagrancy; but, since obviously neither accusation could stand up in court, charges had to be dropped.

When, during an interview with Reade, Kate was asked her motives for adopting male attire, her eyes flashed as she cried, "You want to know the origin of all this mischief? I answer — the injustice of man. Women's labour is shamefully underpaid. That I was not found out by inferior work shows that to refuse me a man's wage because I wore a petticoat was a real injustice." Unfortunately, just as this indignant disclaimer does not sound like any Kate Tozer who ever lived at Cheltenham, it does sound very much like the Charles Reade who was writing the article.

Indeed, the supposed love lyrics of Kate to Nelly bear the same heavy impress as the final word of the supposed Tozer interview: "Asked to analyse her feelings respecting Nelly Smith during the progress of their love affair, a tear started to her eye, and she pondered for a moment, then she rapped out flippantly, 'Well, I suppose the girl supplied a certain want to a childless woman's heart. Perhaps I craved for something to cuddle and cherish, and pet and look down upon. You see, I am accustomed to look up to my husband.'" After this Victorian vindication, there remains only the odd combination of the lubricity and suggestive nuances of Reade's reporting of events and relationships, coupled with his insistence on the essential innocence of all parties concerned; but his sympathy for

Kate is coupled with his round condemnation of homosexual love
(even if he does mention somewhat ambiguously the love of the
biblical David and Jonathan!).

When Reade listed the bases of *The Wandering Heir,* he referred
to the real trial of James Annesley: first, as defendant against a
charge of murder; second, as plaintiff for great estates and titles in
the case of Craig *versus* Anglesey. The first case is to be found in
Thomas Bayly Howell's *Collection of State Trials.* For the second
case, Reade preferred the folio report published by Smith and
Bradley in Dublin in 1744. A third source was the *Memoirs of an Unfortunate Nobleman,* written by James Annesley's attorney, and
mentioned in Reade's novel in Chapter X. Then Reade makes a
startling explanation about how fact becomes fiction: "In the three
books I have now named lies half a plot. But only *invention, of equal
power with the facts,* could make it a whole plot. Therefore I invented Philippa, and all her business, and the whole sexual interest
of the story. I tell you this union of fact and imagination is a kind of
intellectual copulation, and has procreated the best fiction in every
age, by a law of nature" (appendix, *The Wandering Heir*).

A novel that reversed the process of *The Wandering Heir* was entitled *Singleheart and Doubleface* and was published in book form
by Chatto and Windus in December, 1883, after it had already
appeared serially in *Harper's Magazine.* Promptly thereafter, Reade
proceeded to write a dramatic version of the story. To preserve his
rights in the play, he had it produced on June 1, 1882, at the Royal
Princess's Theatre in Edinburgh. The plot was basically as simple as
the title: a woman who is single-hearted falls in love with and is completely loyal to a man who is double-faced.

*Love and Money,* written in collaboration with Henry Pettitt,
followed the more customary Reade pattern; it became the genesis
of a full-length novel. The play was presented at the Adelphi
Theatre on November 18, 1882; the critical reaction, on the whole,
was more negative than affirmative. Clement Scott considered it "a
good, old-fashioned, nervous melodrama, with one fine scene"; but
William Archer asserted that it was "an absurd affair . . . the sensation scene — hero, heroine, and villain imprisoned in a coal-mine —
was a piece of the most dismal clap-trap." To Austin Brereton, the
melodrama was "as conventional and absurd as possible, whatever
the self-satisfied genius who presided at the Adelphi during the run
of the play may think to the contrary."[34]

At any rate, the play provided the grist for a novel, *A Perilous*

*Secret* (1883), which had precisely the same strengths and short-comings as the drama. The novel makes clearer than the play Reade's favorite device of the merging of two streams. Chapter one is called "The Poor Man's Child"; chapter two, "The Rich Man's Child" — and not much prophetic power is required to guess that the obvious advantages of wealth and the grinding disadvantages of poverty will both avail nothing; that the rich man's child will die, and the poor man's child will somehow be substituted, and the promise of the title will thus be fulfilled. Chapter three of the novel contains a game of "Penny, penny, who's got the penny?" that obviously was more at home on the stage, where the audience could see Leonard Monckton secrete the stolen money in Walter Bolton's coat pocket and then, almost immediately after, watch William Hope take it out and hide in it Leonard Monckton's pocket instead.

Clearly marking his preference for the dramatic rather than the novelistic form, Reade remarks in the fifth chapter of the novel that playwrights who must drive on from incident to incident have to eschew the long, boring reflective passages of the novelist. "But we poor dramatists, taught by impatient audiences to move on, and taught by those great professors of verbosity, our female novelists and nine-tenths of our male, that it is just possible for 'masterly inactivity,' *alias* sluggish narrative, creeping through sorry flags and rushes, with one lily in ten pages, to become a bore, are driven on to salient facts, and must trust a little to our readers' intelligence to ponder on the singular situation of Mary Bartley and her two fathers."

Like *Love and Money*, a novel of collaboration between playwright Dion Boucicault and novelist-playwright Charles Reade, *Foul Play* had its first installment in *Once a Week* on January 4, 1868. Very possibly, as Reade pondered writing a novel that would give him the opportunity to denounce the criminal insurance of rotten ships and to capitalize on the contemporary scandal of coffin-ships, he considered that Henry Pettitt and Tom Taylor, who had entered so zealously into the production of other works, were not exactly the collaborators to investigate a contemporary issue. On the other hand, Dion Boucicault had written approximately one hundred and fifty dramas besides acting in and producing many of them. His remarkable productivity and his ability to please precisely the taste of the pit made him one of the most prominent and prosperous of British playwrights. So Reade, for whom the boundaries between the novel and the drama were at best fuzzy, decided to write a novel with a coauthor simply because that writer was a successful playwright. Dickens, about the same time (1869), lamented that Reade "did not stand on his own bottom instead of getting in with Dion Boucicault, etc."[35] The result, in the words of one reviewer, was a creaking amalgam in which the joints were never very well soldered — almost like a coffin-ship itself. "Although nearly every chapter bears unmistakable evidence of the power of the distinguished author of *Never Too Late to Mend*," some of the chapters were "trivial, unnatural, Frenchy," and seem to have been introduced largely as a preparation for a later dramatic version and in order to produce "stagey"[36] effects and situations.

The same year, the joint novelistic effort was dramatized and produced as the four-act drama *Foul Play*, by Dion Boucicault and Charles Reade. After the play's comparative failure at Holborn, Reade decided to write his own dramatic version, which, after a tour of the provinces as *Our Seamen*, was produced in London on April 2, 1877, as *The Scuttled Ship*. Reade's version frankly lumped the expository material Boucicault had spread throughout the first act into a prologue about a note forged on J. Wardlaw's name for two thousand pounds — a forgery ostensibly done by Robert Penfold, Arthur Wardlaw's tutor, an Oxford man and a clergyman. The motivation for Nancy's love of the weak villain is greatly strengthened in Reade's version by her desire for an old house in Chancery Court, one that will cost twelve hundred pounds but that will supply an orchard where she may dry the clothes of her laundry and lodging establishment. The play contains much singing, dancing of sailors, and orchestral use of a musical motif for each character's entrance. "Neptune's Frolic" upon crossing the Equator becomes a major vaudeville event, perhaps as a result of the experienced advice of John Coleman. On the whole, and particularly in terms of exposition, motivation, characterization, and *dénouement, The Scuttled Ship*, is a far better drama by a novelist, than *Foul Play*, by a successful playwright in league with a novelist-dramatist.

Sir Johnston Forbes-Robertson, a member of the cast of the Reade version, provides in his reminiscences, a glimpse of the realistic effects and the playwright's personal activities in the preparation of a play:

At rehearsal he was always ready to show the lover how to make love, or the villain how to "take the corner" in the most effective style. I once saw him teach an actor how to dance the hornpipe! On another occasion he showed the hero how to grapple the villain in the scene of a sinking ship, and actually rolled with him off the ship, over the dusty canvas billows into the trap. The hero was somewhat ruffled, but the old man came up smiling and delighted. The sea in those days was represented by a large piece of canvas painted blue, laid upon the whole of the stage, and shaken by stage hands from the wings. The illusion was hardly convincing, as the drowning men lay quite exposed on the top of the water till they reached, with much struggling, a slit cut in the canvas just above the trap, when they suddenly disappeared. This device however, always evoked rounds of applause from a thrilled audience.[37]

One pities the poor stage manager with an interfering playwright like Reade! On June 20, 1877, the supreme compliment of a parody was paid to *Foul Play* by the appearance at the Queen's Theatre of a burlesque by F. C. Burnand, entitled *Fowl Play, or a Story of Chikken Hazard,* which became immensely popular. During the run of *Foul Play* in Manchester, a satirical journal called the *Mask* published on the first page a repulsive cartoon of Reade and Boucicault and also a violent personal attack in the text upon both authors, accusing them of plagiary from a French drama entitled *Le Portefeuille Rouge.* The author of the critical accusation printed side by side the Boucicault-Reade composition and the text of the French drama. As Reade later pointed out in *The Sham-Sample Swindle,* the two columns actually contained neither the French drama nor the English but a poor translation compared with a paraphrase. Reade insisted that he had never even heard the title of the French play; but John Coleman wickedly suggested that "if his collaborateur had not, I am very much mistaken."[38]

Sometimes other playwrights dramatized Reade's novels quite without the author's permission. When the pugnacious Reade noted the success in America of John Daly's dramatization of his novel *Griffith Gaunt,* he promptly made his own adaptation — a romantic drama in five acts — which was produced at the author's own expense at Newcastle-on-Tyne in 1869. The review in a local newspaper, clipped by Reade and inserted in his voluminous notebooks, suggested that "with judicious condensation and the quickening of the action towards the culmination of the plot the drama will prove eminently successful, for it possesses all the needful elements of success — a vigorous and novel plot, variety of incident and character, and smooth and elegant diction."[39] When the play was later printed (again at the playwright's personal expense), without date or names of publisher and printer, it was called *Kate Peyton: or Jealousy.*

From this second title a confusion has often arisen with the later comedy *Jealousy*, produced at the Olympic Theatre in 1878. At the time, Victorien Sardou occupied the eminent position that had been held previously in the 1850s by Augustine Eugène Scribe. Since everything he wrote was being pirated immediately for the London stage, Sardou was glad to make a financial arrangement with Charles Reade whereby his play *Andrée* was translated and adapted by the British playwright and entitled *Jealousy*. The play was produced by Henry Neville at the Olympic Theatre on April 22, 1878, with all of Reade's usual meticulous attention to the details of production and effect.

Charles Reade not only dramatized his own novels, he also dramatized the novels of other authors living and dead, with and without permission. One of his first dramatic ventures was the adaptation to the stage of Tobias George Smollett's *Peregrine Pickle*, which he prepared in 1851 and produced three years later at St. James's Theatre in November, 1854. The author of the original novel, being safely gathered to his fathers, made no protest. The situation was quite different when Reade laid bold hands on Anthony Trollope's novel *Ralph the Heir*. Trollope's novel was published early in 1872, and the author sailed for Australia about six weeks later. Probably it had not occurred to Reade to dramatize the novel until, unfortunately, Trollope, who alone could give such permission, was well out of the country. Then belatedly, on March 7, Reade wrote: "Dear Trollope, I have been so delighted with 'Ralph the Heir' that I have dramatized the story, — in three Acts. Though the law, as I know to my cost, gives any one the right to dramatize a novelist's story, I would not have taken this liberty without consulting you if you had been accessible. Having done it, I now propose to give the inventor that just honour, which has too often been denied him in theatrical announcements." There followed, in the letter, the pleasant sentiments that this venture of Reade's would "open the theatre"[40] to Trollope and that Trollope ought to make a good deal of money by it if it were produced in Australia under his own supervision. On April 1, 1872, John Hollingshead, manager of the Gaiety Theatre in London, presented the dramatization of Trollope's novel, which Reade had entitled *Shilly-Shally*.

Although Reade had written similar letters to both Trollope and his son Henry, to explain the circumstances of the dramatization and the use of Trollope's name along with his own as coauthor of the play, the father exploded to George Smith, the proprietor of the *Pall Mall Gazette*, enclosing a letter to be published in the *Gazette* (July

16, 1872). Reade replied in a short letter to the editor of the *Daily Telegraph* (August 6, 1872), which had also published copies of the correspondence.

> Permit me a short reply to Mr. Trollope's letter, dated "Melbourne, 1st June." When I wrote him that private letter, the spirit of which, by selection and suppresion, he has misrepresented, Shilly-Shally was to be produced in October next, and meantime any objection of Mr. Trollope's to father his own lines in the theatre would have been law to me. But the theatre demanded the play unexpectedly for a short run in April, and here I was in a difficulty.
>
> Obliged to decide one way or other, I did as I would be done by . . . [and] decided to give Mr. Trollope half the receipts of Shilly-Shally, and, by the same rule, half the credit.
>
> Mr. Trollope decomposes my theory, and objects to his name being connected with the play, though two-thirds of the lines are from his pen.
>
> I submit; and henceforth his only connection shall be with the receipts.
>
> But five years hence, when Shilly-Shally still keeps the boards, and most of its contemporaries, especially the most belauded, have gone to the dogs, I hope Mr. Trollope and his friends will review my judgment with more respect, and my conduct with more kindliness and candour, than they have done up to this date.

In actual fact, the novel was not so intrinsically artistic that the dramatization destroyed its merits. Trollope's *Autobiography* pronounced it to be one of his worst novels, and he expressed surprise that it had attracted a sensational and melodramatic writer like Reade. Besides the unfortunate chronology of the Reade letters, however, and the annoyance their lateness naturally aroused, Reade was scarcely Trollope's choice at any time as a dramatic adapter. "There is no novelist of the present day," wrote Trollope, "who has so much puzzled me by his eccentricities, impracticabilities, and capabilities as Charles Reade."[41]

After *Shilly-Shally* was performed at the Gaiety, the critical blasts and counterblasts echoed throughout London. The issue seems not to have been that the play was very bad, as indeed it was, but that its language was "indecent." The reviewer of the *Times* claimed that "at least three passages spoken by old Neefit were positively indecent, and one by Moggs was a pun upon a place we would prefer not to mention." The *Orchestra* fluted in outraged treble, "He *will* say things in his books and pieces that no gentleman should utter in the presence of ladies . . . a good many of his points and epigrams and descriptive passages are exceedingly ill-bred: they would not be tolerated in a drawing-room, and should not be tolerated on the stage. . . . An aggravation of the offence is that these excrescences of club-room wit should be foisted on an innocent story of Mr. Trollope, of all authors — Mr. Trollope who is so careful never to offend." Richard Lee, the drama critic of the *Morning Advertiser* (review reprinted in the *Times*), warned the playgoing public that

In the matter of taste exhibited in the writing of Shilly-Shally, it is well that intending playgoers — men who propose to take their young sisters, daughters, or sweethearts to the theatre — should know what modest women needs must hear in sitting through this piece. Here are quotations taken down as they fell *viva voce* from the actors' lips: — Mr. Toole as Neefit, squabbles with his daughter Polly. He is made to say, "Why oppose your old father, who has been working for you these thirty years?" To which Polly replies, "Come, father, that can't be, for I'm only 22." And the father's answer is this: "That's no odds; I worked for you" — no, we dare not for decency's sake print the rest.[42]

Reade promptly sued the *Morning Advertiser* for libel. On February 10, 1873, in the course of an all-day trial, Lee stated that he had been "shocked" by the dialogue and expressed particular objection to the use of the word "smock." When Reade's lawyer reminded him of Shakespeare's use of the word, Lee replied, "Ah, *de mortuis!*" The jury brought in a verdict for Reade of two hundred pounds. John Hollingshead hinted that a clever actor can inject a salacious meaning into the most innocent line. Thus he relates that Neefit's question to Polly, "Did you ever hear of a little article called a father's cuss?" literally brought down the house, and the audience continued for some time to rock with delight. Probably it was the talent for comic attitudes of the leading comedian, John L. Toole, that made the simple lines sound like *mots à double entendre*. As the editor of the *Spectator* [43] pointed out, one of the offensive lines — "He must marry her in her smock" — was neither Trollope's nor Reade's line; it was one of the oldest proverbs in the language. After the smoke of critical and legal battle had blown away, and Reade had been mellowed by his victory, he mused on the fact that no critic had ever pointed out a censorable line in Trollope's hundred-odd volumes. Yet, of all the examples of indecency cited against Reade in the comedy, only one was not either Trollope verbatim or Trollope paraphrased.

So far as the actual dramatic adaptation is concerned, Reade had to start with a narrative that, while not quite so complex as *The Last Chronicle of Barset,* had nine lovers; and eight of them, after an interminable game of musical chairs, get married in the closing chapter. Reade eliminated four of the lovers completely: Gregory Newton, Patience Underwood, Mary Bonner, and Augusta Eardham. Then he attempted to pull together Trollope's bulging plot.[44] Instead of focusing on the flimsy and multitudinous conflicts of separated lovers, he emphasized the picturesque character of old Neefit, the heroine's father. But in making the old man the new center for his play version, both the titles become misnomers: Trollope's heir was not Ralph *(Ralph the Heir)* but Robert; Reade's play is not about shilly-shallying lovers who cannot make up their minds. Reade fully exposes Neefit's vulgarity, his tireless scheming to advance the fortunes of his daughter, and his brash self-confidence — but these characteristics are exposed to hearty laughter rather than to ridicule or disgust. Indeed, Reade manages to inject a warm sympathy for the ambitious, hardworking tradesman who wants above all else to make his daughter a "lady" and who will sacrifice his own savings, or even his daughter's happiness, in order to achieve that desire.

Six years after the Trollope squabble, Reade appropriated a novel from across the Atlantic. Mrs. Frances Hodgson Burnett, the American novelist, had written the popular and sentimental *That Lass o' Lowrie's,* and Joseph Hatton and Arthur Matthison had promptly prepared a dramatic version, without, of course, any permission or financial arrangement with the novelist. Although their successful dramatic adaptation was already on the boards, Reade prepared a version of his own in 1878 that had the briefer title *Joan.* During this period, multiple dramatic versions of best-selling novels or sold-out French plays seem to have been the rule rather than the exception. As Reade recorded in *The Eighth Commandment,* two other adaptations of *La Dame de la Halle,* by the French playwrights A. A. Bourgeois and A. M. E. Gaudichot, were currently being performed on the London stage when Reade produced his own version entitled *The Lost Husband* (1852); and no less than seven separate contemporaneous versions of Dion Boucicault's *Corsican Brothers* appeared in London and in the provincial houses.

Although Mrs. Burnett expressed no public indignation at the pirating of her novel by Hatton and Matthison, she was privately outraged that an eminent figure like Reade, who had written so much concerning international literary copyrights, would so coolly appropriate her work. Reade pointed out that, of course, Mrs. Burnett was quite right and that some legal safeguards should exist; but, since they did not, he had simply exercised his rights. In addition, since Mrs. Burnett was an American, he reminded her that all his own novels had been pirated and had sold extremely well in America — quite without profit to the British author.

A year later, on September 10, 1879, the *Manchester Examiner and Times*, perhaps just coming across the literary feud, defended the American authoress and accused Reade of an inconsistency between conduct and expressed belief that amounted to dishonesty. On September 18, Reade rather wearily replied that he had made Mrs. Burnett much the same offer that he had made to Anthony Trollope and that she would receive a share of any profits the drama might produce. Noteworthy is the fact, however, that, after the success of *The Wandering Heir*, his subsequent plays had been uniform failures. In Reade's reply to the *Manchester Examiner and Times*, he also indicated the exemplary nature of his financial arrangements with Messrs. Zola and Busnach for Reade's adaptation, *Drink*, based on Busnach's and Gastineau's dramatization of Zola's novel *L'Assomoir*. Reade did not point out in justification, however, as he might have, that wherever his authorized version was presented, it was preceded by a week or more by E. Romaine Callendar's pirated version *D.T., or Lost by Drink*.

## IV  *Drama Above All*

Even the discreet *Memoir* admits that Charles Reade considered drama to be the apex of all art and to be superior to poetry, painting, sculpture, music, architecture, and especially the lowly art of the novel. Held in the grip of this conviction, Reade had to face the disdainful reception of his first theatrical attempts and the financial drain of most of his later "successes." He struggled valiantly in the toils of what seems, Victorian rhetoric notwithstanding, to have been a real creative agony:

I struggled against this double shuffle [preference of London managers for French adaptations and the works of established playwrights] for about four years, and then I gave it up in despair, and took to novel-writing, against the grain, and left the stage for years. . . .

In 1865 I tried the London stage again under other circumstances, to explain which I must go back a little.

At Christmas, 1852, Drury Lane was in the hands of a gentleman with great courage and small capital. He invested his all in the pantomime; and the pantomime failed so utterly that after one week they took it off, and pitchforked on to the stage a drama called "Gold," which I had flung together in the same hasty way. This drama, though loosely constructed, was English, and hit the time. Not being stolen from the French by any member of the trades' union of playwright critics, it was much dispraised in the papers, and crowded the theatre, and saved the manager.

Afterwards, when the playwright critics drove me out of the theatre, I was obliged to run cunning, and turned many of my suppressed plays into stories. I dealt so with "Gold": I added a new vein of incidents taken from prison life, and so turned the drama "Gold" into the novel — "It Is Never Too Late to Mend."

But lo! the novel being written by a dramatist, naturally presented fresh dramatic features, and tempted me to reconstruct a more effective drama. I offered it to one or two managers. They declined, and gave their reasons — if I may venture to apply that term to the logic of gorillas.

Presently piratical scribblers got hold of the subject, and gorilla logic melted away directly in the sunshine of theft. Managers, both in town and country, were ready to treat for the rejected subject the moment it was offered them, not by the inventor and the writer, but by scribblers and pirates. Several piratical versions were played, in town and country, with a success unparalleled in those days. Saloons rose into theatres by my brains, stolen. Managers made at least seventy thousand pounds out of my brains, stolen; but not one would pay the inventor a shilling, nor give his piece a hearing.

Then I tried the London managers of the day again. I said "My amiable, though too larcenous friends, here is an approved subject, which you can no longer steal; but this is your misfortune, not your fault: why not make the best of a bad job, and put a few thousand pounds into your pockets by dealing with the inventor?"

No; not one would deal with a writer for his own brains. . . .

At last a lady interfered, read my drama, and advised Mr. George Vining to entertain it at the Princess's. He did so, and the drama was brought out with great expectation on the fourth day of October, 1865.

The playwright critics were there in full force, and several of them sat together in the stalls, as usual. But the circumstances under which the play was played were of a nature to disarm hostility. I had not troubled the theatre for ten years; and even now I was only producing, for my own benefit, a play that had been fully discussed, and approved, when played for the benefit of misappropriators. . . .

But, if you want a grain of humanity, or honour, or justice, or manly feeling of any kind, don't you go to a trades' union; for you won't find it there. The playwright critics concerted the destruction of the drama on the first night. They were seen to egg on Mr. Tomlins, the critic of *The Morning*

*Advertiser,* to howl down the prison scenes by brute clamour. Tomlins, being drunk, "his custom ever in the afternoon," ·lent himself to this with inebriate zeal, and got up a disturbance, which with a feeble manager would infallibly have ended in the curtain being let down and the play withdrawn forever. But, for once, the clique ran their heads against a man. George Vining defied the cabal on the stage; and, at last, some fellows in the gallery, shaking off their amazement at the misconduct below, called down, "Turn the blackguards out." Now when the dishonest blackguards in the stalls found the honest blackguards in the gallery had spotted them, they shut up, and prepared their articles for next morning in dead silence.

Next day, of course, they wrote the piece down unanimously. But they had overrated their power. The public got scent of the swindle, rushed to the theatre, and carried the drama triumphantly for 148 nights. The profits were about £8000 of which £2000 came to me on shares. The drama has outlived all the plays that were lauded to the skies that year by the venal clique. It has played in six houses this year, 1873.[45]

## CHAPTER 2

# Novels: Studies of Women

" HE read her a scene from an unfinished drama. She listened as middle-aged women do who have been bored perpetually by authors; not exactly with interest, yet not altogether frigidly.

" 'Yes,' she cried, when he concluded, 'that's good! That's plotting. But,' with a merry stage-laugh, which had become natural to her, 'why don't you write novels?' "[1]

The novels of Charles Reade, whom so sensitive a critic as Henry James called a real master, among the most readable of living English novelists, fall roughly into three thematic groups: the romances — often subtitled "a matter of fact romance" — dominated by heroines (Chapter 2); social studies — dealing with such problems as colonial migration, the Australian gold rush, the solitary confinement system of British prisons, the easy confinement of unwanted relatives in insane asylums, the coffin-ship insurance scandal, and the mounting power of trade unions (Chapter 3). The third thematic division, however, is occupied by only one major work. *The Cloister and the Hearth,* a historical novel with many of the characteristics of both the romances and the social studies.

Thirty-eight years of age when he wrote his first novel, Reade continued to produce novels thereafter at the very high rate of one volume for every eighteen months of his life. As a result, he belongs with the other studious, industrious writers who began writing successfully only in middle life: George Eliot's *Scenes from Clerical Life* was published when she was thirty-nine; Anthony Trollope's first successful novel, *The Warden,* appeard when he was forty; William Thackeray's *Vanity Fair* made him famous at thirty-five. Of course, many of Reade's novels were versions of his earlier plays, as has been observed in Chapter 1.

### I Peg Woffington (*1852*)

*Peg Woffington* was the narrative version of Reade's most famous comedy, *Masks and Faces*, for which Reade had the skilled assistance of dramaturgist Tom Taylor. Thus the novelist dedicated the work "to T. Taylor, Esq. My friend, and coadjutor in the comedy of 'Masks and Faces,' to whom the reader owes much of the best matter in this tale; and to the memory of Margaret Woffington, falsely *summed up* until to-day, this 'Dramatic Story,' is inscribed by Charles Reade. London, December 15, 1852."[2]

The basic plot is a familiar one: Mr. Ernest Vane, a wealthy gentleman from Shropshire, a man of learning, taste, and genuine love of the arts, visits London, goes to the theater, and is fascinated by Mrs. Peg Woffington, who is a great beauty and a comedian of great popularity in the city. He sends letters, flowers, and jewels; but it is his idealistic adoration of the actress and her art that wins her heart, especially when she compares him with blunt sensualists like Sir Charles Pomander, who considers his offer of coach, country house, and pin money a handsome honor. Mabel Vane, his country wife, arrives, just as Peg has decided, rather boldly, to introduce Vane to the love at which he is the merest beginner and to make him love as none of his sex had ever loved, "with heart, and brain, and breath, and life, and soul" (Chapter VII). Peg's furious disillusionment might set the page or the stage for stilettos, poison letters, and barbed female tongues — but Reade found a better way. The mistress and the wife meet (by Peg's posing in an empty picture frame), and they understand and sympathize with each other. But the weaker, simpler rustic persuades the beautiful, talented actress not only to relinquish her husband but to convince him that she has been untrue to him (an irony of which Reade seems entirely unconscious) and thus to return his heart to his wife.

Mabel's impassioned speech is the essence of Victorian effusion:

Oh, yes! you are beautiful, you are gifted, and the eyes of thousands wait upon your every word and look. What wonder that he, ardent, refined and genial, should lay his heart at your feet? And I have nothing but my love to make him love me. I cannot take him from you. Oh, be generous to the weak! Oh, give him back to me! What is one heart more to you? You are so rich, and I am so poor, that without his love I have nothing, and can do nothing but sit me down and cry till my heart breaks. Give him back to me, beautiful, terrible woman! For, with all your gifts, you cannot love him as his poor Mabel does; and I will love you longer perhaps than men can love. I

will kiss your feet, and Heaven above will bless you; and I will bless you and
pray for you to my dying day! (Chapter XIII)

As if this plea were not more than enough, the emotional young
sadist from the country reflects that she ought not to soil a woman's
reputation even to save her beloved Ernest, for "virtue is a woman's
crown." When the overwhelmed actress insists on making the
supreme sacrifice for her newfound friend, Mabel cries, "No, not
friend! sister! I will call you sister." Peg Woffington, now hopelessly
upstaged, cries out in horror "That sacred name to me, from lips so
pure as yours — Mrs. Vane, would you think me presumptuous if I
begged you to — to let me kiss you?"

In the final, enormously long Chapter XIII — as if the editor of
the journal had admonished the author to finish his tale — a husband of dubious value is returned to Mabel Vane, Sir Charles gives
Peg a diamond ring, and Peg returns to her proper setting, the stage.
The author confesses that his story "as a work of art" is over; if the
reader follows him further he is flattered, but the reader does so at
his own risk. This well-merited warning is followed by the Victorian
moral close: Pomander lives the life of a man of pleasure until sixty,
then becomes a man of pain (cause not specified) for eight years, and
dies miserable. Mabel Vane spends the "golden years preparing
herself and others for a still brighter eternity." Peg, engaged by Mr.
Sheridan to play in Dublin, becomes the dramatic toast of that wit-
tiest of cities; but, going to a small London church one Sunday afternoon, she repents of her supposedly sinful way of life and is soundly
converted. She gives herself to charity; and, when appealed to for
aid by a girl who wants to become an actress, she advises her to "fly
temptation." Because Reade could be a Puritan in print about the
actresses he loved all his life long above all other mortals, the story
shifts from a witty farce about the London stage and becomes a final
chapter in a Victorian *Pilgrim's Progress.* "When the great summons
came, it found her [Peg] full of hope, and peace, and joy; sojourning,
not dwelling, upon earth; far from dust, and din and vice; the Bible
in her hand, the Cross in her heart; quiet, amidst grass, and flowers,
and charitable deeds." Then, with a snobbishness that neither birth
in the county gentry nor education at Oxford could eradicate, Reade
closes with a cultured little Latin tag: *"Non omnem morituram."*

This novel, dedicated to a dramatist, straddles Reade's years
devoted to drama and his new and greater career in the novel. But it
shows that Reade kept one foot in each field — although the novel

was a fresh, new breeze blowing in the world of fiction, and although it contains the clear evidence of a new, vigorous, masculine talent, the narrative version nevertheless reflects the glare of the footlights since the best scenes depend upon stage effects. The chapters are really scenes in a play; the preponderance of dialogue appeals to the ear; and the portraiture is the caricature of the farce rather than the subtle suggestion of the novel. The reader easily becomes convinced that he is at a play, even though he does not applaud with the pit; when the volume ends, he feels the curtain drop; and he knows the lights are soon to be extinguished and the hall emptied.

Some scenes are so painfully close to vaudeville that they make little impression when read. When Peg Woffington, masquerading as Ann Bracegirdle, slips from a courtly gavotte with Colley Cibber into a lively Irish jig, she may rouse the gallery of the theater to enthusiasm; but she leaves the reader comparatively cold. The famous scene in which Peg cuts her face out of the lifeless portrait by Triplet and inserts her living head into the aperture, which is barely credible on the stage, becomes utterly farcical and tawdry in the novel. In George Meredith's *Harry Richmond,* Harry effectively substitutes his painted self for an equestrian statue about to be unveiled; but Reade's living portrait must be either a person or a portrait — not both.

Nonetheless, as lively comedy and sharp dialogue, the two scenes are perhaps the best that Reade ever wrote. In the first of the two (Chapter II), Colley Cibber contends that no modern actress can match those of the older generation. Peg Woffington ostensibly sends in an illustrious representative of that generation, Ann Bracegirdle; but Peg is actually masquerading as the aged actress while she slays every reputation past and present, acts several scenes from *The Rival Queens*, and then rebukes her aged contemporary, "Colley, at three-score years and ten, this was ill-done of us! You and I are here now — for what? to cheer the young up the hill we mounted years ago. And, old friend, if we detract from them we discourage them. A great sin in the old!"

In the second scene, the portrait scene (Chapter XIII), art critics arrive to scan the finished portrait. Looking directly at Peg's face in the canvas aperture, Kitty Clive says it is a pretty face and therefore not at all like Peg's; Quin remarks that she cannot know that, for since Peg's face is always painted, who knows what she really looks like? Snarl grumbles that art must represent the truth of life, and since this portrait is clearly not lifelike, it is not true art.

Although *Peg Woffington* bears all the marks of a play adapted for the printed page and marred by that dubious nineteenth-century taste that led Reade to describe Paxton's crystal palace as "the palace of the genii; the brightest idea and the noblest ornament added to Europe in this century — the koh-i-nor of the west" (Chapter XIII), the merits are those of a novelistic Robert Browning — athletic, vigorous, Christian, masculine. Thus, in the opening chapter or scene, Mrs. Triplet, an unsuccessful bit actress, enters her tenement room: "She came in rotatory with fatigue, and fell, gristle, into a chair; she wrenched from her brow a diadem and eyed it with contempt, took from her pocket a sausage, and contemplated it with respect and affection, placed it in a frying-pan on the fire, and entered her bedroom." Vigor of language, naturalistic detail, and gutter humor are evident in such a passage; and it is in no wise damaged by the sequel in which Mrs. Triplet falls asleep, the sausage spits on the fire, and poor Mr. Triplet is disturbed in his sleep by what sounds to the unsuccessful playwright like the hissing of the pit!

Reade's description of Peg as Sir Harry Wildair outraged the proprieties of his readers, not by gutter humor, but by sophistication of point of view: "She used little rouge, but that little made her eyes two balls of black lightning. . . . From her high instep to her polished forehead, all was symmetry. Her leg would have been a sculpter's glory; and the curve from her waist to her knee, was Hogarth's line itself" (Chapter III).

In addition to the values of vigor and humor, three characters of this first novel become portents of future characters by other names but with precisely the same characteristics. Peg is the brilliant, talented, beautiful woman who is enormously resourceful. Although she carries everything before her like a ship under full sail, she leaves all restored to order in the wake of her courageous, passionate passing. Mabel Vane is simple, demure, weak, and deceptively helpless; she leans, she twines, but her strength, like that of a vine, can quietly overcome the immense oak. The lesser in beauty, talent, and brilliance of mind, she always wins a moral victory over her gifted sister-rival.

Last, and certainly least, stands the unworthy cause of all the heroic struggle — the man described by Peg: the "poor heart we have both overrated shall be yours again, and yours for ever. In my hands it is painted glass: in the lustre of a love like yours it may become a priceless jewel." The status and the problem of the male in the triad is thus precisely shown. In the final analysis, even those women who love and labor for his possession are forced to confess that he is not worth the struggle, that, indeed, the only stature he possesses is the reflection of the great love they bear him! And this male deficiency tends to create a plot difficulty. The inconsistency of Vane's character as first presented — manly, humble, sincere, so different from the usual *habitués* of theatrical greenrooms — contrasts sharply with his later identification as the unfaithful husband of Mabel and the treacherous lover of Peg. When he, in turn, demands Mabel's word of honor that she has been and always will remain entirely faithful to him, the reader is disgusted by his hypocritical attempt to vault back into the moral eminence of a saddle already quitted.

Favorably as Reade regarded women, he yet inscribed a keyhole rampant on the coat of arms of the sex. No matter how great their integrity, nobility, purity, or virtue, his females show not the slightest hesitation about listening anywhere or anytime to private conversations. Peg hears her rightful rival's statement of her case while she is hiding within her own portrait; and, not to be bettered by a mere actress, the virtuous wife hides behind a chair in the hall to witness and hear her husband vow that he is willing to renounce credit, character, and indeed all the world to gain Peg.

## II  Christie Johnstone *(1853)*

Like *Peg Woffington, Christie Johnstone* was a one-volume work in an era of three-volume novels. Probably the inordinate length of Victorian novels was not so much a response to public demand as an accommodation to the powerful circulating libraries that fostered the impression that no writer of fiction was important who did not write at length. The padding of prose fiction created one of the paradoxes of nineteenth-century writing: to the intricately interwoven plots inherited from the eighteenth century was added the looseness of construction consequent upon the requirement for three-volume works. Authors were encouraged in their very worst propensities: the enormous galleries of stock characters, the little personal essays of the intrusive author, the riding of ideological hobbyhorses, the novel within the novel, and extensive sermonizing to fill out thin dialogue. From the authors' response to such a circulation demand arose the criticism of Thomas Seccombe that the Victorian novel is overweighted with "moral thesis, plot, under-plot, set characters, descriptive machinery, Herculean proportions, and the rest of the cumbrous and grandiose paraphernalia of *Chuzzlewit, Pendennis,* and *Middlemarch.*"³

By nature rebellious, Charles Reade not only refused to write novels of the expected length but also derided, in *Christie Johnstone,* such efforts. Saunders, Lord Ipsden's valet, "has in the press one of those cerberus-leviathans of fiction, so common now . . . Mr. Saunder's work will be in three volumes; nine hundred and ninety pages!!!!!! In other words, this single work, of this ingenious writer, will equal in bulk the aggregate of all the writings extant by Moses, David, Solomon, Isaiah, and St. Paul!!!" (Chapter XVII).

The plot of *Christie Johnstone* is characteristic in that two stories weave in and out; but it is uncharacteristic in that the aristocratic story (Viscount Ipsden - Lady Barbara) is really an elaborate Victorian frame for the salty, herring-flavored working-class romance (Charles Gatty - Christie Johnstone). Viscount Ipsden, twenty-five, handsome and rich, loves Lady Barbara Sinclair, who considers him a bored and boring dilettante. Dr. Aberford prescribes that the unhappy young lord should live with the poor and help someone every day. In the fishing village of Newhaven, Ipsden meets Christie, identifies with the poor fishermen, does good deeds, proves his manhood, and finally marries Lady Barbara. So much for the frame.

The picture portrays a splendid Nordic fisherwoman, Christie Johnstone, who loves an overmothered English artist named Charles Gatty. When she rescues him from drowning, Mrs. Gatty withdraws her objections to the match and the greathearted fishgirl is married to the finicking, fluctuating artist. The consensus, undenied by Reade's family, is that the Edinburgh fishwife with whom Reade was once in partnership in the operation of a fleet of herring boats may well have been the original of the delightful heroine of the novel. Christie Johnstone is all business in her canny Scottish handling of money but all heart in her impulsive dealing with men — perhaps the best Scottish heroine ever described by an Englishman. In Reade's portraits of the fishwives of Newhaven, women of Danish or Dutch ancestry who seldom intermarried with the native Scots, he delineates two favorite types of beauty that keep recurring in his works:

Of these young women, one had an olive complexion, with the red blood mantling under it, and black hair, and glorious black eyebrows. The other was fair, with a massive but shapely throat, as white as milk; glossy brown hair, the loose threads of which glittered like gold, and a blue eye, which being contrasted with dark eyebrows and lashes, took the luminous effect peculiar to that rare beauty. Their short petticoats revealed a neat ankle, and a leg with a noble swell; for Nature, when she is in earnest, builds beauty on the ideas of ancient sculpters and poets. . . . These women had a grand corporeal tract; they had never known a corset, so they were straight as javelins; they could lift their hands above their heads! — actually! (Chapter II)

This Junesque figure, large, strong, capable, and of a classic rather than a modern mold, seems to have haunted other writers of the period. George Meredith's Diana of the Crossways and Alfred Tennyson's Princess Ida are both tall, formed in the antique cast, and able to meet all alarms and disasters. Tennyson's *Princess* raises a question concerning Reade's view of women. In "Locksley Hall," the laureate calls woman "the lesser man"; at the close of *The Princess*, woman was neither "the lesser man," nor "undevelopt man," nor simply equal to man, but each sex was perfect in its own diversity. It is noteworthy that, in the same poem, the Prince's father accuses Princess Ida of holding the extreme view that woman is "the better man." In Reade's studies of women, he seems almost to agree with the Prince's father — except for the matter of women's capacity to judge men. For example, Peg Woffington had beauty, talent, and integrity; but could she discern the shallowness and falseness of Ernest Vane? No, she was fated, goddess of the stage, to love forever a mere mortal of the pit. Christie — strong, heroic in stature and in spirt, generous to a fault, and incapable of deception — is fated to love Charles Gatty, who is hysterical, contemptible, and vacillating.

When Charles meets and loves Christie, she does everything for him; but when his mother tells him to leave her, he agrees. When her girl friend Jean Carnie shames him into promising to come to Christie's picnic instead of Lady Barbara's, he breaks his promise. Lying in wait for Christie on her return from the party he had snubbed, he wins her forgiveness and all is well again. Why did he lie in wait for her? Because he realized that Christie has saved enough money to keep him while he paints. When her friend Ipsden, at Christie's request, buys a painting from him, thereby making Christie's support unnecessary, Charles leaves her instantly at his mother's command; vacillating, he starts to return; and then, in self-disgust, he swims far out to sea hoping to end his many indecisions. Christie rescues him without knowing his identity, simply because she is a greathearted woman and because an unknown man is drowning in the sea. And this man is the weak idiot that the massive

Christie must love and cherish all her life if Reade has his way! Such a man as Gatty, set beside Christie, makes one suspect that Reade disagreed with John S. Mill's doctrine of equal rights for women simply because he thought they were unspeakably superior in heart, brain, and strength to the heroes whom he commands them to love.[4]

Lady Barbara Sinclair, the other woman in the novel, is a pleasant bluestocking who demands that her lover do something worthwhile and who thereby sets free the latent heroism in Ipsden that she has never before had the wit to discern. She can spurn the pleasant Ipsden, but she is quite unable to fathom the shallow depths of a Carlylean disciple who waxes eloquent about the beauty of the Middle Ages, using as his stock examples Abbot Sampson and Joan of Arc. Through the character of Ipsden, Reade attacks Carlyle's affection for the twelfth century and his doctrine of hero-worship; Ipsden claims that Abbot Sampson and Joan of Arc are not examples of their age, but are the heroic exceptions; and then he classifies Carlyle himself, "with all his talent," as a member of "the class muddle-head" (Chapter IX).

The novel introduces that long procession of Reade's doctors who enliven the wit and tempo of his narratives. Dr. Aberford "was one of those globules of human quicksilver one sees now and then, for two seconds; they are, in fact, two globules; their head is one, invariably bald, round, and glittering; the body is another in activity and shape, *totus teres atque rotundus;* and in fifty years they live five centuries." For the Viscount's ennui and the broken heart consequent to the rejection of his suit for the hand of Lady Barbara, the good doctor prescribes: "Make acquaintance with all the people of low estate who have time to be bothered with you; learn their ways, their minds, and, above all, their troubles . . . fish the herring! Run your nose into adventures at sea; live on tenpence, and earn it . . . one pill per day" (Chapter I).

As for the style of *Christie Johnstone,* the total of nine exclamation marks in Reade's satire of trivoluminous novels is an example of the unorthodox punctuation that outraged critics and irritated the cultivated reader. In Chapter X, when Talbot is invited to play his violin, the complete musical score appears on two pages of the novel. When Viscount Ipsden, on his do-good errands, visits Jess Rutherford, whose husband was disabled by a falling mast, he promises her that she shall never again be in want. Mrs. Rutherford thanks him with an eloquence that rises to an astonishing peroration, both verbally and typographically: "An' O my boenny, boenny lad, may ye be wi' the rich upon the airth a' your days, AND WI' THE PUIR IN THE WARLD TO COME!'' Touching and comic as the words are, critics could not forgive the enormities of exclamation points, musical scores, and solid capitals.

When Charles Gatty and his little band of painters visit Edinburgh (Chapter VI), Charles Reade embarked upon the unfamiliar waters of art criticism. Gatty is a rebel who ironically quotes his academic teachers: "Now look here; the barren outlines of a scene must be looked at, to be done; hence the sketching system slop-sellers of the Academy! but the million delicacies of light, shade, and color, can be trusted to memory, can they?'' The proper reply to the rhetorical question is, of course, that outdoor scenes should be painted out of doors. But Reade ventures beyond this rather pedestrian realism;for, when Ipsden comes to buy a Gatty painting, he speaks with an authority that nothing in his previous experience might seem to justify. His dictum, expressed through Viscount Ipsden, is simply "Art is not imitation, but illusion" (Chapter XII). Perhaps Reade moves at this point ever so slightly from the representational school of art to the impressionism of a Jean Corot or a Joseph Turner.

Even after Reade has tied up all the loose ends of plot and has disposed of every destiny ever mentioned in the narrative, he cannot stop. He adds a four-page essay that is a prescription for happiness in marriage; in it he uses, of all daft examples, the union of that giantess Christie and pygmy Charles; and he ends, of course, describing the other side of Jordan and the bright spirits that walk there. Actually the necessity to include eternity in the future of a happily married couple is an interesting specimen of the era, one that, if used today, would be sensational to the point of outrage. But, if Reade may seem to the reader to have finished at last, the impression is mistaken, for a "NOTE" is appended. The story was written in 1850; the artist of 1853 was tempted to retouch some of the colors; but he finally decided to leave his refutation of Carlyle and his artistic doctrine of impressionism alone, "viz., that of containing genuine contemporaneous verdicts upon a cant that was flourishing like a peony, and a truth that was struggling for bare life, in the year of truth 1850."

When the note was finished, the author still was not through. The *Memoir* preserves an autocriticism in which the author now explains to the critics what an honest man who would avoid excesses of praise or blame should write about his *opus*.[5] The beginning of the essay includes these significant comments:

CHRISTIE JOHNSTONE. A Dramatic Story. The origin of this title appears to be the quantity of pure dialogue in the work. . . . The author of "Christie Johnstone" is full of details — but they are barren details. He deals in those minutiae which are valuable according to the hand that mixes them; but he has not the art of mixing his materials. Hence the compound, with some exceptions, is dry and lumpy.

This is to be the more regretted as the materials are in themselves decidedly good.

We have in this country some dozen ladies and gentlemen who have long ago written themselves dry; but any one of whom would have made a charming story with Mr. Reade's ideas.

The plot, which is of that arbitrary kind that befits a play rather than a story, can be disposed of in few words:

Like all weak plots, it runs in two channels, which are more independent than in rightly constructed fiction, whether story or play.

The remarkable aspect of this autocriticism, over and beyond its egotism, is that it quite accurately foretells the main lines of criticism that actually were taken against Reade's works. True, his novels have an astonishing quantity of pure dialogue. Contemporary and later critics agree that Reade's trust of vivid details and his distrust of his own imagination account for the richness and the lifelessness of his work. Then who but Reade would describe his novel as if it were bad biscuits or poor gravy — "dry and lumpy"? The complacency of the confession that the materials (or the plot structure) of the novel are "decidedly good" reveals Reade's reliance on plot rather than on character, setting, theme, or creativity.

But Reade's criticism also makes clear that he recognized that his plots, so derivative from the "contrived plays" of the French stage, were often arbitrary rather than organic. Instead of the plot being the things that would happen to that kind of person, it becomes a tissue of conventional coincidences, multiclimaxes, hairbreadth escapes, and other machinery of melodrama. In stating that his plot runs in two channels with a regrettable tendency to be too independent of each other, Reade anticipates his critics of almost a century later who noted his tendency to start with one stream; to break off and move to another stream; then quite consciously to call the readers' attention to what was happening; and to bring the two streams together to flow in one channel. Thus, what one might be tempted to dismiss as the *bagatelle* (or, as he preferred, *jeu d'esprit*) of a monumental ego playing godlike games with his own creations turns out to be one of the most factual, objective, and penetrating analyses of Charles Reade ever made.

## III   Art *(1855)*

One of the perplexing literary mysteries about Reade's works is the relationship between the dramas *Nance Oldfield* and *Masks and Faces* and the novels *Art* and *Peg Woffington*. The same year that Reade wrote his first successful drama, *Masks and Faces* (1852), he also wrote or had already written a play called *Nance Oldfield*, which by 1852 had not as yet been produced, although it was later produced in 1855 under the title *Art*. It was itself an adaptation from the French of Fournier's play *Tiridaté*. By 1855, Reade had written a novel taken from *Nance Oldfield* that he called *Art: A Dramatic Tale*; and, since it was only one volume in length, he published it with *Clouds and Sunshine*.

Emerging from the snarled mass of production and publication is the relationship of Nance Oldfield to Peg Woffington, for the two heroines are so much alike that the former seems to be a study for the latter. Indeed, since *Masks and Faces* (*Peg Woffington*) was highly successful as a stage play, and since it reveals in every detail a more sophisticated dialogue and a more essentially dramatic plot line, the writing order might well have been as indicated: first *Nance Oldfield*, 1852; second *Masks and Faces*, later in the same year.

In *Art: A Dramatic Tale*, Reade attempted to establish an artistic theory about the declaration of lines: "Let the stage voice and the dramatic voice . . . be kept apart upon separate stages, and there is no security that the public will not, as far as hands go, applaud the monotone or lie, more than the melodious truth. But set the lie and the truth side by side, upon fair terms, and the public becomes . . . critic; and stage bubbles, that have bubbled for years, are liable to burst in a single night." In order to set such voices "side by side," *The Rival Queens* is presented, within the play *Nance Oldfield*, with Mrs. Bracegirdle, the "stage voice," playing Roxana, and Mrs. Oldfield, "the artistic," playing Statira. Bracegirdle uses all her powers at the beginning, but Oldfield builds gradually to climax by way of contrast, not just by the duration of harsh monotony — and walks into her dressing room the queen of the English stage!

The actual plot of *Art* is quite conventional. Nathan Oldworthy, an elderly attorney of Coventry, sends his son Alexander to London to prepare for the bar. But Alexander has unfortunately written a manuscript tragedy, "Berenice." He goes to the theater, sees Mrs. Oldfield as Belvidera in Otway's *Venice Preserved*, falls in love with her, and returns six nights weekly to see her in all her roles. He rewrites his play as a vehicle for the actress and submits it to Susan, a cousin and dependent of the actress. The theater becomes his real world, and life is only an interlude between its scenes. But, hearing no word from his idolized actress, he falls ill and confesses all to Timothy Bateman, a London attorney whom his father had asked to oversee his education.

When Nathan arrives in London and discovers the cause of his son's inertia, he rudely invades Mrs. Oldfield's privacy; and she finally promises to disenchant his son. She admits the young man when her hair is disheveled and her figure is carefully disguised in an old, baggy dressing gown. She claims she does not understand half of what authors give her to say, asks Alexander if he wants a free pass to the pit, and tells him he must promise to clap hard. When he confesses his adoration, she tells him he can be one of her twenty beaux. She offers him snuff, which he declines, but which she uses copiously. When he inquires about his tragedy, which she has sincerely admired without realizing that he is the author, she replies in words that must have occasioned an autobiographical twinge in Reade's breast, "Plead, Alexander, plead, and rhyme no more!" (*Art*, p. 20).

Alexander is cured of his stagestruck adoration by this harsh treatment, but he sinks into a decline; and Reade must, of course, now play the game the opposite direction: Nathan pleads with Anne Oldfield to be kind to his son. Meanwhile, she has discovered that Alexander had been her rescuer in a coach accident. When she invites the young playwright to discuss his play with her, his father practically has to carry him to her home. She plays to the poet the role he had prepared for her so superbly that, as Reade puts it, "Love, taste, and vanity were all gratified at once." Using the modern psychiatric technique of dramatic therapy, Anne casts Oldworthy as the inexorable consul about to curse his son, Susan as the jealous Tibulla, and Alexander as Tiberius. Then she bundles them, all cured and happy, out of her house at the stroke of three because plays began in those days at five and she has to prepare for her performance in *The Rival Queens*. Although Alexander remains her admirer, the poet and the actress do not marry (shades of Reade's Mrs. Seymour!). Instead, as a good and lifelong friend, she persuades him to foresake dramatic authorship and to return to law. He lives to be eighty-six; she dies at forty-seven; noblemen and gentlemen vie to hold her pall as they bear her to Westminster Abbey to be interred near the poets "whose thoughts took treble glory from her, while she adorned the world" (*Art*, p. 288).

From this plot analysis, it is apparent that the plots of both works are only loosely related, although Reade's favorite double *fausse sortie* is used in each: in *Masks and Faces*, not only must the actress relinquish the husband, she must also disenchant him; in *Nance Oldfield*, Nathan pleads first that his son be disenchanted for the sake of his professional career and then that his son be reenchanted for the sake of his health. But it is also apparent that Nance and Peg are closely related portraits — so closely related that, if they are not mother and daughter, they are at least sisters under the skin.

### IV    Clouds and Sunshine (*1855*)

Charles Reade published the story "The Box Tunnel" in the November issue of *Bentley's Miscellany* in 1853, and *Art: A Dramatic Tale* followed in the December and January issues. *Clouds and Sunshine* was serialized in four installments during the summer of 1854. "The Box Tunnel" might be considered a short story, but *Art* and *Clouds and Sunshine* are clearly novelettes. Four years later, in his source books for fiction and other literary projects, Reade jotted down his attitude, dated 1858 toward short fiction in a "Digest," under the heading "memoranda agenda" (59): "The short story of the nineteenth century is one of the blunders of the age: it is a flabby anecdote generally without a true anecdote's backbone. . . . This gap in fiction I mean to try and fill, with the aid of others: and I shall use the aid of others, for I hope to stir up an original writer in this kind, for I have hardly time or fertility to fill so large a gulf." In *Christie Johnstone*, Reade ridiculed the prevailing "trivoluminousness" of the circulating libraries. The rebellion in *Clouds and Sunshine* is milder, perhaps because the champion of fictional brevity is growing tired of rowing against the current. Reade lets ridicule dwindle to one feeble joke — paper is not absolutely valueless, whatever the "trivoluminous" may think.

The novelette *Clouds and Sunshine* is essentially a pastoral romance in which the biblical imagery of the dramatic version — *Rachel the Reaper* — is thoroughly eclipsed by the solid British reverence for property. The story begins in the rural setting of *It Is Never Too Late to Mend* (1856) and, astonishingly, stays there. The hero never departs on a journey; instead, the heroine is the one who travels from afar. Excitement in the tale is generated by the thrill of property ownership. Will Rose marry the son of her tenant farmer and thus raise his economic status? Will Aunt Clayton leave her property to Rachel, thereby making it worthwhile for Hickman to marry the heiress already carrying his child? Can Squire Phillips be forced to disgorge Uxmoor Farm, which rightfully belongs to Rose Mayfield? When Jack White, the graceless nephew, ungratefully demolishes the house bequeathed by his aunt, her true will leaving all to Rachel is discovered in a tottering wall. Now no word is spoken of her affair with Hickman, and no problem raised about the birth of an illegitimate child — all has been hallowed by the sanctifying touch of property: a good broad farm and two thousand pounds in the bank!

One odd characteristic of the story is that nothing is ideal. Vivacious Rose is a widow; pale Rachel has borne a child out of wedlock, Hickman is an adventurer; White is a ne'er-do-well. Robert (the hero) is a first-rate curmudgeon, and his self-righteous father really cares only that his son marry a woman of property. Somehow the cast of characters and the moods of the hero and the heroine sound more like those of Thomas Hardy's Wessex novels than the usually Simon-pure innocents of Charles Reade.

Reade novels that begin briskly and weave exposition into breathtaking narration often come to a slow close. At the beginning of Chapter X, Reade states the undeniable truth that, "when everybody sees how a story will end, the story is ended." Nevertheless, there follows a prolonged authorial essay addressed to the impatient reader, that is climaxed by a benediction in the last paragraph of the book almost identical to the one delivered by the old Jew Levi in Reade's drama *Gold.* "Friendly reader, (for I have friendly as well as unfriendly readers,) I do not wish you a day without a cloud, for you are human, and I, though a writer, am not all humbug. But in ending this tale, permit me to wish you a bright afternoon, and a tranquil evening, and above all, a clear sky when the sun goes down."

## V   White Lies: A Story (1857)

*White Lies*, published by Trübner in December, 1857, continued the conformity to the trivoluminous style that Charles Reade had established with *It Is Never Too Late to Mend* (1856). As he related in *The Eighth Commandment*, the novel was built on his play, *The Double Marriage* (not produced until 1867), which in turn was based on a play by August Maquet entitled *Le Château Grantier*. When *White Lies* first appeared in the *London Journal*, the editor, Mark Lemon, doubtless hoped to repeat Richard Bentley's enormous success with the publication of Reade's *It Is Never Too Late to Mend*.

But *White Lies* was an entirely different sort of story, as Robert Louis Stevenson observed when he likened this tale of bigamy set against the background of the French Revolution to a foretaste of the style and subject matter of the novelist Ouida. Reade was quite frank about the genesis of the novel and also about the reason why it was written at that particular time. He considered both *White Lies* and *Love Me Little, Love Me Long* to be nothing more than potboilers: the former was written to defray the expensive lawsuits against the pirates of his drama *Poverty and Pride*; the latter, to provide the money to publish *The Eighth Commandment*. "I sat down," he said, "to write a pack of fibs. . . . One or two honest fellows came about me, animated with a friendly warmth, to bid for the coming fibs. I bled them."[6]

*White Lies* opens with a melodramatic scene that in style is pure Victor Hugo. When the Governor reads his list of French soldiers who have defected to the enemy, he finds there the name of Captain Camille Dujardin. The rusty scarecrow standing before him is the captain, and the governor contemptuously regards the traitor. But the scarecrow draws off his coat and shows a white scar on his shoulder, a long cicatrix on one arm, and a raw wound on his chest. He demands to know if the governor can read this history that tells of capture and imprisonment as something that is not treachery. "The wounded man put his rusty coat on again, and stood erect, and haughty, and silent. The general eyed him, and saw his great spirit shining through this man." In reply to the governor's more respectful questions, the hero explains that he has suffered cold, hunger, darkness, wounds, solitude, sickness, despair, and prison. Indeed, he would have died a dozen deaths but for one thing: "I had promised her [Josephine] to live." Considering the Gallic setting, it is only natural that both Reade's earlier French dramatic translation, *The Ladies' Battle*, and the opening scene of the novel *White Lies* should be strongly indebted to French playwrights and novelists.

*It Is Never Too Late to Mend* marked Reade's first use of the hero away from home — a situation that made possible two separate series of incidents and that specialized in the heroine who is caught in the Enoch Arden dilemma of thinking the hero is dead but being uncertain about the time and place of his demise. This pattern, which is of occasional usefulness to the most sophisticated of novelists and playwrights, is important to the dynamics of *Peg Woffington*, *It Is Never Too Late to Mend*, *White Lies*, *The Cloister and the Hearth*, *Hard Cash*, *Griffith Gaunt*, *Foul Play*, *Put Yourself in*

*His Place, A Simpleton, The Wandering Heir* — to practically all of Reade's major works. But in *White Lies*, Reade even has the colossal bad taste to play the game of *fausse sortie* four times over with the same quartet of characters.

Dujardin is captured in battle and imprisoned. His betrothed, Josephine, is led to believe that he has forgotten her and has become a traitor to France. His commandant, Raynal, marries Josephine out of a sense of duty to his former friend and subordinate, Dujardin. Just after the newly married Raynal rides off to duty in Egypt, Dujardin, of course, comes tottering down the long drive of Beaurepaire. Then, after he has been nursed to health, and after Madame Raynal has admitted that she still loves him although she has married his friend, official word arrives that Raynal is dead in Egypt; and Madame, a widow, marries Dujardin privately but legally. Then a letter arrives from Egypt explaining that the commandant is recovering nicely from a wound received in battle and has just been promoted to colonel. At this point, the confused Dujardin obeys Josephine's plea to leave the house forever. Just after his departure, Josephine becomes aware that she is pregnant; and Colonel Raynal returns to find her playing with Dujardin's child, who has been born in secrecy. Asked for an explanation, Josephine's sister Rose claims the child is the fruit of a secret *amour* of her own, thus saving Josephine, destroying her own reputation, and revealing just how many times Charles Reade was willing to play the game of *fausse sortie*.

The extended war passage in which Dujardin destroys the immense gun, Long Tom (Chapter XXI), is as sentimental and melodramatic as the incidents of the French Revolution and the taste of the Victorian era. Charles Reade claimed to be a sensational writer; and the broad canvas, the vivid colors, the abrupt contrasts, the supernaturally good heroine, the superhumanly brave hero, and the startling effects and hairbreadth escapes of weekly fiction certainly justify his claim. Although one senses that these are little boys playing with toy soliders, they are nevertheless having a wonderful time. The callousness with which Mark Twain's Connecticut Yankee at King Arthur's court destroyed fifteen thousand knights in armor like mere sardines sealed in their own tin cans is akin to the marvelous dexterity of Charles Reade's underground tunnels, his logistics of battle, and his total forgetfulness that, in order for the marvelous strategy to work, thousands of men must lose their lives. But, as is characteristic of the sentimental Victorian novel, the death of a single hero must be strung out and wrung dry of every lachrymose possibility, although thousands may perish unnoted and unsung. This element is all of a piece with the marvelously histrionic canvas battles that covered the walls of public and private buildings in the nineteenth century, in which the horses roll their agonized eyes; the hero, classically disrobed, is wounded and nobly dying; and the bugles call to further action. All is decorously enclosed in a rich gold frame with an inner velour border.

Reade seems always to have conceived of his novelistic characters as actors in a drama taking place on the frontal lobes of his brain, yet he was quite capable of changing a role disastrously in midscene. Josephine is the daughter who never thinks of herself, asks only how she can please others (Lucy Fountain, *Hard Cash*; Arabella Bruce, *A Terrible Temptation*), and finds rich pleasure in obeying those she loves. But when Perrin, the notary, affronts her mother, the baroness, the dove instantly becomes a falcon:

Josephine de Beaurepaire came from her chair with one gesture of her body between her mother and the notary, who was advancing with arms folded in a brutal, menacing way — not the Josephine we have seen her, the calm languid beauty, but the demoiselle de Beaurepaire — her great heart on fire — her blood up — not her own only, but all the blood of all the de Beaurepaires — pale as ashes with great wrath, her purple eyes on fire, and her whole panther-like body full of spring. "Wretch! you dare to insult her, and before me! *Arrière misérable!* or I soil my hand with your face!" . . . The towering threat and the flaming eye and the swift rush buffeted the caitiff away: he recoiled. She followed him as he went, strong, *for a moment or two*, as Hercules, beautiful and terrible as Michael driving Satan." (Chapter IV)

Reade was always very fond of the Junoesque type; since he neglected to include one who met the usual specifications in the *dramatis personae*, he simply transformed one of the other characters, a most unlikely one, into Juno, albeit he ran into some confusion of gender with references to Hercules and Michael. The author had the grace to recognize the magnitude of the transformation required, however; and he admitted that Josephine is not the woman previously seen but is, instead, the incarnate spirit of her family and race.

Reade was often, and perhaps exaggeratedly, praised for his understanding of the female point of view. Women, he opines in Chapter XIV, are good for the short run but ill-equipped for the long

haul. Thus, "do not look for a Bacona, a Newtona, a Handella, a Victoria Huga." Some American ladies, Reade claimed, consider this
defect to be produced by a limited and limiting education. But the
British expert on women replies that it is a defect of nature: "They
can bubble letters in ten minutes that you could no more deliver to
order in ten days than a river can play like a fountain." After that
comforting metaphor assuring men that they are rivers and that
women are only playful little fountains, the male sage on women
continues: "They can sparkle gems of stories; they can flash little
diamonds of poems. The entire sex has never produced one opera
nor one epic that mankind could tolerate; and why? these come by
long, high-strung labour. But, weak as they are in the long run of
everything but the affections (and there giants), they are all over-
powering while their gallop lasts. Fragilla shall dance any two of you
flat on the floor before four o'clock, and then dance on till the peep
of day." However, the stalwart male, the evening before flat on the
ballroom floor, rises in the morning, goes to work as usual, and could
go on again to dance the following night. But flighty Fragilla? "She
who danced you into nothing is in bed, a human jelly tipped with
headache."

## VI   The Bloomer (1857)

Charles Reade wrote not only a number of studies of women but
at least one and possibly two works on feminism. Appearing first in
Bentley's *Miscellany*, Reade's *Bloomer* was later included, along
with *Art: A Dramatic Tale*, and *Clouds and Sunshine*, in the volume
published by Richard Bentley in 1857 under the general title *The
Course of True Love Never Did Run Smooth*. The historical origin of
the book lay in the agitation of Mrs. Amelia Bloomer, *circa* 1850, of
Seneca Falls, New York, for sensible clothing for women. Editor of
the *Lily* and wife of an eminent lawyer, Mrs. Bloomer had the sang-
froid not only to wear her ghastly garments but to recommend them
to others: a short skirt, loose trousers buttoned around the ankle, and
a broad-brimmed, low-crowned hat.[7] Reade, however, either had
some misapprehension concerning the nature of the costume
recommended and its difference from the garments worn by his
heroine, Caroline Courtenay, or redesigned it himself for the very
good reason that the costume as originally suggested by the lady
from upper New York was entirely indefensible. Caroline's costume
looks quite unlike the bulbous monstrosities people who attended
public school during the 1920s and 1930s called bloomers; "she

stood in the threshold erect yet lithe, the serpentine lines of youthful female beauty veiled yet not disguised in vest, and pantaloons of marvelous cut — neat little collars, dapper shoes, and gaiters, delicious purple broad-cloth" (Chapter III).

Reade called his novelette a *jeu d'esprit*, written for amusement only, without any of the usual intention to improve, instruct, or elevate. Yet this light little book, a return to the briefer form with which Reade was originally most at home, is one of the most delightful, brisk, and downright funny works he ever wrote. It recaptures the high spirits of *Peg Woffington* and *Christie Johnstone* without having either the hairbreadth escapes of the latter or the moral platitudes of the former.

In this novel, Richard Courtenay, the younger son of a good Devonshire family, migrates to America and by putting his little inheritance into commerce, dies far richer than the elder son who had inherited Courtenay Court. Richard's son John, a staunch republican who likes to twist the tail of the British lion and who grows richer still, decides to buy the ancestral estate in England when he sees it advertised for sale in an American newspaper. He is welcomed at the lodge gate by an old man who sings out (Chapter II) — "Oh! Master John, how like you be to Master Richard sure*ly*." He sleeps in the ancestral chamber, advises the county gentry on American investments, becomes a justice of the peace, and, dying, leaves everything to his young daughter Caroline, who lives in New York. She remains there until she meets young Reginald Seymour, heir of the neighboring estate, who is on a tour of the States. She falls in love with Reginald, but knows she will alienate him by her promise to wear bloomers at a forthcoming ball. As an apologia-in-advance, she presents a witty little pageant proving that trousers can be highly feminine (by the example of Turkish women) as well as far more practical and graceful than ball gowns. Through this dramatic means she also comments on the British custom of exposing the shoulder and bosom but carefully covering the ankle. She carries off her demonstration with flair and bravado, but Reginald has to admit that his prejudice is stronger than his love, and he leaves for England.

The Reverend James Tremaine, curate of Conyton, and a friend of both families, breaks the deadlock. Calling upon the young Seymour heir when he assumes residence in his English estate, Tremaine first suggests the study of geology as the sure cure for a broken heart. Just as Tennyson in *The Princess*, published ten years earlier, had recommended the study of geology and evolution to enlarge the minds of women, the curate claims that science "lifts you out of this ignorant present, and transports you into various stages of this earth's existence: you learn on its threshold what a mushroom in this world's great story is the author of the pyramids." Then, rushing on with the zeal of an enthusiast, he exults:

> You find that the earth was red hot for millions of years, and spouted liquid stone like a whale: in that stone look for no sign of vegetation, and still fewer of life. Then for millions of years the heat of its upper crust has been cooling, and water depositing rubbish which has coagulated into stone; and in this stratified stone you shall find things that lived or grew very late in the world's history, in fact within a few million years only, at least I think so, since the flesh of mammoths had been found in ice in our own day, and was eaten by our contemporaries the wolves. (Chapter V)

So Reade makes his claim to march with the scientific avant garde.

When the clergyman visits the American heiress, he follows an even more inspired course of logic. He tricks her by seeming to say that Mrs. Bloomer would set one-third of the women of a nation at variance with the other two-thirds. When Caroline falls into the trap by insisting that Mrs. Bloomer wished to dress all the women in bloomers, the curate slyly demurs,

> No, excuse me, how would old women, and fat women look in a Bloomer? How would young matrons look, at that period, when a woman is most a woman? No, the dress for women must clearly be some dress that becomes all women, at all times and occasions of life. There are plenty of boys of sixteen or seventeen, who could be dressed as women, and eclipse all the women in a ball room; but it would be indelicate and unmanly. You, with your youthful symmetrical figure, could eclipse most young men in their own habiliments: but it would be indelicate and unwomanly. Forgive me, I distress you! (Chapter VII)

She replies, that he has convinced her; but when the cleric sends her lover to seek forgiveness, Caroline waits for him at the bridge, dressed in — a bloomer! Of course the reference to beautiful boys sounds daringly Renaissance, and the reference to the symmetrical slenderness of his hostess's form is as daringly un-Victorian. But both Tennyson in *The Princess* and Reade in a number of works expressed surprising interests in transvestism. The most Victorian note is the high status of a clergyman in the world of the Evangelical Revival, and such clergymen are very different from the eighteenth-century clerics of Richardson and Fielding, who are scarce a step above the butler who meets them at the door and the chambermaid who prepares their rooms.

One of Reade's convenient coincidences saves the day: the bridge breaks; Reginald falls into the stream. Caroline laughs; then, seeing Reginald is drowning, she leaps in and is able to save his life — all because she is wearing a fitted bloomer instead of a voluminous dress. The pace of the narrative is breakneck; interest never flags; yet many of the scenes are the kind of slapstick that is more effectively viewed on the stage than visualized on a printed page. An example is the comic scene in the kitchen when Elisa, the cook, wants to wear pantaloons or bloomers for perfectly practical reasons, and Mrs. Trimmer the housekeeper tells her to leave her employment immediately. "Hold your tongue — no woman shall stay a day in this house who thinks to put on that *im*moral, *on*delicate, *on*decent ah! ah! ah!' Trimmer screamed, put her nose out straight in the air — put on her spectacles and screamed again. Miss Courtenay stood at the door in a suit of propria quae maribus!!!"Chapter III.

### VII   Griffith Gaunt: or Jealousy *(1866)*

In January, 1866, the first installment of *Griffith Gaunt* appeared in *Argosy*, a monthly periodical edited by Mrs. Henry Wood. Illustrated by William Small, the serial run concluded in the November issue; by that time, the novel had already been published the previous month in three volumes in England by Chapman and Hall and in America by a long-standing agreement with Ticknor and Fields, who used it serially in the *Atlantic Monthly* before issuing it in book form. Of this novel, Reade claimed that "the whole credit and discredit of 'Griffith Gaunt,' my masterpeice, belongs to me, its sole author and original vendor." ("The Prurient Prude" *Readiana*, p. 432). It is certainly true that the novel was written in the period when he was at the top of his form, for *The Cloister and the Hearth* had been completed only five years before, and *Hard Cash* was the only novel written in the interval between *The Cloister* and *Griffith Gaunt*.

Other writers and critics of the period were inclined to agree with the author's estimate of *Griffith Gaunt*. Algernon Charles Swinburne claimed that "no language can overpraise what hardly any praise can sufficiently acknowledge — the masterly construction, the sustained intensity of interest, the keen and profound pathos, the perfect and triumphant disguise of triumphant and perfect art, the living breath of passion, the spontaneous and vivid interaction of character and event, the noble touches of terror and the sublimer strokes of pity, which raise this story almost as high as prose can climb towards poetry, and set it perhaps as near as narrative can come to drama."[8] W. L. Courtney pointed out in 1889 the practically pleasing consideration that Messrs. Chatto and Windus, who produced the popular edition of Reade's works, could probably testify that, at the time of their publication, no novel commanded a better sale in America and the British colonies, as well as in England.[9]

The novelist of sensation did well to choose for this novel those emotions that are strong enough to survive the overwhelming bulk of incident beneath which they are usually buried in the fiction of the time. Reade's subtitle is *Jealousy*, and the writer portrays this emotion from the first scene, in which Griffith Gaunt shows Kate "the livid passion of jealousy writhing in every lineament of a human face," to the last scene, in which Gaunt shows the same "ugly and agonized expression of countenance" to a young surgeon who, with the zeal of a medical enthusiast, proposes to transfuse some of his own blood into Kate's veins to save her from sure death. Thus the book falls into that comedy of "humours," *à la* Ben Jonson or Jean Baptiste Molière, in which a single obsessive human passion is not so much explored as repeatedly exhibited.

It may perhaps seem strange to treat a book entitled *Griffith Gaunt* in a chapter entitled "Studies of Women." But the title of the novel might much more appropriately have been "Catherine Peyton," since she is clearly the dominant character, as well as the one through whose eyes all the events are seen. The author falls into the laudatory judgment of women and the pejorative judgment of men that he had shown from the very beginning of his career. Just as Peg Woffington shone both in the novel and in the drama, and just as Christie Johnstone glowed on her native brine, so Kate Peyton casts all others in the shade from the first excellent paragraphs of description:

Miss Catherine Peyton was a young lady of ancient family in Cumberland, and the most striking, but least popular, beauty in the county. She was very tall and straight, and carried herself a little too imperiously; yet she would sometimes relax and all but dissolve that haughty figure, and hang sweetly drooping over her favorites: then the contrast was delicious, and the woman fascinating.

Her hair was golden and glossy; her eyes a lovely gray; and she had a way of turning them on slowly and full, so that their victim could not fail to observe two things: 1st, That they were grand and beautiful orbs; 2d, that they were thoughtfully overlooking him instead of looking at him.

So contemplated by glorious eyes, a man feels small and bitter. (Chapter I)

Just as Reade has a Juno — brilliant, splendid, full of noble passions and generous pride — he has to have a Phoebe as her foil, a woman simple, tender, extremely feminine. Peg Woffington was matched with Mabel Vane; Christie Johnstone with Lady Barbara; and Kate has her Mercy Vint — although Mercy is also a rather large, capable woman. In Reade's third study of bigamy (*Peg, White Lies,* and *Griffith Gaunt*), the confrontation in the first one of the dominant fiancée-heroine Peg Woffington and the true wife Mabel Vane is repeated in the prison conference of Catherine Gaunt and Mercy Leicester; but the episode is reversed. In each case, the true wife must win the struggle in order to preserve the Victorian proprieties, but the female types are switched: Mercy is the Mabel type, but she must lose because she is a bigamous wife; Kate is the Peg type, and she must win because she is the true wife.[10]

Perhaps because the female rivals in *Griffith Gaunt* are so well matched in their obvious strength and subtle weakness, the author establishes as the center of their tumultuous passions a lone, contemptible man who is utterly unworthy of all the tumult. Griffith Gaunt, a tongue-tied squire, hunter, drinker, and bon vivant, gets so much more than he ever deserved that he has no comprehension of how prodigally he has been blessed. Gaunt, then, stands in the ignoble tradition of Ernest Vane and Charles Gatty; but Sir George Neville, the man Kate obviously ought to have married, is a more masculine, less languorous Lord Ipsden.

Just as the old sexual triangle is reestablished, so a dual line of action is predicated: the hero and the heroine, and the hero and Mercy Vint. These lines weave in and out until the confrontation occurs between the two women who engage in Reade's usual feminine battle for the custody of the worthless male. Of course, Reade's overworked Doctor Number One always bleeds his patients to the brink of death, or even over the brink; but Mercy is there to follow Reade's homeopathic prescription of wine and soup, so there is no need to call on the services. of Doctor Number Two. The two Catholic clerics — Father Francis and Brother Leonard — Reade handles very well for a Protestant writer in an Evangelical period.

Father Francis, the practical cleric of Browning's "Bishop Blougram's Apology," counsels Kate, when she decides to settle her choice between two lovers by rejecting both and taking to the veil: "we want no poor nuns . . . you must marry . . . the heir to your husband's estates [the richer of the two candidates, of course] will be a Catholic, and so the true faith get rooted in the soil." But, beyond the blunt honesty of the practical churchman, Father Francis is a warm, firm characterization, a balanced personality of real attractiveness and power.

When he is replaced by Brother Leonard, however, Kate is both frozen by his function as spiritual adviser and thrilled by his power as a preacher. Later, after Griffith has left his wife in jealous anger at her supposed infatuation with the priest, Father Francis returns and bluntly states the healthy and needed truth that it was Kate's fault for letting a young priest just out of seminary, five years her junior, interfere between husband and wife and withdraw her from the world and her husband's companship. He turns upon the self-righteous wife with full force — if one adds Leonard's romantic notions of women to Kate's romantic idea that all priests are angels, the consequence is that a truly dedicated, sensitive, and spiritual priest ends by being in love with his parishioner's wife!

Interestingly enough, this novel is almost never discussed as a study of mixed religious marriage, which it certainly explores in far more depth than the jealousy theme that provides the springs of action. The treatment of the doomed, romantic infatuation of the celibate priest for the married woman is handled in a manner that suggests Reade's own problem of an Oxford living that was his only until he married and of a housekeeper-friend who was married to someone else. This autobiographical twinge, which adds passion to the romance of Catherine and Gerard in *The Cloister and the Hearth,* gives at least fervor to the entirely discreet situation in *Griffith Gaunt.*

Passages in the novel once again proclaim Reade's rather extraordinary courage in hazarding some of the taboos of his time. Caroline Ryder, Kate's maid, is in love with Griffith. Just as Father Leonard is often described in diction that has the connotation of effeminacy, so Caroline, a perfectly normal and healthy young woman, has what Reade considers to be masculine traits — in particular, roving eyes and a roving heart. A married woman, she has been separated from her husband and has had many lovers in her short life. She appears to be decent, respectable, and gracious; but Reade sums her up as "a female rake; but with the air of a very prude" (Chapter XVIII). She is bold enough to counsel the priest that, since he is suspected of evil, he might as well enjoy its reality (Chapter XXIV). When Kate falls on the stairs, Reade describes Griffith as, sexually speaking, "a widower." Later, when Gaunt returns to his rightful wife, she woos him in the day, the wines seduce him at night, and he ends up in her bedchamber instead of the guestroom he had occupied the night before. As a result, the servants treat him once again with respect because he has proved "he was the master of the house" (Chapter XXXIII). Finally, when Caroline Ryder confesses her love to Gaunt, Reade philosophizes that "scarcely one man out of a dozen, sick, sore, and hating her he loved, would have turned away from the illicit consolation thus offered to him in her hour of weakness, with soft seducing tones, warm tears, and heart that panted at his ear" (Chapter XXIV).

Although many critics applauded Reade's effort in *Griffith Gaunt*, others, and some of the same as well, had striking criticisms to make. *Blackwood's* review, otherwise extraordinarily laudatory, insisted that the conclusion ruined the book. Gaunt should have died somewhere out of sight of the reader, disappeared into some nameless grave; but he ought not to have returned after betrayal, denial, and bigamy, and settled right back into being the master of his wife's house. "When Kate, who has had to defend herself from the charge of murdering him, returns home, her husband turns up too after a while, very penitent, and headachy, and miserable, and after various scenes, which are very artificial, a perfect reconciliation ensues, with babies galore, and the other orthodox evidences of conjugal beatitude."[11]

The same reviewer raises the quite cogent question of Reade's disposition of Mercy Vint, Gaunt's bigamous wife. Could "the proud Sir George Neville, who has been Kate's chivalrous and respectful 'servant' for ever so many years, fall in love with the publican's daughter, and bring her, as Lady Neville, to the immediate neighbourhood of the man with whom she has been so fatally connected?" The reviewer also points out that, if there is some question about the innkeeper's daughter's making an acceptable Lady Neville, is there not also the same question in *Christie Johnstone* about Christie's making just the ideal wife for a painter? Perhaps Mrs. Gatty had, after all, the better part of wisdom in questioning the relationship of fish and paint. And as for her relatives, much though Charles Gatty admired the physical perfection of his wife's young brother Flucker, Gatty was a born snob who would scarcely relish those occasions when Flucker, the mate of a merchantship, came to call, and, as soon as he was within hailing distance of the house, would shout his arrival in such roars as to bring all the neighbors to their windows in scandalized amazement.

Even Swinburne, after his words of praise, noted one point at which the author's psychology seems badly muddled. Griffith Gaunt is legally bound to a wife whom he believes to be unfaithful. Inadvertently, he has won the heart of a young, simple country woman who has nursed him back to health. Recognizing her essential innocence and knowing that he cannot offer her marriage, he honestly decides to leave. But in the process of his departure he is taunted by an old suitor of Mercy who now hopes to reoccupy his former place in her affections. "Instantly, rather than face the likelihood of a rival's triumph the coward [Griffith Gaunt] turns back and offers his hand to the girl, whose good offices he requites by deliberate betrayal of her trust and innocence to secret and incurable dishonour. This is no more an act of jealousy than murder by slow poison is an act of impatience. It is an act of envy; and one of the basest on record in fiction or in fact."[12]

Another contemporary critic saw the novel in a different light. Justin McCarthy regarded *Griffith Gaunt* as a grim and dreary book — in fact, a tiresome book. "I regard [it] as a falling off, because it is a sour, unpleasant, and therefore inartistic book . . . but I saw nothing in it which could with any justice be said to have the slightest tendency to demoralize any reader."[13] The last comment brings into focus the furious charges against the book, which are hard to believe at this remove in time and place. When the book was published in America, didactic moralists were in such a state of hysterical indignation that charges of indecency and immorality were hurled at the book before it was on the booksellers' shelves. As usual, Reade rushed to his own defense, this time with a splendid statement by the inspired title "The Prurient Prude." The force of the rebuttal can be suggested by the opening of the article: "Sir, — There is a kind of hypocrite that has never been effectually exposed, for want of an expressive name. I beg to supply that defect in our language, and introduce to mankind the PRURIENT PRUDE. . . . 'Doctor Johnson,' said a lady, 'what I admire in your dictionary is that you have inserted no improper words.' 'What! you looked for them, madam?' said the Doctor. Here was a 'PRURIENT PRUDE,' that would have taken in an ordinary lexicographer" ("The Prurient Prude," *Readiana*, p. 442).

Very succinctly, Reade stated his case as author.

I have produced a story called "Griffith Gaunt, or Jealousy." This story has, ever since December, 1865, floated *The Argosy*, an English periodical, and has been eagerly read in the pages of *The Atlantic Monthly*. In this tale . . . I have to portray a great and terrible passion, Jealousy, and show its manifold consequences, of which even Bigamy (in my story) is one. . . . I fill my readers with a horror of Bigamy, and a wholesome indignation against my principal male character, so far as I have shown him. Of course "Griffith Gaunt," like "Hard Cash," is not a child's book, nor a little girl's book: it is an ambitious story, in which I present the great passions that poets have sung with applause in all ages; it is not a boatful of pap; but I am not paid the price of pap. ("The Prurient Prude," *Readiana*, p. 427)

In his own period, such a reply must have broken new critical ground since the invariable touchstone seems to have been, "Would I like to have my young daughter read this book, or see this play?"

Then, having quite adequately met any reasonable criticism, Reade hurls himself into a headlong and impetuous attack upon his attackers: I am "well accustomed to that sort of injustice and insolence from scribblers who could not write my smallest chapter to save their carcasses from the gallows, and their souls from premature damnation . . . scribblers whose lives are loose, and their conversation obscene; they take my text and read it, not by its own light, but by the light of their own foul imaginations; and having so defiled it by mixing their own filthy minds with it, they sit in judgment on the compound." Such a pen needs no other champion; it attempts to defend the author by obliterating the critics ("The Prurient Prude," *Readiana*, p. 427).

But when as eminent a champion as Charles Dickens did arise, his horn sounded an uncertain note; for he wrote about the novel to his and Reade's friend, Wilkie Collins:

I have read Charles Reade's book, and here follows my state of mind — *as a witness* — respecting it.

I have read it with the strongest interest and admiration. I regard it as the work of a highly accomplished writer and a good man; a writer with a brilliant fancy and a graceful and tender imagination. I could name no other living writer who could, in my opinion, write such a story nearly so well. As regards a so-called critic who should decry such a book as Holywell Street literature, and the like, I should have merely to say to him that I could desire no stronger proof of his incapacity in, and his unfitness for, the post to which he has elected himself.

Cross-examined, I should feel myself in danger of getting put on unsafe ground, and should try to set my wits against the cross-examiner, to keep well off it. But if I were reminded (as I probably should be, supposing the evidence to be allowed at all) that I was the editor of a periodical of a large circulation in which the Plaintiff himself had written, and if I had read to me in court those passages about Gaunt's going up to his wife's bed drunk and that last child's being conceived, and was asked whether, as Editor, I would have passed those passages, whether written by the Plaintiff or anybody else, I should be obliged to reply No. Asked why? I should say that what was pure to an artist might be impurely suggestive to inferior minds (of which there must necessarily be many among a large mass of readers) and I should have called the writer's attention to the likelihood of those passages being perverted in such quarters. . . .[14]

The young daughter upon the judgment seat of literature has been replaced in Dickens's criticism by "inferior minds" — but, whether childish or inferior, the tacit agreement is that literature must always be limited in its scope to those areas and expressions that could not possibly be misunderstood by juveniles or perverted by inferiors. Considering the strong affirmative note of the first paragraph of Dickens's letter and the dreadful hedging and backtracking of the last, one understands why Reade decided to be his own champion. At any rate, notoriety inspired galloping sales. In New York, within a few weeks of publication, Augustin Daly staged an adaptation of the story with John K. Mortimer and Rose Eytings in the leading parts. The play was so successful that managers vied with one another in offers to get the notorious money-maker to their own theaters.

VIII   A Terrible Temptation: *(1871)*

When Charles Reade, who rarely used anything from his own experience as the setting for a novel, returned to those country houses in the vicinity of Ipsden that he must have known well, he did so with a plot so jarring and so ahead of its time that his enemies leaped to battle and his friends scarcely knew how to defend him. *A Terrible Temptation* is a tale about a London rake and his mistress, his reformation and his retributively childless marriage, his philoprogenitive monomania and his wife's desperate remedy for their childlessness. The situation is not so impossible, but the subtle approval of the rake as hero, the strong and sympathetic characterization of the mistress (a Peg Woffington type!), and the ingenuous pleasure with which the housemaids examine the male infant outraged those readers and critics who insisted that at least in the world of the novel, if not in the world of the day, the wages of sin should be death.

But even more flagrantly, in breezy, casual violation of public and private mores, the details of a swapped pregnancy are presented with the same nonchalance with which a journalist would describe a local masquerade. With utter simplicity Reade refers to the secret facts of life entirely without noble euphemisms but in what he called "the homely expressions of Scripture" — a statement that should have triggered a belated scriptural defense in the great age of Evangelical study of the Word. After all, the biblical Sarai says to her husband Abram, "Behold now, the Lord hath restrained me from bearing: I pray thee, go in unto my maid; it may be that I may obtain children by her" (Genesis 16). And the biblical Rachel is even more explicit: ". . . when Rachel saw that she bare Jacob no children, Rachel envied her sister; and said unto Jacob, '. . . Behold my maid Bilhah, go in unto her; and she shall bear upon my knees, that I may also have children by her' " (Genesis 30).

The astonishing fact is that *Cassell's* family magazine should have published such a story by Reade serially, to its bitter end. Even Reade questioned his luck; for he wrote on October 30, 1870: "I have lately signed with Cassell, and am languidly working on a weekly serial. Have written one number. Rather smart, I think, but also rather loose. I fear it will offend the mothers of families. Indeed, query, will Cassell publish it? Yet, is it really wrong to tell the truth soberly — viz. that young men of fortune have all mistresses; and that these are not romantic creatures, but only low, uneducated women bedizened in fashionable clothes?"[15] At this point the author is deceiving himself or his correspondent; for, though Rhoda Somerset may be uneducated, she is beautiful, infinitely crafty, and histrionic in the grand manner; indeed, she is every bit as sympathetic a picture of Reade's Juno type who can do everything and do it well as is Peg Woffington herself. But perhaps Reade does penance for this deceit of the creative imagination, when, in the fashion of Daniel Defoe's heroine Moll Flanders, he has the courtesan of the first volume become the charitable and indefatigable street-preacher of volume three, whose sermons sound remarkably like the diction and sentiments of George Eliot's Dinah Morris (*Adam Bede*).

After the *Times* published a decidedly acid review of the novel,
the author ironically awarded its pages the credit for the tale's origin
— and indeed one can well believe him, because Reade's plots frequently came from his copious collections of newspaper clippings of
the bizarre, the criminal, and the sensational. In a letter to the
*Times*, written August 26, 1871, Reade claimed that the "leading
idea" of *A Terrible Temptation* came from the report of a particular
trial heard in the Central Criminal Court on February 3, 1870, in
which William Skepelhorne and his wife Sarah were charged with
conspiring with Louisa Julia, wife of Thomas John Ironside, to
deceive the latter gentleman into believing that his wife had given
birth to a daughter.

At any rate, as is often the case with attempted censorship, the
charge of immorality served as a potent stimulant, rather than a
block, to circulation and sales. Reade boasted that in the United
States three publishers sold three hundred and seventy thousand
copies of the novel or, according to his own estimate, about thirty
times the circulation of the *Times* in the United States and nearly six
times its English circulation. With that slap, the author, who needed
no one else to spring to his defense, must have sat back and chuckled
at the pleasant sound of money clinking into the till. But the
notoriety did affect his subsequent British financial arrangements,
for Reade lamented that Mr. Frederick Chapman would give only
six hundred pounds for a three-volume edition of fifteen hundred
copies. By comparison, Chapman had paid fifteen hundred for
limited copyrights to *Griffith Gaunt,* and Bradbury and Evans had
given two thousand pounds for *Foul Play.*

Just as Reade returned to his family background for the setting of
his novel, so he used his own family names for characters in *A Terrible Temptation.* The Bassett family is derived from the name of the
largest wood on the Ipsden estate. Compton, the name of one of
Reade's brothers, had come down in the family from the historical
incident of a gallant boy of nineteen who had defended the estate
against the cannon of Fairfax. This name also appeared in *Hard
Cash;* Ipsden is the hero of *Christie Johnstone;* and Dodd, the name
of one of Reade's father's tenants, appears in three novels: *It Is
Never Too Late to Mend, Love Me Little, Love Me Long,* and *Hard
Cash.* Indeed, Reade claimed that "there is more real invention in 'A
Terrible Temptation' than in most of my stories, and that it deserves
a high place amongst *them* at all events."[16]

Yet the basic plot design is his old favorite of two interweaving streams. The handling is tighter in this instance because — instead of starting one stream then switching to the other, and finally bringing the two together, Reade sets them side by side from the very beginning of the novel and continues them together to the very end. Miss Arabella Bruce of Portman Square is wooed by cousins, Richard Bassett and Sir Charles Bassett. The cousins live next to each other, and Richard hates Charles because he thinks that Charles's inheritance was stolen from him. His impassioned sense of dispossession is blurted out in a speech that ends with a hilarious Victorian appellation: "Oh, Miss Bruce! you can't conceive what a disinherited man feels — and I live at the very door: his old trees, that ought to be mine, fling their shadows over my little flower-beds; the sixty chimneys of Huntercombe Hall look down on my cottage; his acres of lawn run up to my little garden, and nothing but a ha-ha between us!" (Chapter I).

Richard lives with a certain degree of cautious decorum, watching for the main chance; but Charles has been an abandoned rake at Eton, at Oxford, and now in London. The contrasting houses, set side by side, are a castle and a simple farm gatehouse, respectively. The supposed son of Sir Charles lives; the indubitable son of Richard dies. Later Lady Bassett bears a legitimate male heir the very same day that Mrs. Bassett bears a daughter. And the final double irony that welds the two contrasting houses and their inimical inmates together is that Sir Charles's supposed heir is none other than Richard's illegitimate son and that Sir Charles's legitimate son and Richard's daughter are wed in the final chapter of the third volume. The real achievement of the novel — by far Reade's best balance of characterization and action — is never mentioned by the author, who seemingly cared only for some casual symmetry between the all-important plot and the insignificant people caught in its web. Other notable elements of the novel are the unique self-portrait of the author as Mr. Rolfe the writer, the continuation of the exposure found in *Hard Cash* of the evils of private asylums (see page 000) and a latter-day study of the problem of dominance in marriage that Geoffrey Chaucer had handles so amusingly in *The Wife of Bath's Tale.*

Critics seem to have been annoyed at the portrait of Reade not only as a writer but as a novelist who was capable of doing freelance detective work as well as psychological counseling. Readers today are indurated to the writer-sleuth who practices a remarkably successful branch of psychiatric therapy. Mr. Angelo, the athletic

young cleric, who in the tradition of Brother Leonard is deeply in
love with his lady parishioner, recommends an author to help deal
with the kidnapping of Sir Charles and his incarceration in a lunatic
asylum. "He is a writer, and opinions vary as to his merit. Some say
he has talent; others say it is all eccentricity and affectation. One
thing is certain: his books bring about the changes he demands. And
then he is in earnest; he has taken a good many alleged lunatics out
of confinement" (Chapter XXI).

Other than claiming that Mr. Rolfe believes in "The Importance
of Being Earnest" and that his novelization of government blue
books had some sociological effects, his belief does not seem unduly
high self-praise. Indeed, Reade's self-portrait becomes even less
flattering: ". . . he looked neither like a poet nor a drudge, but a
great fat country farmer. He was rather tall, very portly, smallish
head, commonplace features, mild brown eye not very bright, short
beard, and wore a suit of tweed all one color. Such looked the writer
of romances founded on facts. He rolled up to the window; — for, if
he looked like a farmer, he walked like a sailor, — and stepped into
the room" (Chapter XX).

The description in the novel of the study at Albert Terrace is even
more revealing to those interested in the work habits of writers. After
an extended description of mirrors, views, and woodwork, the author
arrives at the heart of the matter:

There was a collection of solid quartos, and of smaller folio guard-books
called Indexes. There was "Index rerum et hominum," and a lot more; indeed, so many that, by way of climax, there was a fat folio ledger entitled
"Index ad Indices."

By the side of the table were six or seven thick pasteboard cards, each
about the size of a large portofolio, and on these the author's notes and ex-
tracts were collected from all his repertories into something like a focus for a
present purpose. He was writing a novel based on facts. Facts, incidents, living dialogue, pictures, reflections, situations, were all on these cards to
choose from, and arranged in headed columns, and some portions of the
work he was writing on this basis of imagination and drudgery lay on the
table in two forms, his own writing and his secretary's copy thereof, the
latter corrected for the press. This copy was half margin, and so provided for
additions and improvements, but for one addition there were ten excisions,
great and small.

Lady Bassett had just time to take in the beauty and artistic character of
the place, and to realize the appalling drudgery that stamped it a workshop,
when the author, who had dashed into his garden for a moment's recreation,

came to the window and furnished contrast No. 3, for he looked neither like a poet nor a drudge, but a great fat country farmer. (Chapter XX)

In chapters XVI - XXIII, Charles Reade dramatically exposes the evils of private lunatic asylums. Among the counts against them is first of all, the ease of commitment.[17] Richard Bassett, possible heir or administrator to the Bassett estates occupied by his cousin, Sir Charles, hears that the latter has had an epileptic seizure and has been left with some thickness of speech and some haziness of memory; he has him visited by alienists in disguise, gets a writ of commitment, and kidnaps his cousin to deliver him to the lunatic asylum. In this somewhat more moderate treatment than the highly sensational exposure in *Hard Cash*, Reade admits that there are good and bad asylums. Dr. Suaby of Bellevue House is a doctor who need have no fear of surprise visits by inspectors. The good doctor is "a pale, thoughtful man, with a remarkably mild eye; is against restraint of lunatics, and against all punishment of them" (Chapter XXIII).

The second count against private lunatic asylums is that, although it is easy to obtain commitment, it is extremely difficult to arrange release. Thus Dr. Suaby, convinced that Sir Charles is completely cured, writes Richard to that effect. When no answer arrives, he writes again three weeks later. Suddenly a reply arrives that remands Sir Charles to an institution under the direction of the brutal Burdoch. Thus the third count is that affidavits from the chief doctor of one institution that a patient is cured may be foiled by frequent removals to other and worse institutions where there is a tacit understanding that the commitment is for life and that the heirs will make it worthwhile to the keepers to hear nothing more from their unfortunate relatives. Thus Mr. Rolfe, much to Mr. Reade's joy, is forced to recognize that, persuasion and lawfulness having availed nothing, the only recourse now is to a melodramatic rekidnapping of the victim, this time by his loving wife.

The two most striking weaknesses of the novel stem from the playwriting background of the author and from the odd pattern of male-female love about which he sometimes chose to write. The first is the technique of the thin disguise which is, however, marvelously effective. It is difficult enough to believe that Sir Charles never recognizes his former mistress Rhoda Somerset when, disguised as a nun, she nurses him back to health (Chapter VI). It is possible to assume that he spent most of that time in either a raging fever or a comatose stupor. But when Sir Charles has recovered his health and she visits once again, still in nun's garb (Chapter VIII), it is incredible that her former lover-patient should find her voice only strangely familiar! Rhoda weakly explains that she, a holy nun, is the sister of his former mistress.

The other glaring problem is the old one of the weak hero. Sir Charles is introduced as a charming, pleasant young rake who is languorous and diffident from his excesses. He courts a young woman who asks only to become some man's slave, but he refuses to master her. When he thinks his mistress sent the anonymous letter that poisoned his relationship with his fiancée's family, he falls into convulsions. When his sweetheart is bundled off to Baden by her irate father, he can only sit, head in hand, and lament her loss until his former mistress tells him to be a man and go after her. When married, he is unable to produce a natural heir, and the author hints that he cannot because of his youthful excesses. When he is thrown by his horse at foxhunting, he is taunted by his cousin, and falls into the epileptic fit that provides the basis for his commitment to an asylum.

Although Sir Charles is certainly not a figure of romance, and is a weak enough hero, his weakness is somewhat less striking than that of the hero in other books because Lady Arabella, his wife, is also a quiet, loving, mild sort of woman. "Her figure was tall and rather slim, but not at all commanding . . . she would take up or put down her own scissors half-timidly, and look round before threading her needle, as if to see whether any soul objected" (Chapter I). The chief problem for Arabella Bruce is that, after her rearing by an irascible father had made her afraid of her own shadow and fearful of seeking a relationship with any person (except how best to please that person), life did not give her a sturdy oak about which to twine gracefully; instead, she has a weak and ailing husband whose only strong desire is to have a son to inherit his lands but who lacks the physical vigor to sire one. Thus the weak is forced to fight, and the pleaser of others has to scheme and plot for herself. In some ways this situation makes Arabella, as she attempts to cope with forces obviously too strong for her, more attractive to the reader than the great-legged, thundering females Reade admired, for they were in severe danger on entrances and exists of knocking over scenery as well as supporting actors. No Peg, Christie, or Kate, Arabella is far more in the tradition of Lucy Fountain (*Love Me Little* and *Hard*

*Cash*). As such, she matches her mate well and does not, by contrast, make conspicuous his guillibility and inability to deal with the complications of his title and estate.

When the *Daily Globe* of Toronto had quoted the strictures of the periodical, *The Round Table*, on the morals of *Griffith Gaunt*, Charles Reade doughtily accused them of "second-hand libel." Now Goldwin Smith, an old Magdalen College acquaintance,[18] whom Reade had referred to obliquely as a "Canadian or British liar," found his opportunity for revenge. He launched an attack upon *A Terrible Temptation* far more savage than anything the American moralists had written about the earlier novel. He objected to the glorification of that "scarlet woman," Rhoda Somerset. He pointed out that Reade's choice of hero had required him to marshal the reader's sympathies on the side of a rake who had once kept a mistress. He was disgusted by the "succulent suggestiveness" of the scene in which a healthy wet nurse gives suck to Sir Charles's supposed son. And he so erred in a no doubt hasty reading of the novel as to suggest that Lady Bassett was depicted as a wife tottering on the brink of adultery.

Although Henry Kingsley, among contemporary writers, considered Reade's *Terrible Temptation* "the worst novel ever written by a man of ability," it is only fair to place against that criticism his other literary judgment that George Eliot's *Mill on the Floss* was the best.[19] But Swinburne dashed to Reade's rescue:

Such attacks on it [*A Terrible Temptation*] as I remember to have seen were not generally based on the simple fact that it contained a remarkably lifelike and brilliant study of a courtesan — ultimately transfigured by conversion into a field-preacher: they were based on the imputation that the married heroine of the story was represented as hovering more or less near the edge of adultery. . . . It requires not merely a vigorous effort of charity, but a determined innocence in the ways of the world of professional moralists, to believe that any reader of the book, at any stage of the story, can have really mistaken the character of the "terrible" and most natural temptation which besets the tender and noble nature of the heroine: a temptation, not to illicit love [with the Reverend Mr. Angelo], but to legal fraud instigated by conjugal devotion.[20]

Reade's reply to this charge of immorality was of an unexpected type. In a notebook of the period he neatly pasted an American notice describing him as "a slimy, snaky, poisonous literary reptile"; his book as "this mass of brothel garbage"; and himself again as "a

gatherer of offal for the hyenas of the human race."[21] Some authors
collect such notices to read, with laughter, to their friends; but
Reade took the most insignificant writer, the most preposterous
onslaught, pathetically to heart. His reply to his critics was sadden-
ing because, with all the books and plays Reade had written, he was
so essentially unsure of himself and of his place in literature that he
had to point to material possessions to sustain his self-esteem as a
writer:

> I leave this on record for the instruction of those who complain that
> authors work for money instead of contenting themselves with the meed of
> praise they receive.
> Was anything of mine ever praised as heartily and eloquently as here an
> excellent and innocent story is abused?
> Through my whole career it has been so: a little faint, reluctant praise.
> Bushels of insolent vituperation.
> But with the proceeds of a pen that never wrote a line till I was 35 years
> of age I have got me three freeholds in the Brompton Road, a leasehold in
> Albert Terrace, a house full of rich furniture and pictures and a few
> thousands floating, and so I can snap my fingers at a public I despise, and a
> Press I know and loathe. To God alone my thanks are due who gave me my
> good gifts and the sense to see that literature is a trade and that an author is
> a being secretly despised and who can only raise himself above contempt
> by
> Riches,
> or *je vise au solide*.
> 8th June 1872.[22]

This note is, perhaps, from the Charles Reade who distrusted the imagination and the life of the artist, who clipped newspaper items of
bizarre crimes and sensational trials, who considered these to be the
"warm facts" of life, and who built his stories laboriously on an
edifice of garbled journalism. Furniture, deeds, stock — "*je vise au
solide*" — these are so real and solid that the least eminent Victorian
could not brush them off as fancy.

One turns from the author's note with regret, and returns to the
warm confident element of cheerful Christianity that gave so much
health and vigor to his tales. Toward the end of the third volume of
*A Terrible Temptation*, Mrs. Richard Bassett is invited by Lady
Bassett to call on her in her illness. Richard Bassett instructs her to
decline, but she surprisingly refuses.

". . . I have been a better wife than a Christian this many years; but there's a limit. And, Richard, I should never have married you, if you had told me we were to be at war all our lives with our next neighbor, that everybody respects. . . . Not that I complain: if you have been bitter to them, you have always been good and kind to me; and I hope I have done my best to deserve it; but, when a sick lady, and perhaps dying, holds out her hand to me — write her one of your cold-blooded letters! That I WON'T. Reply? my reply will be just putting on my bonnet, and going to her this afternoon . . . She is a lady, a real lady, every inch. But it is not that altogether: no, if a sick woman called me to her bedside this week, I'd go, whether she wrote from Huntercombe Hall, or the poorest house in the place; else how could I hope my Saviour would come to *my* bedside, at my last hour?" (Chapter XLII)

### IX A Simpleton: A Story of the Day *(1873)*

*A Simpleton* began its serial course in *London Society* in August, 1872, and ran concurrently in the United States in *Harper's Magazine*. This period was an enormously busy one for Reade: he was grinding out newspaper articles in the tradition of Defoe and Swift; he was involved in all the litigation and unpleasant correspondence consequent upon the dramatic version of Trollope's *Ralph the Heir;* he was still writing *The Wandering Heir* and preparing a dramatic version of it; and the Tichborne case, which was in the courts and newspapers, was to Reade of both particular current interest and future usefulness. Not surprisingly *A Simpleton* seems to lack that gusto, pace, and vigor that were ever Charles Reade's authorial signature.

During the winter of 1871 - 1872, Reade went into three months of isolation at Oxford; but he produced only the first two rather lethargic chapters of this novel. When his publishers began to evince unmistakable signs of impatience about the appearance of the first issue in August, Reade knew he had to complete the task; and with a great burst of intensive effort, he brought the novel to a close. The mark of this period of concentrated writing is evident in the tone and mood of the book. Even Swinburne, who loyally called it a "brilliant story," also admitted that it contained passages of deadly dullness. Perceptively, considering the manner of composition, he claimed that the second half of the book redeemed and rectified "the tedious excesses and excursions of the first" ("Charles Reade," *Miscellanies*, p. 275).

A Reade notebook called "Mareria Novae Fabulae" contains mis-

cellaneous notes that Reade evidently used for *A Simpleton*. A large
amount of material concerns the geography of the Cape area of
Africa and specifically the diamond fields. Most of this material is in
the handwriting of S. Langley, evidently a hack writer or scholar
whom Reade employed to collect such information for him in the
British Museum. So many notes of the 1870s are in Langley's un-
gainly, jagged handwriting that it is fair to assume that he filled the
position during this period that the "university hacks" had in the
early 1860s. In Reade's own handwriting is the enigmatic notation:
"For the second woman use Boucicault's second character in
Hunted Down; and perhaps the little actress in Caste with particulars of class."

This entry attests to Reade's old habit of turning plays into novels
and, even if the initial play did not exist, of visualizing his characters
as if they were first seen on the stage. His relaxed manner of drawing
characters not from life but from the plays of his contemporaries
prepares one to discover that the charge of plagiarism was leveled
against him once again. In the preface to *A Simpleton* he replies
clearly and cogently to the criticism by making a rather interesting
distinction:

> It has lately been objected to me, in studiously courteous terms of course,
> that I borrow from other books, and am a plagiarist. To this I reply that I
> borrow facts from every accessible source, and am not a plagiarist. The
> plagiarist is one who borrows from a homogeneous work: for such a man
> borrows not ideas only, but their treatment. He who borrows only from
> heterogeneous works is not a plagiarist. All fiction, worth a button, is
> founded on facts; and it does not matter one straw whether the facts are
> taken from personal experience, hearsay, or printed books; only those books
> must not be works of fiction.

The author thus fends off the charge of plagiarism by the shield of
his favorite thesis — facts make great fiction; and, whatever their
source, facts are always in the public domain.

He confesses engagingly that, for the preparation of his tales, he
used a vast amount of heterogeneous material — from conversations,
journals, blue books, histories, biographies, law reports, and so on. "I
rarely write a novel without milking about two hundred heterogeneous cows into my pail, and . . . 'A Simpleton' is no exception to
my general method; that method is the true method, and the best,
and if on that method I do not write prime novels, it is the fault of
the man, and not of the method" (preface, *A Simpleton*).

In regard to his sources, Reade had the assistance of two practical

seamen for nautical knowledge: William Barrington Reade and
Commander Charles Edward Reade, R.N. For the background and
setting of the South African scenes, he used, besides the notes of his
busy hacks, "Mr. Day's recent handbooks; the old handbooks;
Galton's 'Vacation Tourist;' 'Philip Mavor; or Life among the Caf-
fres;' 'Fowwer;' 'Notes on the Cape of Good Hope,' 1821; 'Scenes
and Occurrences in Albany and Caffre-land,' 1827; Bowler's 'South
African Sketches,' 'A Campaign in South Africa,' Lucas; 'Five Years
in Caffre-land,' Mrs. Ward; etc., etc., etc." But his principal obliga-
tion in this area was to Mr. Boyle, the author of some letters to the
*Daily Telegraph* that were afterward reprinted in a volume. "Mr.
Boyle has a painter's eye, and a writer's pen, and if the African
scenes in 'A Simpleton' please my readers, I hope they will go to the
fountain-head, here they will find many more."[23]

As to the plot and the characters, these were invented. The title, *A
Simpleton*, was not quite new, for a French play had been entitled
*La Niaise*. But *La Niaise* is in reality a woman of rare intelligence
who is taken for a simpleton by a lot of conceited fools, and the play
is built on their blunders and her unpretending wisdom. "That is a
very fine plot, which I recommend to our female novelists. My aim
in these pages," wrote Charles Reade in his preface, "has been much
humbler, and is, I hope, too clear to need explanation."

The title of the tale describes Rosa Lusignan, who is called a
simpleton by her father, her friends at school, and herself — and
only her lover is too fascinated to join in the general consensus. One
of Reade's dark beauties, she has "coal-black hair, and glorious dark
eyes, that seemed to beam with soul all day long; her eyebrows,
black, straightish, and rather thick, would have been majestic and
too severe, had the other features followed suit; but her black brows
were succeeded by long silky lashes, and sweet oval face, two
pouting lips studded with ivory, and an exquisite chin, as feeble as
any man could desire in the partner of his bosom" (Chapter I).

Phoebe Dale, Reade's "second woman," is his more usual type of
Saxon beauty.[24] "Her figure and face both told her breed at once:
here was an old English pastoral beauty . . . with broad, full bust and
massive shoulder, and arm as hard as a rock with health and constant
use . . . a face honest, fair, and rather large than small; not beautiful,
but exceedingly comely; a complexion not pink and white, but that
delicately blended brickdusty color, which tints the whole cheek in
fine graduation, outlasts other complexions twenty years, and
beautifies the true Northern, even in old age" (Chapter IV).

This Juno figure par excellence, Phoebe, is destined to fall in love with a weak male not worth her little finger. Reginald Falcon is "an egotist . . . cheek like delicate wax . . . fair hair like silk . . . pale, handsome face and fascinating manners. . . . He was feeble as a child. . . . Telling her a pack of arrant lies . . . he borrowed twenty pounds of her" (Chapter IV). Much like Reade's other plots, this one hinges on an exciting and seemingly tragic ocean voyage and a hero thought to be dead. The Phoebe-Reginald combination travels from Essex, to London, to South Africa; but the journey always intersects at some significant point with the Rosa-Christopher combination.

Dr. Christopher Staines, twenty-eight, marries Rosa Lusignan, nineteen, instead of waiting for the right woman, Lady Cicely Treherne, who shortly appears. After gaining her father's respect by taking out a six-thousand-pound insurance policy, the doctor discovers that he is wed to a charming child who cannot manage money or household. Driving a cab at night still does not balance the budget, so he sails on the *Amphitrite* as doctor and guardian of the ailing sixteen-year-old Lord Tadcaster. News is brought that Christopher has fallen overboard just before Rosa bears a fine son. Assumed dead, Christopher is rescued by Captain Dodd *(Hard Cash)*, placed in a hospital at Cape Town, and then taken as a guest on the farm of the secondary couple, Phoebe and Reginald Falcon.

Deciding to let Rosa enjoy his insurance money, the doctor goes to the African diamond fields while Reginald ships off to woo and marry Rosa, bigamously, for her money. The villain kidnaps Rosa's son, then returns him to act the role of hero and rescuer. Rosa consents to marry Reginald out of gratitude. But when she is about to escape her dilemma by suicide, the doctor returns, rich, saves his wife, whips Reginald, pays back the insurance money, and the couple live comfortably with Rosa's well-to-do Uncle Philip.

Other resemblances to Reade's earlier novels include social problems, such as tight corsets and the difficulty of beginning a medical practice, as well as the desirability for a family man to have life insurance (see *Put Yourself in His Place*). Women kiss with the violence only Reade seems to have noted and cringed at: "In flowed Florence; they both uttered a little squawk of delight, and went at each other like two little tigresses, and kissed in swift alternation with a singular ardor, drawing their crests back like snakes, and then darting them forward and inflicting what, to the male philosopher looking on, seemed hard kisses, violent kisses, rather than the tender ones to be expected from two tender creatures embracing each other" (Chapter VI).

Reade is a drawer of sharp, dramatic contrasts with little admixture of neutral gray. When the Simpleton, Rosa Lusignan, has all but ruined the young physician Christopher Staines's career by her extravagance, making it necessary for him to drive a hack incognito at night, the author states the situation in measured opposites: "the man all industry, self-denial, patience; the woman all frivolity, self-indulgence, and amusement; both chained to an oar, only — one in a working boat, the other in a painted galley" (Chapter IX). But the sharp contrast serves to make a new element clear. Like the heroes in *Hard Cash* and in *Put Yourself in His Place*, Christopher Staines is a man far superior to his wife, Rosa — so much so that one can only wish that, instead of marrying her when he was twenty-eight and she nineteen, he had waited until Lady Cicely Treherne appeared. The male's superiority to his wife is quite a change from Reade's other studies of women; but in the sentimental conclusion, Staines turns out to be the simpleton and Rosa the most desirable wife a man could find. This reverses the thesis and logic of the text, and at the end of the book Reade uses Uncle Philip to express his paradox:

"The great sweetener of a man's life," said he, "is 'a simpleton.' I shall not go abroad any more; my house has become attractive: I've got a simpleton. When I have a headache, her eyes fill with tender concern, and she hovers about me and pesters me with pillows: when I am cross with her, she is afraid I am ill. When I die, and leave her a lot of money, she will howl for months, and say I don't want his money: 'I waw-waw-waw-want my Uncle Philip, to love me, and scold me.' One day she told me, with a sigh, I hadn't lectured her for a month. 'I am afraid I have offended you,' says she, 'or else worn you out, dear.' When I am well, give me a simpleton, to make me laugh. When I am ill, give me a simpleton to soothe me with her innocent tenderness. A simpleton shall wipe the dews of death, and close my eyes: and when I cross the river of death, let me be met by a band of the heavenly host, who were all simpletons here on earth, and too good for such a hole, so now they are in heaven and their garments always white — because there are no laundresses there'. Arrived at this point, the Anglo-Saxon race will retire, grinning, to fresh pastures, and leave this champion of 'a Simpleton,' to thunder paradoxes in a desert." (Chapter XXIX)

In the midst of *A Simpleton*, an old friend reappears when Captain Dodd (*Love Me Little, Love Me Long,* and *Hard Cash*) rescues the doctor from the sea. The author's special interest in doctors and in the practice of medicine is revealed in the ironic twist by which Dr. Staines is brought to full recovery by the use of his own prescription — a beef-tea bath. The ship's surgeon had read in the *Lancet* medical journal an article by a Dr. Staines concerning the recovery of a starved child by that extraordinary means. Moreover, Reade's prescription for unusual success in hunting diamonds is precisely the same technique that had stood his heroes in good stead in the gold-fields of *It Is Never Too Late to Mend:* when some prospectors are sieving the streams, Reade's heroes seek the matrix from which the small fragments have been washed downstream. By digging in the large humps of earth, nuisances to the Boer farmers, they discover the remains of hot-earth bubbles, hot enough to have formed diamonds deep within the stony rubble.

A Reade book would be strange without any hint of disguises. So Reginald Falcon, having absconded with the diamonds on pretense of selling them in London, woos Christopher's supposed widow, and passes himself off as the last benefactor and friend of her supposedly deceased husband (Chapter XXVII). Once again the innocently can-did Reade, seemingly without any desire to shock or offend, includes a story sequence too strong for Victorian stomachs. After Reginald Falcon has repeatedly betrayed Phoebe Dale's love and trust, she still continues to follow him and rescue him. He has even proposed to another woman, but she forgives; he is being taken to prison for debt, and she pays his debt and sets him free. She cannot take him back to her paternal farm because she is ashamed of the pseudo-gentleman with whom she has the misfortune to be in love, so she goes with him to a village five miles away. "On the road down he was full of little practical attentions; she received them coldly; his mellifluous mouth was often at her ear, pouring thanks and praises into it; she never vouchsafed a word of reply. All she did was to shudder now and then, and cry at intervals. Yet, whenever he left her side, her whole body became restless; and when he came back to her, a furtive thrill announced the insane complacency his bare con-tact gave her" (Chapter IV).

This kind of obsessive love, obviously sexual in nature and totally unrelated to the intrinsic worth of the person loved, was indeed strong stuff for Reade's time and place. W. Somerset Maugham could make sensational coin of such a degraded obsession many years later in *Of Human Bondage*, but even he used it to describe the love of a man for a woman. Reade, far more boldly, in an age that liked to think of unmarried women as entirely innocent and un-touched, and of married women as "angels in the house," let the sublimely healthy Phoebe, the buxom Saxon picture of decency and sanity, become the victim of a sexual obsession for a man she could never admire or respect but to whom she is tied forever by a mysterious mixture of passion and loathing.

Charles Reade treasured the occasional passages of his works that revealed the poetic side of his creativity. Of course they were not so important to him as the ingenious plot or the highly patterned characterization, and they obviously meant less to his readers than the hairbreadth escapes and the melodramatic confrontations, but they are still there; and, when Reade thought of himself as an artist, it was usually to these few vagrant passages that he retreated for confirmation. One such passage may be found in Chapter XVIII when the Falcon family is making the long trek from the cattle market back to its kloof: ". . . suddenly a golden tinge seemed to fall like a lash on the vapors of the night; they scudded away directly, as jackals before the lion; the stars paled, and with one incredible bound, the mighty sun leaped into the horizon, and rose into the sky. In a moment all the lesser lamps of heaven were out, though late so glorious, and there was nothing but one vast vaulted turquoise, and a great flaming topaz mounting with eternal ardour to its centre" (Chapter XVIII).

The value of such a passage lies less in its attestation to poetic style than in the masculine vigor of the writer who takes the tired nouns of conventional nature poetry and couples them with verbs of remarkable force and vividness: "fall like a lash," "scudded away directly, as jackals before the lion," "with one incredible bound," "Leaped . . . and rose," "Vast . . . flaming . . . eternal ardour." Even the rising of the sun above the African veld becomes the climactic scene of a stage melodrama in which sharp, abrupt action sinks to rest in moral platitude. The entire story is comparable in a way, for all the violence of misunderstanding, cross purposes, supposed deaths, and disguised villains can be enjoyed like the mimic warfares of childhood.

## X  The Jilt: A Novel (1877)

The heroine of this little tale, Ellen Ap Rice, the loveliest girl in Wales, fits into the same character gallery as Rosa Lusignan, the "Simpleton." The thinnest and yet in some ways the most exotic of his tales, *The Jilt* exhibits many of the Reade techniques that by this period in his life had become quite automatic. In this novel, Lieutenant Arthur Greaves falls in love with Ellen, the spoiled daughter of the mayor of Tenby. She accepts engagement, with the understanding that they will not be wed until Arthur is at least a postcap-

tain. After Arthur has reported to the Royal Navy ship *Centaur* for a
two-year duty, Edward Laxton, the immensely rich owner of a
beautiful private yacht, arrives in Tenby harbor, The wealthy, handsome, extremely eligible young Edward is lionized by fathers and
mothers with available daughters, but he is interested only in Ellen.
He persecutes her; and, because of his persistence and the social
pressure of her family and friends, she becomes his bride.

Just as coincidentally as Arthur was called to duty at the moment
of his engagement, he comes home at precisely the right time to hear
that his fiancée has just sailed away with a richer suitor-husband.
The lieutenant falls ill of fever and is left with recurrent jaundice.
After reappointment to active duty, he sails on the *Phoebe*, bound
for Hong Kong, where he is to rejoin the admiral under whom he
had previously served. On the way, the ship is overtaken in a calm by
a beautiful pirate ship, operated by Edward Laxton, who is masquerading as a corsair and who is well on his way to insanity. His
bride, Ellen, manages to get a message explaining all to Arthur
Greaves; her husband is carried off in irons for piracy, but is committed to a lunatic asylum rather than to court martial or prison.
After Edward promptly and conveniently dies of a broken blood
vessel, Ellen Ap Rice, the indestructible loveliest girl in Wales, is left
a wealthy widow and the possessor of enough sense to marry Arthur
Greaves.

Reade seems to suggest that he might be planning to continue the
book for some few pages and at least one more volume when he introduces the issue of marital sovereignty. Since Ellen was first the
victim of a tyrannical husband, is it not only fair that her second husband should now be the victim of a tyrannical wife? But some vague,
undelineated rational solution seems to have been found, and Reade
drops the whole project, if it were a project at all.

A similar issue was raised when, in the fifth chapter of *A
Simpleton*, Rosa was married to Christopher. At the beginning of
chapter six, the author raised the question of whether or not it is appropriate to write further about their lives together. "And here,
methinks, a reader of novels may perhaps cry out and say, 'What
manner of man is this, who marries his hero and heroine, and then,
instead of leaving them happy for life, and at rest from his uneasy
pen and all their other troubles, flows coolly on with their adventures?' " To this question the author can only suggest an experiment.
"Catch eight old married people four of each sex, and say unto them,
'Sir,' or 'Madam, did the more remarkable events of your life come

to you before marriage or after?' Most of them will say 'after,' and let
that be my excuse for treating the marriage of Christopher Staines
and Rosa Lusignan as merely one incident in their lives; an incident
which, so far from ending their story, led by degrees to more striking
events than any that occurred to them before they were man and
wife."

At any rate, *The Jilt* is a standard Reade romance. There are two
lovers, one of whom has to be away; while he is away, the other gets
involved elsewhere; the ocean voyage plays an important part in the
plot; the remarkable gravitational pull of coincidence puts the hero
on a ship attacked by the villain; true love triumphs; and the pair
originally plighted at the beginning finally marries at the end. And
the Victorian compromise operates so well that, through their mis-
takes and infidelity, they gain the financial wherewithal not only to
marry but to live together afterward in all the overstuffed and over-
draped comfort of Victorian wealth.

## XI  Singleheart and Doubleface: A Matter of Fact Romance *(1884)*

When *Singleheart and Doubleface* was ready to appear in
England as a serial in *Life* and in the United States in *Harper's
Magazine*, Reade almost automatically set about his customary
course of writing a dramatic version. Doing so preserved his rights to
the play; but, in order to preserve his rights for stage production, he
had it produced on June 1, 1882, at the Royal Princess's Theatre,
Edinburgh.

In *Singleheart and Doubleface*, Reade twice comments on the
comparative brevity of this realistic study of a good woman's love for
a n'er-do-well husband. In returning to his natural bent for the com-
pact narrative rather than for the extensive novel, he claims that he
has "sworn not to be trivoluminous"; and, in passing over a three-
year period of time with little comment, he explains that they were
"three years whose incidents I have decided not to particularize, and
so be trivoluminous, not luminous" (Chapter V).

Reade begins this exceedingly thin novelette with the usual jux-
taposition of two different types of women; but this time they are
sisters: Deborah — big, redheaded, quick, but illiterate; Sarah —
literate, small, brown-haired. Sarah has been courted by Joe Pinder
since she was nineteen — and the reader knows immediately that Joe
is the man she ought to marry; something may happen so that she
will not, but she will marry him in the end! She marries, of course,
the flashy, shallow, and irresponsible James Mansell — on the Reade

theory that all the strongest and best British women are irresistibly attracted by weak or villainous men. Mansell becomes an alcoholic, incapable of even self-support; and he is told so by Sarah in a statement remarkable for its comprehensive brevity, "You are neither a husband, nor a father, nor a man" (Chapter III).

In a perfectly nauseating fourth chapter, Pinder and Sarah vie in telling each other how wonderful they are. After Mansell's abortive attempt to rob the safe in his own wife's shop, he blusters the situation out with the police and sails to America to make his fortune. Thus Reade has arranged, in his traditional fashion, to have the husband away from the wife for an undesignated period. When Mansell returns to Sarah and his daughter Lucy — one of Reade's dreadfully cute children — Deborah quite perceptively says that he has returned garbed as a gentleman to get the same things he once tried to obtain when dressed as a burglar. But Deborah can perceive these things because she is neither wholly good nor the heroine. With rather startling frankness, Reade describes the return of the vagrant husband and the consequent "renewal of conjugal ardor" (Chapter VI).

On the pretense of investing Sarah's accumulated four hundred pounds in American securities, Mansell takes his family to New York, promptly deserts his wife and daughter, and returns to the American woman he had "married" on his previous trip. When Reade once again plays in this novel his favorite game of bigamy, the power of coincidence is so great that Sarah, looking for her husband, quite by chance ends up wearily sitting on the front steps of his American wife's lodging house — no small feat, even in the New York City of the 1880s.

Given lodging in the house, Sarah recognizes the voice of Elizabeth Haynes's husband; she steals back the money she had stitched into his vest in England for safety in America; then, slipping into their bedroom, she stands watching Mr. and Mrs. Haynes sleeping together. When the loss is discovered, Elizabeth suspects Sarah; but she faces a bankrupt husband with a frank proposition: "I will undertake to keep you, if you will only spend your evenings with me" (Chapter IX). When Sarah sails for England with both her daughter and her money, but without her husband, Reade arranges a melodramatic scene in which Mansell is standing on the shore and is amazed at the meek wife on the deck who, with burning eyes, brandishes her daughter on one arm and has her money clutched in her other hand.

When she returns home, the reticent Sarah tells nothing about the events of her trip, not even to admit to her own sister that her suspicions had proved to be absolutely correct. Meanwhile, Solomon B. Grace marries the former bigamous wife, Elizabeth Haynes. Solomon is one of Charles Reade's corny Yankees; " 'Don't ye now, don't ye,' he snivelled; 'you'll make me cry enough to wash a palace car' " (Chapter XI).[25] As for Sarah, she gives Joe Pinder affection but will not consider divorce from James. Finally Joe, like Thackeray's Dobbins *(Vanity Fair)*, regains his self-respect and decides to move to London. But the long hand of coincidence reaches clear across the Atlantic Ocean, plucks up the brand-new Mr. and Mrs. Solomon B. Grace, and has them arrive in the nick of time to inform Sarah that Mansell has died in a New York hospital. Of course, in the Evangelical era, he died penitent . . . Elizabeth pardons him . . . Sarah pardons him. Now what one knew from the beginning must happen, does happen — Sarah marries Pinder at the point at which no reader could possibly care less. This novel is surely one of Reade's worst, for it is so mawkish, contrived, and thinly motivated that the woman who christens herself "singlehearted" ends up loving another man!

### XII  A Perilous Secret *(1884)*

*A Perilous Secret*, a two-volume novel that was perhaps a kind of compromise between one-volume "luminosity" and "trivoluminousness," was drawn from a play[26] that Reade had based on an idea suggested to him by Henry Pettitt.[27] The highly sensational plot of the novel implies that Reade had been reading about tracheotomies and the possibility of drawing electrical energy from harnessing the tides (Chapters III, XXVII). Chapter titles vividly express the melodramatic mood and the study in contrasts afforded by the novel: "The Poor Man's Child," "The Rich Man's Child," "Two Fathers," "Mary's Peril," "The Course of True Love," "Lovers Parted," "The Knot Cut — Another Tied," "The Clandestine Marriage," "The Serpent Let Loose," "Lover's Quarrels," "Apologies," "A Woman Outwits Two Men," "Buried Alive," "Retribution," "Strange Turns," "Curtain." The book was designed for serial publication, for each chapter heading reads like the title of a melodrama of the stage or that of a penny-shocker to be read in the attic! But in the twentieth century one ought to recognize in quite demonstrable ways the indebtedness to Victorian melodrama of the modern detective story and the fiction of violence.

A *Perilous Secret* abounds in *dramatis personae* with multiple sets
of heroes, heroines, and villains. Inventor William Hope, who is
traveling from Liverpool to Hull with his motherless daughter
Grace, meets Richard Bartley, shipbroken and commission agent,
whose dying daughter Mary inherited from her mother twenty thousand pounds that will pass to Walter Clifford if she dies. Because of
their "remarkable resemblance, Grace can be substituted for the
moribund Mary. When the substitution is discovered by Leonard
Monckton, one of Bartley's clerks, he is sent to jail for fourteen years
for supposedly robbing Bartley's safe.

Colonel Clifford, the village squire, has been selling parcels of his
estate to keep his race horses. So Bartley, at Hope's recommenda-
tion, is able to rent, along with the mineral rights, one of the
colonel's farms where Hope has observed coal outcroppings. Walter
Clifford, the colonel's son, falls in love with Mary (Grace Hope)
Bartley, and Percy Fitzroy and Julia Clifford form a comic alliance.
Both Colonel Clifford and Richard Bartley object to Walter's suit for
Mary; so, in despair, the young man leaves England, only to be
recalled immediately by a telegram from Mary announcing that
Colonel Clifford is dying. Mary and Walter are married secretly just
about the time that the villain Monckton is released from jail. His
former wife, Lucy, bigamously remarried, pays him to stay away.
But he returns for revenge on Bartley and Clifford and rather in-
cidentally makes Lucy's son, Augustus Braham, his heir. Only after
Monckton's death is it discovered that under his true name, Louis
Carruthers, he had unknowingly been heir to large estates. Thus,
ironically, he enriches his unfaithful wife and her illegitimate son
Augustus, and makes possible the return to well-financed
domesticity of her second husband, the father of that son.

The great sensation scene is played by William Hope, his
daughter Grace (Mary Bartley), and a subvillain, Ben Burnley,
henchman of Monckton, when they are trapped in a caved-in mine.
Of course, Burnley must be drowned, and William and Grace must
be rescued. Bartley becomes a white-haired old gent who putters
around with fruit trees, the colonel, who did not die after all, is
reconciled to Walter's marriage, Percy and Julia are happily married,
and financial redress is made to all.

The young heroine Grace, introduced at the somewhat noncommit-
tal age of four, is described as "fair." Thus, when the reader later
meets the villainess, Lucy Muller, he expects her to be tall, dark, and
handsome — and he is not disappointed. Julia Clifford, the other·

romantic ingenue, is an heiress who is tall and black-browed and who has that winsome black down on her upper lip. William Hope is one of Reade's universal geniuses: linguist, mechanic, mineralogist, draftsman, inventor. The only things he cannot do are make or keep money, a singular omission in a mercantile culture. Coincidence plays its usual important role when the poor man's living daughter Grace is discovered to be remarkably like the rich man's dead daughter Mary.

When Bartley finally decides that it is safe to introduce William Hope to his own blood daughter, now called Mary Bartley, Reade explains lamely why he does not describe the reunion: "we poor dramatists, taught by impatient audiences to move on, and taught by those great professors of verbosity, our female novelists and nine-tenths of our male, that it is just possible for 'masterly inactivity,' *alias* sluggish narrative, creeping through sorry flags and rushes, with one lily in ten pages, to become a bore, are driven on to salient facts, and must trust a little to our readers' intelligence to ponder on the singular situation of Mary Bartley and her two fathers" (Chapter V). Here, in one condescending cluster, are the writer's allegiance to the techniques of the stage, his scorn for George Eliot's "glacial movement," and his apologia for his headlong pace of narration — something that he clearly felt needed no apology.

Hope manages to rescue Mary from a rather improbable drowning — one more of Reade's melodramatic rescues. Hope performs a more dramatic rescue when he gets Mary out of a collapsed mine — Reade's big "sensation" scene. Ben Burnley, Monckton's fellow-felon, is discharged on Hope's orders for smoking in the mine (Reade had earlier used this same incident in *Joan*). Later Burnley is paid by Bartley to see that William Hope does not get out of the mine alive. By mistake, Burnley is trapped along with his victims, Mary and her father. After six days, Burnley is reduced to cannibalism and even Hope cries out, "IS GOD ALL APATHY?" When the former felon punctures a tank containing thirty tons of water, he is drowned; and the Hopes are rescued from above (Chapter XXIII).

In addition to the usual melodramatic elements, there is a good bit of humor in this novel; for example, the thoroughly delightful comic dialogue between five-foot Percy and his beloved five-foot, eight-inch Julia (Chapter XVII). At the close of a battle of wit, the resolute little Percy marches off singing; Julia seems to relent, and calls him coaxingly, "Percy, *dear*." Percy, who congratulates himself on his firm skill in handling the fair sex, returns to receive the kiss he is sure will be bestowed. But if Percy knew his creator better, he would know that the end of a chapter is an excellent location for the French comic trick — the *fausse sortie*. " 'Well,' said he, with an air of indifference, and going slowly back to the gate. 'What is it now?' said he, a little arrogantly. She soon let him know. Directly he was quite within reach she gave him a slap in the face that sounded like one plank falling upon another, and marched off with an air of royal dignity, as if she had done the most graceful and lady-like thing in all the world." Slapstick, of course, and quite literally so, but produced with great verve and gusto.

When the *dénouement* is past and only the resolution remains, Reade muses on the irony that, as much as people insist upon a happy ending to romances, "it seems to be a rule of life, and in fiction, that interest flags when trouble ceases" (Chapter XXVII). Another bit of irony transforms Bartley, the power of evil who made everything happen in the novel, into a soft, senile old gentleman, now quite vague and harmless. It is also a striking irony that when Lucy's first husband, Monckton-Carruthers, dies, she uses part of her son's inheritance to invite her second husband, his actual father, to return home from the United States.

Quite abruptly, at the conclusion, when Reade has long since dismissed Lucy as a decidedly secondary character of little importance to the novel, Reade himself points out the irony that Lucy, former mistress and then wife of the villain, is now a faithful wife to her bigamous second husband, a tender mother, a kind mistress to her household, and therefore, via a string of moral failures, has arrived at the medium state of the good life. Since she is healthy and sober in eating and drinking, this latter state will probably continue for a longer period than her early life in the service of evil.

Why all this tardy fuss about the early era *versus* the late, and the emphasis upon a medium condition of life? Some of the critics of Reade's day had been objecting to the custom of sensational novelists and dramatists to neglect what Shakespeare had called "the middle humanity." Probably Reade was distorting their objection to the all-good heroes and the all-bad villains of melodrama, but he flings Lucy Monckton in their teeth as an embodiment of "moral mediocrity." However, since there had been no previous hint in either exposition or complication that Lucy was to be the representative of "middle humanity," this statement can only be a bit of impromptu bravado on Reade's part, an attempt to make one think that the character was far better worked out and more philosophically oriented than she was. Then, having adduced his shaky evidence for this doubtful thesis, Reade abandons the argument entirely and lets one know what was really suspected all along — that Lucy is only a lay figure of evil, female gender, and that the novelist's real interest lies with his good and heroic characters. Reade considered fiction to be the parent of history, and would never place the parent below its child. His real admiration is never for median states, but for those superior men and women who make life beautiful and who raise the level of all humanity. They are the figures, he writes at the close of the novel, whom he enjoys depicting; and they are the only ones he leaves at the end of the last chapter with regret.

With such a complacent flourish, Reade ends his book and, looking about, discovers himself standing side by side with his arch foe, Thomas Carlyle; for both writers joined assiduously in "hero-worship." Of course, had Reade so desired, he could with justice have cited no less an an authority than Socrates-Plato to the effect that the writers of the ages had to depict noble and heroic men doing noble and heroic deeds if the populace were ever to be trained in the highest morality. No poet who persisted in depicting the gods engaged in ungodlike activities would be left uncensored in the *Republic,* and since dramatists required effeminate male characters who flaunt their fortune and cry aloud in their sorrows, then drama would not be allowed in the republic of wisdom at all.

CHAPTER 3

# Novels: On Social Issues

THE last sentence of *Put Yourself in His Place* reveals Charles Reade's intention for his novels about current social issues: ". . . I have taken a few undeniable truths out of many, and have laboured to make my readers realize those appalling facts of the day which most men know, but not one in a thousand comprehends, and not one in a hundred thousand realizes, until fiction — which, whatever you may have been told to the contrary, is the highest, widest, noblest, and greatest of all the arts — comes to his aid, studies, penetrates, digests the hard facts of chronicles and blue-books, and makes their dry bones live." Reade's friend Wilkie Collins collected all the remarkable police cases and judicial narratives he could find; and, out of the vast accumulation of bizarre criminal facts, he chose the bricks to go into the solid fabric of his mystery stories. As the author of *Woman in White* and *The Moonstone*, Collins was ever on the alert for perplexing criminal oddities; but the author of *It Is Never Too Late to Mend*, *Hard Cash*, and *Put Yourself in His Place* cast himself in the pleasing romantic role of knight-errant who went striding across a kingdom to find those legal or social wrongs that he believed only the writer of fiction could redress.

Reade was by no means alone in such an attempt. Charles Dickens struck at the dark places of society with lavish outpourings of comedy, eccentricities galore, involved and coincidental plots, pathos and bathos; he buried his social criticisms in so rich a tissue of humanity that they tended to become particular peccadilloes rather than a general indictment.[1] Harriet Martineau made up her characteristically dry little stories about the application of morality to social economy, and Benjamin Disraeli bound together scurrilous gossip of high society with excerpts from his own parliamentary speeches and called them "social novels." For Reade, all the facts had to be there on the printed page; but he so fused them with plot and character that to tell the story or to describe the character's predicament was automatically to expose social abuse. He was not always successful, however, in producing exactly the proper fusion of fact and fiction.

Unfortunately the social novel, in the hands of whatever practitioner, tends to become the story of colorless people set in elaborately accurate staging. Although Reade was unquestionably, in this department of literary activity, a forerunner of Emile Zola and of the realistic and naturalistic movements, he nevertheless often assured that the "facts" of his blue books and newspaper accounts necessarily became the "truth" of literature. Indeed, it is interesting to note that Zola was doing editorial and translator's work for the French firm of Hachette et Frères at the very time that the company was publishing pirated translations of Reade's novels for the French reading public. Reade's information was always valuable, delightfully available, and necessary to his forensic purpose; but he often permitted it to degenerate into the clutter that jumbled Victorian architecture, crowded Victorian parlors, and finally became so eccentrically eclectic that it ruined Victorian taste. Nonetheless, his factual novels suited an age suspicious of poetic fancy, enamored with the ideal of scientific observation, and busy collecting every kind of monstrosity and knickknack as if it were all authentic treasure.

In 1940, George Orwell addressed himself to the factuality of Reade's novels and at the same time estimated that three of his works (*Foul Play, Hard Cash,* and *It Is Never Too Late to Mend*) would outlive the entire works of Meredith and George Eliot:

What is the attraction of Reade? . . . it is the charm of useless knowledge. Reade was a man of what one might call penny-encyclopaedic learning. He possessed vast stocks of disconnected information which a lively narrative gift allowed him to cram into books. . . . If you have . . . the sort of mind that likes knowing exactly how a medieval catapult worked or just what objects a prison cell of the eighteen-forties contained, then you can hardly help enjoying Reade. He himself, of course, did not see his work in quite this light. He prided himself on his accuracy and compiled his books largely from newspaper cuttings, but the strange facts which he collected were subsidiary to what he would have regarded as his "purpose." For he was a social reformer in a fragmentary way, and made vigorous attacks on such diverse evils as blood-letting, the treadmill, private lunatic asylums, clerical celibacy and tight-lacing.[2]

Years before the Goncourts coined the expression "the human document," Reade was busily compiling large volumes and cards of newspaper clippings and personal testimony of persons who had worked or lived in highly specialized surroundings. Before writing novels about sheep raisers, gold miners, and fishermen, he read the standard travel books and collected special accounts from individuals who could speak from experience. Members of his own family could brief him on nautical matters;[3] he kept hack writers busy at the Bodleian Library and in the British Museum culling facts and writing up cases for his files.[4] As he so bluntly put it, he milked about two hundred cows into the pail of each story and thus created a highly mixed but not very homogenized product.

As for what his elaborate system of cards, notes, clippings, research writers, travel diaries, and much, much more did for Reade, the answer has never been better and more fully stated than by Walter Frewen Lord in 1906:

"In the course of that career he wrote very well indeed about Australia without having been there; he wrote in great detail about banking without having been in business; he wrote of strikes and "rattening" as if he had been a picketed operative; he described accidents and incidents in coal-mines much better than most men who pass their lives in that kind of work. . . . His knowledge of prison life makes one marvel how it could have been acquired except as a warder or an amateur convict. Lunatic asylums had a special attraction for him; they were fruitful . . . of blood-curdling melodrama where almost every page contains not only a judicious thrill, but a valuable piece of information (laboriously acquired by the author) and a handsome moral. It is inconceivable that any man could write the sea-fight in *Hard Cash* without having himself commanded, and fought, a merchant vessel. . . . He is equally at home with respectability and with crime; and when he tells us of a forgery it is our own fault if we cannot go away and do likewise . . . he laboured over detail to an extent that far out-distances any other writer of his time.[5]

I    It Is Never Too Late to Mend: A Matter of Fact Romance *(1856)*

On June 10, 1852, Charles Reade had finished the novel *Peg Woffington*, which was based on his play *Masks and Faces*. Almost immediately, he sketched, in a great burst of energy, the plot outline of *Gold*, the genesis of his novel *It Is Never Too Late to Mend*. By December, 1852, Reade had begun, between the demanding productions of *Masks and Faces* and *Gold*, to write *Christie John-*

*stone*. He finished this work in the early summer and at once began the familiar task of making a novel out of *Gold*. This novel, first called "Susan Merton," was later given the proverbial title Swinburne so deplored — *It Is Never Too Late to Mend*. When the two-volume work was published on August 1, 1856, it was reviewed in *Bentley's Miscellany* as "incomparably the best novel of the season";[6] other major critics (with the exception of the writers for the *Saturday Review*) were unanimous in its praise, but each had some minor criticisms to make.

Much comment was made by these critics about the seeming independence of the two halves of the book: Berkshire is the beginning and the end, but English prisons and Australian goldfields are sandwiched in between. The explanation for this cleavage is that Reade meant to use his melodrama as the mere frame for a terrifying picture of prison life in England of the time. Reade's source for the inserted material came from "a noble passage in the *Times* of September 7th or 8th, 1853"; and with it, Reade set out, somewhat grimly, to test the lines of procedure he had for long accepted intellectually but had as yet hardly used. On June 20, he wrote: "I propose never to guess where I can know." Since his story crossed the sea to Australia and plunged the reader into gold mines there, Reade began to make lists of the necessary preparations for the author. "To be consistent with myself I ought to cross-examine at the very least a dozen men that have farmed, dug, or robbed in that land. . . . Failing these I must read books and letters and do the best I can. Such is the mechanism of a novel by Charles Reade." After this complacent boast, he faces the potentialities of success and failure: "Now, I know exactly what I am worth. If I can work the above great system there is enough of me to make one of the writers of the day; without it, NO, NO."[7]

Other than the usual objections to the use of unwieldy and proverbial titles, not enough attention has been given to the title of this novel as a clue to its central meaning. It may, in addition, have been a prophetic double entendre that Reade aimed at himself, for he was forty-two at the time and may have felt very much a failure so far as both drama and the novel were concerned. But an analysis of the patterns of characterization indicates that this novel is clearly an Evangelical study of the conversion experience. If a person sees the error of his ways, no matter how old nor how hardened in them he may be, if he truly repents, can he really begin afresh on a new path

108                                        CHARLES READE

and can he maintain it? The central character was probably meant to
be Tom Robinson, who, in the first section of the book, is a free man
but is despaired of by the decent people who know his past. The second section depicts him in prison among other criminals, where he
meets a saintly chaplain who does not despair of Tom's possibilities
for reform. The third section, which portrays the new life of the
redeemed man, is honestly enough presented to admit a temporary
fall from grace in Sydney, which is followed by a humbled and fearful return to the path the chaplain had laid out for him. Reade treats
this solemn theme with enough lightness to show how indignant a
reformed thief can become when someone has stolen a hard-earned
fortune from him!

But what is true of Robinson is also true to a lesser degree of the
other characters. When Robinson is being taken to the Black Hole,
he screams at the new chaplain (Mr. Francis Eden): "Do you see
this, you in the black coat? You that told us the other day you loved
us, and now stand coolly there and see me taken to the black hole to
be got ready for the mad-house? D'ye hear?" The chaplain replies,
gravely and gently, "I hear you" (Chapter XIII). Thus, all Mr.
Eden's inspired preaching will do no good until he "gravely and
gently" accepts the responsibility of making his idealism work in the
lives of the prisoners and in the conduct of a British prison.

Even the resolutely good *émigré* George Fielding, in Australia to
earn enough to marry Susan, has to learn the odd lesson that mere
goodness is not enough. Robinson ponders about the case of Fielding
with amazement, for here is an honest man who never prospers. Is
this the unrewarded honesty to which he has been converted? Reade
permits the former felon to come to an astonishing but nevertheless
honest conclusion: success in the world does not come from goodness
alone, but from the combination of virtue with that cluster of circumstances which is generally called "luck." George, who left
England cursing his fate and feeling like a British Job suffering un-
merited punishment, must come to a humbler definition of self.
When George is at last glad just to be alive, the tide turns, and he
begins to receive his due reward.

The novel has been criticized not only for the two somewhat
se parate halves but also because it seems to have no single hero. If it
is only a romance, this lack is a real difficulty; but, if it is a book
written to illustrate the title, enrichment results from three very
different heroes — thief, good man, and saint — since for each of

them "it is never too late to mend." Reade's stubborn extension of
this thesis to the bitter end is illustrated by the departure abroad of
the thwarted villain Meadows, his mother, and her servant. Not
satisfied to send him away with all his schemes awry and his life in
ruins around him, Reade tells his readers that Meadow's mother has
plans to make him repent his evil past and to lead him to conversion.

Dedicated, oddly enough, to the president, fellows, and demies of
Magdalen College, Reade's "attempt at a solid fiction" is an almost
complete denial of academic posture. The story claims that
knowledge comes from experience, not from books; that self-
knowledge is not everything; and that human personality can un-
dergo remarkable transformations through the power of the Gospel.
The thesis rejects idea, ideal, and theory until each has proved its
adequacy by operating successfully in the real world. Of course, the
nature of the book cannot help but suggest the author's great admiration for Charles Dickens. Like his master, Reade seizes upon
some glaring public and social evil, footlights it with the dramatic
techniques he had learned from the stage, and holds the illuminated
and magnified evil up to public indignation. Just as *Bleak House* exposes the glacial cruelty of the Court of Chancery, *Hard Times*
shows human life strangled by the red tape of officialdom, and *Little
Dorritt* reveals the hopelessness of imprisonment for debt, *It Is
Never Too Late to Mend* presents a powerful and unforgettable picture of the bestial inhumanity with which prisoners were treated in
some nineteenth-century British jails.

Beyond mere choice of topics, many Dickensian touches are
noticeable in character, dialogue, and incident. In Chapter XI,
Reade echoes Dickens's insistence on the influence of environment
on character by claiming that prison treatment harmed Robinson's
"soul more than had years of burglary and petty larceny." It is a
highly Dickensian feast, both as to irony and menu, to which Mr.
Williams, the prison overseer, sits down after deciding that the
prison gruel was too thick and rich: soup with tapioca, salmon,
lobster patties, rissoles, turkey, tongue, mutton, pigeon, greengage
tart, yellow custard, iced pudding, Stilton cheese, salad, muscadel
grapes, guava jelly, and wines. Dickensian also is the death of
prisoner Edward Josephs, aged fifteen, who hangs himself in his cell
by his own pocket handkerchief; Dickensian are the sentimental
references to mother and friends; Dickensian is the quiet malice of
the public indictment. While a fifteen-year-old lad is hanging

himself, the author appends the soothing refrain "ILS EST DEUX
HEURES: TOUT EST TRANQUILLE: DORMEZ, MAITRES,
DORMEZ!"[8]

Reade, with his legal training, often slips into the highly effective
rhetoric of legal indictment:

Thus in the nineteenth century, in a kind-hearted nation, under the most
humane sovereign the world has ever witnessed on an earthly throne . . .
Edward Josephs has been done to death in the queen's name, in the name of
England, and in the name of the law. . . . For the present, the account
between Josephs and the law stands thus: — Josephs has committed the
smallest theft imaginable. He has stolen food. For this the law, professing to
punish him with certain months imprisonment, has inflicted capital punishment; has overtasked, crucified, starved — overtasked, starved, crucified —
robbed him of light, of sleep, of hope, of life; has destroyed his body, and
perhaps his soul. (Chapter XXVII)

The versatile author then turns to the technique of the financial ac-
countant: "Sum total — 1st page of account —

| Josephs | The Law |
|---|---|
| a larcenist and | a liar and |
| a corpse. | a felon." |

*Never Too Late* (or as even Reade, oppressed by the excessive
length of its title, called it in his notebooks, "Sera Nunquam") is,
like many of Dickens's works, a study in contrasts. Isaac Levi, the
righteous but unforgiving Jewish usurer, balances John Meadows,
the Christian but unrighteous Gentile usurer. Contrasted are the two
unfavored lovers: William Fielding fights temptation by staying
away from Susan Merton, but John Meadows feeds his desire by
hovering closer and closer to the flame. Two prison systems are contrasted: The old higgledy-piggledy massing of all levels of criminals
in large dormitory accommodations provided not only dangerous exposure of all to the worst but also comforting warmth of contact with
others suffering the same penalties. Solitary confinement, the new
system, which sounds sensible because of its careful classification of
prisoners, is actually inhuman because of the intolerable loneliness it
inflicts.

A contrast also exists between the visiting prison chaplain from the
north of England, the Reverend James Lepel, who gets along splendidly with the sadistic governor, Mr. Hawes, and Mr. Francis Eden,
who sets himself resolutely to break Hawes's illegal discipline and to
reform the prison administration. The small cells and the tiny fields

of tight little England, contrast with the vastness of space in the sub-continent of Australia. In England, propertied villainy, in the form of Mr. Meadows, is victorious; in Australia, with its extreme flexibility of economic status, the virtuous triumph and are able to return to triumph in England. Of course, the most striking contrast is between the two Robinsons: the thief who in England helped to destroy George's standing in his home community, and the partner who in Australia was a tower of resourcefulness and the molder of his fortune.

As usual, elements of melodramatic excess hurt the emotional motivation of the characters. Mr. Eden is one of Reade's fainting heroes: he writes a "stiff memorial" to the secretary for the Home Department demanding an inquiry into the conduct of the jail; sends a copy to the prison governor Hawes, directs and seals his own copy, and then falls onto a sofa in a dead faint. This melodramatic swoon gives the author an opportunity for a melodramatic rescue, for Susan arrives with her Aunt Davies and posts the letter (Chapter XVII).

When Robinson has been committed to the dark hole and is about to lose his mind after six hours of incarceration, he hears the voice of the new chaplain comforting him with the word "brother." This scene is quite believable and even acceptable to modern readers, but it becomes incredibly effusive when Robinson, in an access of emotion, cries to his comforter: "I am kissing your dear hand. There! There! There! I bless you! I love you! I adore you! I am kissing your hand, and I am on my knees blessing you and kissing. Oh, my heart! my heart! my heart!" (Chapter XV).

Once again, this Reade novel is rich in irony. It is comic irony that the villainous Mr. Hawes hates Simon Legree (villain of Harriet Beecher Stowe's *Uncle Tom's Cabin*) and fervently hopes that his cruelty will be punished. It is heroic irony that Robinson should discover large "sheets of gold" in the roof and walls of the very tunnel the villains laboriously dug to rob the hero of his little hoard. Rhetorical irony echoes from Isaac Levi's revelation that he had fitted Meadow's house with piping that carries the sounds of every word spoken to Levi's house: "You had no mercy on the old Jew. You took his house from him, not for your need but for hate. So he made that house a trap and caught you in your villainy!" (Chapter L).

Reade also found it pleasant to indulge in some of his old sensational tricks. He enjoys substituting little pictures for words — a bit like rotogravure pages for children — and so he draws for the reader a picture of a little nugget of gold balanced for scale on the end of a prospector's knife. As enamored as ever with the disguise technique, he dresses his villain in donkey skins and has him wear a donkey head, but that villain is quite capable, even in this ponderous costume, of crawling on his hands and knees with a dagger held between his teeth. The French technique of the false *dénouement* is dragged out again when Susan is given false news of George's marriage abroad, thus setting her free to marry Meadows as an expression of her appreciation for his kindness and because of family pressure. One of the incredible moments of melodrama occurs when Tom Robinson is able to identify all his stolen money — seven thousand pounds — because he had memorized the serial numbers on the bills.

The Victorian earnestness responsible for Reade's inception of the work also marked it completion. In the twenty-second chapter of volume two, Reade extols the Victorian doctrine of progress and its consummation in the nineteenth century: "When we write a story or sing a poem of the great nineteenth century I give you my sacred word of honour there is but one fear — not that our theme will be beneath us, but we shall lack the comprehensive vision a man must have from heaven to catch the historical the poetic the lasting features of the Titan events that stride so swiftly past IN THIS GIGANTIC AGE!!!"

One of the things about "Sera Nunquam" that struck contemporaries was the marvelous factuality of the Australian settings, the cattle-raising country and the gold-mining areas. In an essay about Henry Kingsley, written when Henry James was only twenty-two, the critic cited Reade to make his point:

It is one of those rudimentary truths which cannot be too often repeated, that to write a novel it is not necessary to have been a traveller, an adventurer, a sightseer; it is simply necessary to be an artist. Mr. Kingsley's descriptions of Australia are very pretty; but they are not half so good as those of Mr. Charles Reade, who, as far as we know, has never visited the country. . . . Mr. Reade went to Australia — that is, his imagination went — on purpose to compose certain chapters in "Never Too Late to Mend." Mr. Kingsley went in the flesh; but Mr. Kingsley in the flesh is not equal to Mr. Reade in the spirit.[9]

Australian writers have questioned James's judgment; but most agree that, whether on the stage or in a novel, whether through the eyes of experience or the reading glasses of the study, Reade's descriptions were always "vivid."

In 1858, Reade published a volume, *Cream*, which included "Jack of All Trades: A Matter of Fact Romance," and "The Autobiography of a Thief." Readers of *It Is Never Too Late to Mend* discover in Volume II that the chaplain Eden sets the thief Robinson to the task of writing an honest account of his past life: "He was not to white-wash, and then gild himself, nor yet to vent one long self-deceiving howl of general, and therefore sham penitence, but he was to be, with God's help, his own historian and sober critic." Accordingly, Thomas Robinson writes his jail epistle, "The Autobiography of a Thief," and at first Reade planned to include this novelette in the longer novel. To resign this plan was a struggle because he considered the account "the central gem of my little coronet." Since the printer had warned Reade that the novel manuscript was, by his calculation, enough for five ordinary volumes without the autobiography, he decided to omit it. When explaining this omission, however, he preened his artistic feathers and said in the prefatory note to "The Autobiography of a Thief" that "a story within a story is a frightful flaw in art."

In some mysterious manner, Reade seems really to have convinced himself that his autobiography of a thief was an actual autobiography written by a real thief. He confesses humbly that the novel presented Thomas Robinson "tinted in water-colours by me," but in the autobiography he would be "painted in oils by himself, and retouched by Mr. Eden." The autobiography proper runs about forty-eight pages, and then Reade does the oddest thing of all. Under headings A., B., C., etc., he comments on the paragraphs of the confession, and these comments are not primarily about facts but about language, connotation, and denotation. At one point he is annoyed by Robinson's phrase " 'collected and took with me.' No such thing. 'Stole' is the word that represents the transactions. Always be precise! Never tamper with words: Call a spade a spade and a picklock a picklock — that is the first step toward digging instead of thieving." The moralizing tendency is clear, but perhaps what is not clear is the imitation of the factual imposture of Jonathan Swift and Daniel Defoe. By criticizing his own prose when he writes in the person of an imaginary thief, Reade manages to distance the thief and make him seem somehow separate from his creator.

But unfortunately the sensationalism of the confession did not quite fulfill the anticipation built up by the advertisement. The "central gem" of Reade's little coronet sparkles very little, nor would it have livened the novel from which it was — very wisely — omitted.

## II   Love Me Little, Love Me Long *(1859)*

Malcolm Elwin called *Love Me Little, Love Me Long* a "milk-and-water story" noteworthy only as a mawkish prelude to *Hard Cash*. Probably written in haste to provide money to publish *The Eighth Commandment*, Reade's pamphlet against copyright abuses, *Love Me Little* hardly fits with novels written primarily about social issues, but it does concern marriages between persons of different social classes. On the other hand, this novel is not simply a "matter of fact romance" because there is no dominant female character; and the hero, David Dodd, not only does not faint easily but is a thoroughly dominating, swashbuckling character in the best tradition of the adventure novel. David, the perfect figure of upright masculinity, is poor but worthy; and he must carve a career for himself. Amid persons of languid and fastidious boredom, he alone is vital: he can play the violin melodiously, and he can tell sea stories entrancingly. Drawn by the plot into a group that is playing at lovemaking and marriage, he alone is capable of real passion and its appropriate manly expression.

Lucy, the heroine, is a very unselfish girl who wants only to please and to be loved; but she is unfortunately also intelligent. As a result, when "Fountain [her bachelor uncle] kept showing and proving Mrs. Bazalgette's [her aunt] egotism; and Mrs. Bazalgette kept showing and proving Mr. Fountain's egotism; Lucy ended by seeing both their egotisms as clearly as either could desire" (Chapter XXV). The play of these two egotists and the skillful but sad manner in which Lucy thwarts them without ever being rude or unpleasant to either makes delightful drawing-room comedy. Indeed, these scenes make the reader suspect that this, too, is a novel quickly transposed from an earlier drama or dramatic sketch, although no such documentary evidence is available to indicate its dramatic source.

Indeed, Reade appears to have taken *Peg Woffington*, with its marvelous verve and audacity of dialogue, to have split it down the middle, and to have inserted one single sensational episode near the French coast — a thrilling rescue in the best seafaring tradition, with elaborate use of nautical language and technicalities. Also, the inspiration for the characters of both the hero and the heroine may have been within Reade's own family, representing a biographical link rare in a Reade novel.

When Charles Reade was a child, he was largely reared by his second sister, Julia. The boy developed a strong attachment to his sister and managed to include in his affection her husband, Captain Allen Francis Gardiner, Royal Navy, whom she married in 1823. The *Memoir's* rapturous references to the grace and beauty of Julia and to the splendid manhood of Allen presumably represent a family tradition that Charles Reade heartily shared. Malcolm Elwin, as biographer of Charles Reade, suggests that, when Julia died after only eleven years of marriage, Reade consciously or unconsciously sought an opportunity to memorialize her in fiction, and may have done so in 1863 in the figure of Lucy Dodd; and even her captain husband may have served for the portrait of the gallant Captain David Dodd.

So capable, brave, and ingenious is David Dodd that he barely misses being the "Admirable Crichton" that Robert Penfold becomes on the desert island of *Foul Play*. Not only is this Reade tale an unusual romance because of the courage and dominance of the hero, but it is even more unusual because of the development of its characters. The problem with both his romances and social novels is that characters in the romances are presented and then tend to be arrested and static, and characters in the social novels are blown about like paper dolls by great social issues. But David Dodd matures from the yearning hero who bursts into tears when refused by his fair lady to the David Dodd who will not accept the command of a ship through her influence without the proffer of her hand in marriage. And Lucy begins as a cool, self-contained young lady who desires no husband but rather the continuance of her pleasant single state; barely able to comprehend David's passion, she is totally incapable of sharing it. In the end, however, she is able to appreciate the true, strong passion of a real man for a woman.

Generally, the other characters deteriorate: John Fountain and Mrs. Bazalgette are revealed as self-centered, self-seeking leeches who care nothing for the real happiness of their ward but who use her as an instrument of their own comfort, a pawn against an adversary, or even as a victim with whom to punish the object of a mild flirtation. When the story concludes, Lucy, who has come to appreciate real persons and real love, has to be separated from these unreal creatures of pettishness and sharp little irritations. The only member of the Fountain-Bazalgette family who grows is Uncle Bazalgette; at the beginning, he is a cipher whose only function is to hand out money, but he becomes at the close a strong balance between his wife's petty infatuations and his niece's future happiness.

When Reade introduces the banker Mr. Hardie, an unsuccessful candidate for Lucy's hand, he takes the opportunity to display his erudite research in a whimsical little essay about the nature of the older style of banking: "The Hardies were goldsmiths in the seventeenth century; and when that business split, and the deposit and bill of exchange business went one way, and the plate and jewels another, they became bankers from father to son." Mr. Hardie's chief traffic was in deposits that bore no interest, a transaction that was known in that period as "the legitimate banking business." Reade ridicules this title as one that could not have been invented by the customers for a system entirely "destitute of that reciprocity which is the soul of all just and legitimate commercial relations." As Rea rather overdramatically asserts, its principle was, "You shall lend me your money gratis, and I will lend it out at interest: such is legitimate banking — in the opinion of bankers" (Chapter XI).

Abandoning the imposture of lofty disdain of Hardie's business transactions, Reade penned a disquisition about the bank failures of 1831 for the length of two chapters, XI and XII, or about forty pages. This kind of disquisition led even Reade's great admirer Swinburne to refer to his besetting sins as "pretention and prolixity."[10] Although Reade was generally concise in method of narration and in authorial comment, he could be "tediously prolix" in discussing tangential matters that happened to catch his attention; in including extraneous material he happened to come across in his voluminous notecards and could not resist using, or in taking a wild ride on his latest hobbyhorse, whether or not it could be fitted into any stable of that particular novelistic landscape. Scissors, which have occasionally been applied to the novels of Dickens, Richardson, and Scott, might to equal advantage snip away those interminable "facts" with which Reade "enriched" his work and that later generations consider to be padding, ostentation, or worse — failure of the creative imagination.

Yet Reade can scarcely be blamed for being a part of that literary landslide from François Chateaubriand to Honoré de Balzac — that movement from the Romantic idea of literary power as a heaven-sent gift of invention and creation that needed no test of verisimilitude to establish its value and relevance, to Balzac's attempt to present a sociological study, rich in environmental factors, family heredity, interpersonal relationships, economic pressures, and obsessive motivations. Reade's suspicion of fancy and his confident reliance upon solid fact as stammered forth in the municipal courts of London and reported in the daily press constituted his enthusiastic assent to the naturalistic movement on the Continent and his pioneering efforts on its behalf in England. Rather than create a world, he felt that the world would create its own fiction — a fiction solidly based upon fact, educational in its exactness, and elevating in its moral value.

At the close of his novel, Reade addressed a warning to male readers: "No male will understand Lucy Fountain, who does not take 'instinct' and 'self-deception' into the account." Perhaps this statement is a lame explanation for the somewhat ambiguous title, as well as for his heroine. Lucy seems that odd kind of woman who is quite satisfied to be the spectator at other men's feasts, to live as a ward in two homes, and to spend her life running errands for two ungrateful egotists. She really does not want to marry, and men with their erotic demands and their inconsiderate dislocations of her pleasant routine sincerely annoy and mystify her. So, at the beginning, she has little love to offer; but this little represents a willingness to learn and to grow, and thus finally to love, not little, but long. At any rate, Reade seems to have again been engaged, first, in apologizing for the comparative brevity of his study: "But with those two clews you cannot, I think, fail to unravel her; and will, I hope, thank me in your hearts for leaving you something to study, and not clogging a languid narrative with a mass of comment and explanation." But, second, he is, as usual, referring to his conviction of the inferior place of prose fiction to that of drama, in which there is no temptation to clog the dialogue with masses of comment and explanation.

Reade began *Love Me Little, Love Me Long* with a preface that almost promised a sequel: "Should these characters, inbedded in carpet incidents, interest the public at all, they will probably reappear in more potent scenes." The author evidently recognized that *Love Me Little, Love Me Long* had a rather "languid narrative," and this humbling recognition must have driven him to promise that, when the reader next met the characters in *Hard Cash*, (1863), they would "reappear in more potent scenes."

### III   Hard Cash *(1863)*

Between August and December, 1858, Reade zealously collected evidence against the corrupt conduct of private asylums in England. He shared with the public the first fruits of his sociological labor in "Our Dark Places," a series of letters to newspapers. Five years later, the evidence supplied the basis of the novel *Hard Cash;* and eight years later the material was utilized for several scenes in *A Terrible Temptation.* Thus an attempt to revive the art of the literary pamphlet, as formerly wielded by Swift and Defoe, resulted in sensational social novels; indeed, critics of the period feverishly debated whether or not the examination of prisons and madhouses provided suitable subject for the art of fiction. Swinburne insisted, concerning the prison episodes in *It Is Never Too Late to Mend*, that "there is not, however, in all the range of his work, another as flagrant instance of passionate philanthropy riding roughshod over the ruins of artistic propriety." He somewhat modified his harsh strictures, however, in regard to *Hard Cash* in which "the crusade against the villainous lunacy of the law regarding lunatics was conducted with more literary tact and skill — with nobler energy and ardour it could not be conducted."[11]

After referring to the critical controversy about *Hard Cash*, *Blackwood's Magazine* opined that fiction "has a right to every spot on which men struggle and suffer, with the one only proviso that her powers are equal to it — and no man can complain of Mr. Reade that he has failed to vindicate his capability of treating one of the most painful subjects within the ken of man."[12] Dr. Orestes Brownson, in his usually conservative *Quarterly Review*, went so far as to claim that "Mr. Reade has done a braver deed in his exposure of these asylums than Dickens did by his exhibiton of Dotheboy Hall, and he has avoided the manifest exaggeration which Dickens is never able to escape."[13] Although *Love Me Little, Love Me Long* had reverted to Reade's natural length for a romance of one volume, *Hard Cash* (or *Very Hard Cash* as it appeared piecemeal in *All the Year Round*) was once again trivoluminous. Despite Dickens's personal admiration, the serial was none too successful and was rumored to have lowered the circulation of the magazine by three thousand copies; at least the loss was so serious that Dickens had to ask his assistant, Wills, to perform the delicate task of requesting Reade to cut the story short.

In writing a sequel, an author takes a certain risk in introducing the same set of characters after an interval of twenty years; and, although Reade surely meant the chief *personae* to come off well, it is not certain that they did. With tongue in cheek, Reade referred to the marriage of David Dodd and Lucy Fountain as a "misalliance" and reiterated his earlier insistence that, when she married him, she was not "in love with him," but became "her husband's lover after marriage, though not before." At sea, the captain capably sails his ship through storm, survived an attack by pirates, and withstands the peccadilloes of difficult passengers; on land, David Dodd ends in a lunatic asylum and has to be rescued by his own son from a fire; and he totally loses his memory until resuscitated from supposed death by the bite of a fly! Lucy, too, seems to have suffered some by the passing of the years. The ample hospitalities of Fountain Abbey were somehow more appropriate to her chatelaineship than the tea parties of Barkington; and the sense that she is living amid an inferior class has absorbed her in her family to the exclusion of a vulgar, pushing world that could not claim her as equal.

Richard Hardie also deteriorates with the years. In *Love Me Little, Love Me Long* he was handsome, absorbed in making money, but honorable and a gentleman of integrity. In the later volumes, he invests in a "bubble" he knows is certain to burst, embezzles from his own firm, steals the deposit of his successful rival for Lucy's hand, dips into the trust funds of his own children, keeps a mistress in the same house as his severely Evangelical daughter, lies to his son, curses him, and locks him up in an asylum with the intention of keeping him there until death!

W. L. Courtney, in his judgment that there is "very little trace of Oxford in Charles Reade," seems to have missed the very spirited account of the Henley Boat Race to which Reade devotes not only an exciting first chapter in *Hard Cash* but also a second even more moving one concerning the hospitalities that followed the race. However, Courtney admitted that there was "an indefinable air of Eton and Oxford in Alfred Hardie."[14] Hardie's enforced incarceration in lunatic asylums not only permits him to exhibit the infinite resourcefulness of a well-educated mind but gives the author an opportunity to see those dark places of England through his ardent, youthful eyes. However, the episode also permits the author to fall into his favorite pattern of the hero who is mysteriously away from home. To his father, Hardie becomes a dangerous foe capable of escaping even the most expert vigilance and of upsetting all his financial plots; to his sister, his absence is sad and absolutely inexplicable; to his fiancée, his involuntary departure on the eve of his wedding brands him as a deceiver who enjoyed playing with her affections.

Just as the character of Alfred Hardie falls into well-traveled creative paths for the author, another of Reade's corny Americans and one more of his Negro escapees from a Christie minstrel show reappear. Joshua Fullalove is a Methodist parson, but in order to express that practical genius which was already the stereotype of the American, Reade makes him also an engineer, an inventor, and a dedicated maker of money. Through Fullalove, the author enjoys taking an oblique and sardonic glance at the American institution of slavery: "he [Fullalove] played at elevating the African character to European levels. With this view he had bought . . . Vespasian [a Negro companion] for eighteen hundred dollars; whereof anon. American is fertile in mixtures: what do we not owe her? Sherry-cobbler, gin-sling, cocktail, mint-julep, brandy-smash, sudden death, eye-openers. Well one day she outdid herself and mixed Fullalove: Quaker, Nimrod, Archimedes, philanthropist, decorous Red Rover, and what not" (Volume I, Chapter VII). As for Vespasian, Fullalove's Negro companion, he is the stock comic figure: he uses long words, has a great sense of humor, but is subject to unaccountable rages. The Reverend Mr. Fullalove expresses his humorous dejection about the Nego character in Reade's concept of Yankee speech: "Darn the critter! he's fixed my flint eternally. Now I cave. I swan to man I may just hand up my fiddle, for this darky's too hard a row to hoe" (Volume I, Chapter X).

As stock Reade characters appear, the stock novelistic construction is also used. The elder hero away from home, Captain David Dodd provides the much-admired battle against two pirate ships in which the captain of the *Agra* is wounded (Volume I, Chapter VIII). Another sensational moment is the battle with a mighty tempest in which the "hard cash," Captain Dodd's fourteen thousand pounds, is lost, but is then miraculously recovered in a bottle attached to a bladder bobbing about with the other flotsam from the *Agra*. Reade's familiar habit of developing two streams of narrative that converge at a climactic moment into one unified stream is referred to quite frankly as " 'love' and 'cash,' the converging branches of this story, [which] will flow together in one stream" (Volume II, Chapter XIV).

Fond of satirizing the medical profession, Reade includes not one but three doctors: the Scottish Dr. Sampson (based on Dr. Dickson who was listed in Reade's notebooks under the topic "Dickeybird-iana") with his "chronothairmal" system of diagnosis is surely one of the most infuriating and endearing doctors in literature; the learned quack, Dr. Osmond, thinks Alfred has the "incubation of insanity"; and Dr. Wycherley, although his bonnet contains its own bee, is both amiable and admirable: "Dr. Wycherley, you see, was a collector of mad people, and collectors are always amateurs and very solemn connoisseurs. His turn of mind co-operating with his interests led him to put down any man a lunatic whose intellect was manifestly superior to his own. Alfred Hardie, and one or two more contemporaries, had suffered by this humour of the good doctor's" (Volume II, Chapter XXX).

Edith Archbold, with her dark hair and bushy brows, falls into the steroeotype of Reade's "other woman"; but the frank description of her amorous nature is startling in the Victorian era. Of powerful frame, she is the head nurse at Silverton Grove House where Alfred is an involuntary inmate. Her exterior mirrors her interior: all is vigorous, strong passion, strong self-control, and strong will. She is attracted to Alfred by his extraordinary energy and the tenacity of his purpose to escape. She sees him fighting against seven or eight men and, after almost beating them, surrendering voluntarily to her. Maintaining perfect control over her appearance, she yet permits her fancy to smolder into passion. When Alfred is transferred from Dr. Wycherley's comparatively enlightened sanitarium to Drayton House, Dr. Wolf's veritable prison, Mrs. Archbold, dressed magnificently, is there ahead of him and complacently confesses she is Wolf's new matron. But there her control is swept away by passion, as with "one grand serpentine movement she came suddenly close to him, and, standing half behind him, laid her hand softly on his shoulder, and poured burning love in his ear. 'Alfred,' she murmured, 'we are both unhappy; let us comfort one another. I had pity on you at Silverton House, I pity you now: pity *me* a little in turn; take me out of this dreadful house, out of this revolting life, and let me be with you. Let me be your housekeeper, your servant, your slave.' "

When Alfred tried to quiet her panting confession, she persists: "I, like you, am warm and tender; at my age a woman's love is bliss to him who can gain it; and I love you with all my soul, Alfred; I worship the ground you walk on, my sweet, sweet boy." Then, turning to him even more ardently, she proposes to gain his freedom: "Say you the word, dearest, and I will bribe the servants, and get the keys, and sacrifice my profession forever to give you liberty. . . . Give me a chance to make you mine forever; and, if I fail, treat me as I shall deserve; desert me at once; and then I'll never reproach you; I'll only die for you; as I have lived for you ever since I first saw your heavenly face" (Volume III Chapter VIII). Some strange switch of masculine and feminine roles has apparently taken place; Edith Archbold woos, and her language is the immemorial diction of males who seek to persuade their mistresses. She does not require marriage; she will be housekeeper, servant, or slave. She does not even require a vow of constancy; if her skill in the making of love does not make him completely hers, then the failure will be her own fault, and she will deserve desertion. To make the female ardor even more unmistakable, Reade writes: "The passionate woman paused at last, but her hot cheek and heaving bosom and tender, convulsive hand prolonged the pleading." Then the author moralizes about the low threshold of sexual temptation for most men; "I am afraid few men of her own age would have resisted her; for voice and speech and and all were burning, melting, and winning: and then so reasonable, lads; she did not stipulate for constancy" (Volume III, Chapter VII).

When Alfred rejects Edith's proposition, she tells him he is a fool not to have accepted her offer of freedom and then run away from her the very next day. But now she will show him "what an insulted woman can do. A lunatic you shall be ere long, and then I'll make you love me, dote on me, follow me about for a smile; and then I'll leave off hating you, and love you once more, but not the way I did five minutes ago." When Alfred threatens to kill her before any such thing should happen, she replies, "If you don't do it very quickly, you shall be my property, my brain-sick, love-sick slave" (Volume III, Chapter VIII).

After having the extraordinary courage or naiveté to paint so passionate and earthy a female, Reade makes amends to offended taste in the conclusion by having Edith Archbold become a widow and marry poor little Frank Beverley, whom she had described as following Alfred around like a little dog, the very figure of the doting idiot she planned to make out of Alfred. Poor Frank is restored to his property but is handed over in savage domesticity to muscular Archbold! Not at all distressed at the prospect, the author, complacently meditates about the wedding; saved by the Victorian conversion pattern, "So you see a female rake can be ameliorated by a loving husband, as well as a male rake by a loving wife" (Volume III, Chapter XXII). The second half of the conversion pattern Reade expanded into *A Terrible Temptation* (1871), in which a male rake is rehabilitated (except for his power to sire children) by a loving wife. And so the author goes offstage, grinning triumphantly after having flouted and satisfied tradition in almost the same blow; but he leaves the loving male lamb Frank in the tender mercies of the ameliorated tigress Edith.

The author varies the narrative style of *Hard Cash* by telling some of the story through the entries in Jane Hardie's and Julia Dodd's diaries, as well as by submitting the former to the ironic comments of her caustic brother, Alfred. The plot is thoroughly milked for every last drop of sentiment in the gushy, ghastly deathbed scene of Jane Hardie;[15] and the pathos of banker Hardie's senile last days as his own's son's unwitting pensioner is exploited. For vigor, the book can have few rivals; but the total effect is marred by Reade's bad logic in assuming that, if an episode works well once, it works better twice or even thrice in the same volume.

## IV  Foul Play (1868)

Samuel Plimsoll, the Liberal member of Parliament from Derby, directed his reform efforts largely against what slangily were called "coffin-ships." Such ships were unseaworthy and overloaded vessels, often heavily insured, in which unscrupulous owners risked the lives of their crews with the double indemnity that, if all went well, the ordinary profits of a voyage with a full cargo would be gained; and, if the ship sank, the insurance would bring a handsome return on the total investment. In 1872, Plimsoll published a study, *Our Seamen*, which exposed this social evil and made a great impression throughout the country. On his motion in Parliament, a royal commission was appointed the following year. When a government bill was introduced in 1875, Plimsoll supported it, although he was convinced of its inadequacy. On July 22, 1875, when Benjamin Disraeli announced that the bill was to be dropped, Plimsoll, shaking his fist in the speaker's face, called the members of the House "villains" because he assumed that the bill had been stifled by shipowners. Eventually he apologized for this outburst, but popular sentiment rallied to his side and forced the government to pass a bill that gave the Board of Trade stringent powers of inspection. As a memorial to his efforts, the line beyond which a ship may not be loaded is generally called the "Plimsoll mark."

Four years before parliamentary reformer Plimsoll wrote his influential study, Reade had heard of the scandalous practice, and he determined to use it in a novel.[16] The dramatist Dion Boucicault collaborated with him on the novel, *Foul Play;* which appeared in *Once a Week,* beginning in January, 1868. After the authors had squabbled their way through a dramatic version that pleased neither and was a comparative failure at the Holborn Theatre, Reade decided to make a dramatic version of his own. With the new title *The Scuttled Ship,* the play was produced on April 2, 1876, with considerable success at John Coleman's new theater in Leeds.

Robert Penfold is the noble but victimized hero of *Foul Play*. As the Reverend Mr. Penfold, he is tutor to Arthur Wardlaw and is falsely accused of a two-thousand-pound forgery that was perpetrated as a jest to prove that a forged signature would not be discovered. Although the forgery is done by other persons in jest, Penfold nevertheless becomes the victim and goes to jail. Once released, he becomes James Seaton and signs on as seaman aboard a Wardlaw ship — "a good, sound vessel," the *Proserpine*, which is to be scuttled by the mate, Joe Wylie, at John Wardlaw's orders for the needed insurance money. Ironically, Helen Rolleston, Arthur Wardlaw's aristocratic fiancée, ends up on the ill fated *Proserpine* because the other Wardlaw ship, the *Shannon*, had to be overhauled in Sydney harbor.

When the *Proserpine* begins to leak, Seaton pleads with Captain Hiram Hudson to abandon ship. When the ship sinks, Seaton is set adrift in an old lifeboat with Helen. Although the heroine has a limited life expectancy because of consumption, she and Seaton (now the Reverend John Hazel, missionary) do splendidly on a desert island, a "Robinson Crusoe" episode that continues for twenty-four chapters (XXIII - XLVII). Pluck and virtue are richly rewarded; for Helen, under the influence of South Sea sunshine, recovers completely. Robert Penfold is enriched by pearls and pirate gold from the island; Arthur goes insane with frustrated malice; and Robert and Helen are united in marital bliss. Economically speaking, the novel describes how the poor but deserving youth Robert Penfold overcomes financial fraud and amasses the capital to be able to afford marriage to Helen, the daughter of Sir Edward Rolleston, general of a crack regiment of the Horse Guards.

A comparison of Reade and Boucicault's novel and Reade's subsequent dramatic version displays the relative strengths and weaknesses of the two genres. Although Reade frequently referred to his preference for the crisp brevity of the dramatic form, his novel permitted time and space for much more adequate motivation of the action than did his play. The first nine pages of the novel are pure exposition, all of which had to be dispersed throughout the drama. The explanation of the arrest of Robert Penfold for forgery is much better in the novel than in the play where it is dragged in largely as a device for the introduction of a new character. Chapter VI of the novel contains the note that the *Shannon* had to be overhauled in Sydney harbor because its pumps kept running night and day; therefore, the novel offers Helen Rolleston adequate motivation to travel on the other Wardlaw ship, the *Proserpine*. The novel gives early warning that Helen is consumptive; the drama mentions this salient fact just before her exposure to the sea in a small boat.

The play employs the exceedingly melodramatic device of having Arthur Wardlaw drop dead on the stage from hate and rage; but the novel presents a more plausible reason, insanity, as the cause of his demise. Nevertheless, the novel closes each chapter with melodramatic curtain lines that would have been more effective for delivery on the stage. Oddly enough, both drama and novel are visited by characters and titles from *Hard Cash:* the ship mentioned in the novel in Chapter XLIV is named the *Julia Dodd;* Joshua Fullalove is its skipper (the Methodist parson?) and Vespasian·is still his Negro companion.

The Robinson Crusoe section of the drama, with its setting on a desert island, is greatly expanded in the novel. Perhaps every romantic wants someday to try his hand at an island idyll and to create an Admirable Crichton who attempts everything and fails at absolutely nothing. Reade was evidently not amused when F. C. Burnand published his skit-parody *Chikkin Hazard* in *Punch*. Even the inoffensive joys of a derelict chair that yields castor oil and of capers cut by a ready hero for the sauce did not amuse Reade — perhaps because Reade, like his admirer Swinburne, wrote his own best parodies — and *Foul Play* is clearly one of them. One must remember, however, that for Reade the romantic interest and the desert island setting were both subordinate to the important novelistic exposé of the scandal of coffin-ships. Orwell's favorite Reade novel was *Foul Play*, although when he suggests that it is not an attack on anything in particular, we can only assume that he had read it a long time before!

Of all men who ever lived, he [Reade] was the best fitted to write a desert-island story. Some desert-island stories, of course, are worse than others, but none is altogether bad when it sticks to the actual concrete details of the struggle to keep alive. A list of the objects in a shipwrecked man's possession is probably the surest winner in fiction, surer even than a trial scene. . . . He [Reade] was the kind of man who would have been at home on a desert island himself. He would never, like Crusoe [*Robinson Crusoe*], have been stumped by such an easy problem as that of leavening bread, and, unlike Ballantine [*Coral Island*], he knew that civilised men cannot make fire by rubbing sticks together.

The hero of *Foul Play*, like most of Reade's heroes, is a kind of superman. He is hero, saint, scholar, gentleman, athlete, pugilist, navigator, physi-

ologist, botanist, blacksmith and carpenter all rolled into one, the sort of
compendium of all the talents that Reade honestly imagined to be the normal product of an English university. Needless to say, it is only a month or
two before this wonderful clergyman has got the desert island running like a
West End hotel.[17]

Even so staunch a supporter as *Blackwood's* was forced to admit
that Robert Penfold is not one of Reade's successes in characterization. His information is too universal, and his powers too boundless;
moreover, the novelist's power of convincing characterization simply
could not keep up with his hero's powers of achievement. The
periodical points out, nevertheless, the interesting critical idea that,
in a choice between Thackeray's "unheroic model, the man un-
distinguished by any special ideal or attempt at excellence," and
Charles Reade's more than life-size hero, the approval of idealism is
all on the side of the latter's failure in attempting excellence.[18]

Reade probably felt that the ultimate compliment had been paid
to his novel-drama when his invention was copied by real life. The
*Times* of November 29, 1872, described a case tried the previous
November in Boston, Massachusetts, before Judge Lowell. A ship
was abandoned at sea in June, 1871, while on a voyage to Hong
Kong; the crew, after spending three days and nights in their boats,
arrived safely at Fayal. The master was charged by the crew with
scuttling the ship by boring holes in her. After a three-day trial, the
judge observed, in his summation: "The witness Bruce [a sailmaker],
who had been reading a novel of great power, goes to sea, and finds
all the prominent details of the plot of that story worked out in fact
by the master and his accomplices. The great improbability of this
happening is pointed out; and he comes and says the master is in the
habit of reading 'Foul Play' during the voyage, and that he often saw
the book lying about the poop. This conduct on the part of the
master would be equivalent to leaving a printed confession in sight
of his crew."[19]

## V  Put Yourself in His Place *(1870)*

The *Memoir* states that since 1859 Reade had been considering
the subject of trade unionism in a growing industrial town. Materials
in his notebooks provide evidence that he had begun collecting
newspaper clippings on the topic at least by 1862.[20] Invariably the
champion of the underdog, who had faced legal action and public
opprobrium for his exposures of British prison conditions, British
asylums, and British coffin-ships, Reade planned a kind of David-

Goliath study of a single man who faced and defeated the giant of trade unionism.[21]

After the first installments of *Put Yourself in His Place* appeared in the *Cornhill Magazine* during March, 1869, Reade moved, during the summer, from Bolton Row to 2 Albert Terrace, Knightsbridge; and there he remained for twelve years. Mrs. Seymour, his housekeeper and lifelong companion, died there; and all novels subsequent to these opening chapters of *Put Yourself in His Place* were written there (except for *A Perilous Secret*). The continuing ardor of his reformer's zeal is manifested by the final claim of the book: "I have drawn my pen against cowardly assassination and sordid tyranny." With this stirring declaration, the author ends three volumes that, like many other of his works, begin bravely and briskly but strike an obstacle and fall apart as coherent narrative. The opening chapter presents an excellent contrast between the industrial city of Hillsborough and the lovely site on which it was built. The city is "all ups and downs and back slums"; its streets are "wriggling, broken-backed." The very houses "seem to have battled in the air, and stuck wherever they tumbled down dead out of the mêlée." The city is pockmarked with public houses and bristling with chimneys that, in defiance of the law, belch such volumes of black smoke that the very "air of Hillsborough looks a thing to plough, if you want a dirty job." This infernal city is only a short distance from Cairnhope Mountain, which rears its craggy head from the purple heather. There stands a deserted but not ruined church; and it and the factory in the city provide the twin poles of tension in the splendid dynamics of place in this novel. Eventually, the church becomes a forge — and the industrial revolution has won over its last bastion of feudal defense.

Henry Little; a wood-carver and inventor of tools and machinery, is the David; the Hillsborough (perhaps Sheffield) trade unions are the cumulative Goliath, hostile to individual enterprise and careless about safe working conditions. Driven out of the city by threats, beatings, warning letters, and explosions, Little sets up a small forge in the ancient, unused country church. The trade-union ruffians, hired to drive him away or to kill him, are frustrated by the timely arrival of fendal-squire Raby and his Old English Yuletide mummers. Up to this point, the locations have been used symbolically, the plot has crackled with energy, and the thinness of character delineation has been more than compensated for by the absorption in event.

But Little, who suddenly determines to sell his patents in America, leaves without any word, except for a sheaf of unposted letters. His departure permits the author his favorite device of the hero far from home and presumably dead. It also permits the usual black-hearted but indecisive Reade villain to steal his letters, plant part of a corpse in the river, wreck the factory chimney, supplant the hero in the graces of the heroine, and even marry her at a ceremony performed by an imposter who is not really in holy orders. For this last incident and the false *corpus delicti,* the clippings of the notebooks must be blamed, but the author is responsible for the needlessly complicated plot. From this point on, the social crusade becomes a minor issue, and the drama of sensation creaks tastelessly from contrived scene to pre-conceived ending. By his own unconscious self-parody, Reade invites outside parody, such as was provided in America by Bret Harte's perceptive skit *Handsome Is as Handsome Does.*

Many stock Reade characters appear in their usual order. Henry Little, the "Resourceful Hero," can do anything and everything[22] except make the story come quickly to its sensational close. The "Odd But Good-Hearted Doctor" Reade calls a "corpulent lunatic," but he borrows from him the title-motto, "Put yourself in his place." For good measure, two villains, Coventry and Grotait, aristocrat and plebian, respectively, command a goodly number of subordinate henchmen. And the dual heroines of which Reade was so determinedly fond are Jael Dence — the "Strong, Natural Girl" — and Grace Cardin — the "Domestic Innocent."

In *Griffith Gaunt,* so that everybody might be nicely paired at the end, the tavern keeper's daughter marries the elegant and chivalric Sir Neville. In *Put Yourself in His Place,* presumably for the same reason, hard-working farm-girl Jael Dence marries the lord of the manor, Guy Raby. She does so in spite of the evidence that Squire Raby is enormously proud of his family lineage, absolutely intolerant of his sister's *mésalliance* to a manufacturer, and in every fastidious way alien to the "strongest woman in the county." Since this novel has no "Dark Passionate Woman," Reade compensates by permitting his ladylike heroine Grace Corden to fly at villain Frederick Coventry with a stiletto in her hand and to yell like "a furious wild beast" — actions quite out of character for such a spoiled, sheltered lady.

*Put Yourself in His Place* joins the host of novels of the period that portray the decay of the aristocracy and the rise of the mercantile or manufacturing middle class. When Guy Raby's sister Edith marries an insolvent and finally suicidal builder, he turns her portrait to the wall with the sentiment GONE INTO TRADE written across the back. The aristocratic villain Frederick Coventry is forced by his dissolute habits and his taste for luxury to sell Bollinghope House, the park, and the forest in order to raise the money to live in Paris. Raby offers to make Henry Little his heir, but the rising workman-inventor must decline in order to make his fortune and his place in the world without hereditary aid.

Perhaps the best statement of the origin of the facts that Reade could make into solid fiction can be found in his letter of appreciation to the editor of the *Times:*

For eighteen years the journal you conduct so ably has been my preceptor and the main source of my works; at all events of the most approved. A noble passage in the "Times" of September 7 or 8, 1853, touched my heart, inflamed my imagination, and was the germ of my first important work, "It Is Never Too Late to Mend." Some years later you put forth an able and eloquent leader on private asylums, and detailed the sufferings there inflicted on persons known to you. This took root in me, and brought forth its fruit in the second volume of "Hard Cash." Later still your hearty and able but temperate leaders on trades unions and trade outrages incited me to an ample study of that great subject, so fit for fiction of the higher order, though not adapted to the narrow minds of bread-and-butter misses, nor of the criticasters who echo those young ladies' idea of fiction and its limits, and thus "Put Yourself In His Place" was written. Of "A Terrible Temptation" the leading idea came to me from the "Times," viz., from the report of a certain trial, with the comments of counsel, and the remarkable judgment delivered by Mr. Justice Byles.[23]

## VI   A Woman-Hater *(1877)*

The first number of Reade's *Woman-Hater* appeared in the June issue of *Blackwood's* at the same time *Belgravia* was publishing the first of his *Good Stories of Man and Other Animals*. A number of features of the *Woman-Hater* make it unique in Reade literary annals for it is the most international and fashionable of his works and is reminiscent of the locale, character, sophistication, and subtlety of human relationship of Henry James. As a novel that defies single classification, it is certainly a romance, dedicated to the social issue of the education and equality of talented women. The novel is set in the world Reade must often have inhabited — fashionable Europe and English country houses — but about which he wrote so little.

Although a social novel, the narrative is not dominated by male characters; although a romance neither is it dominated by female characters. The genders are remarkably balanced in this plea for the equality of the sexes! In addition, after all the years of successful writing of novels, Reade chose for some crochety reason to remain anonymous in the serial publication of this one. But, Reade's style was so well known that, within the first week of the publication of the first issue, no less a contemporary than Mrs. Margaret Oliphant, herself a novelist of note, wrote to the editor a letter identifying the anonymous author. Thus, when *Blackwood's* published *A Woman-Hater* in three volumes early in June, 1877, Reade's name appeared on the title page. The price he was paid for publication by Harper's was a thousand pounds — more than twice as much as the same publishers gave Thackeray for *The Virginians* and a third more than Wilkie Collins received for each of his two most famous thrillers.

Reade's delight with his own production is evidenced in the marvelous verve of the book, which never flags in energy nor fails in invention but goes on with greater and faster involvement to a well-wrapped-up Victorian ending. With excited, but calculated, deliberation, Reade wound tightly the threads that bind:

1. Ina Klosking, a noted contralto opera diva, deserted by, but still very much in love with,
2. Edward Severne, her utterly charming husband, who
   a. gambles compulsively although systematically,
   b. borrows from friends by the use of forged collateral,
   c. flirts with every female in sight,
   d. faints so cataleptically that on one occasion he is rescued from supposed death by
3. Rhoda Gale, an American girl who can find nowhere to practice medicine and is found starving in Leicester Square by
4. Harrington Vizard, who
   a. is infatuated with music and la Klosking,
   b. tries to reform Severne by exposure to rural life in Barfordshire,
   c. employs Rhoda to practice preventative medicine in his village Hillstoke (*cf.* Stoke Row near the Reade manor at Ipsden)
5. and has a half-sister, Zoe, who falls in love with Ned Severne, who wishes to marry her for her wealth, but is already married to Ina Klosking; moreover; Zoe has a better suitor, Lord Uxmoor, who proposes by letter, is rejected by word of mouth, but better luck next time!

The incredibly complex plot winds through gambling spas on the Continent, the polluted water and muck heaps of a model English village, and the vagaries of English country inns. The tale concerns itself with German opera and English oratorio, and produces all the sensational thrills available from premature interment, attempted bigamy, achieved forgery, disguised detectives, amazing anecdotes about animals, women's rights, and the education of talented females. The banal and the unique lie close together, as do the serious and the trivial; and the author seems to care nothing for their disparities. He only takes insane joy in twisting them all together in one bundle of life.

From the sociological rather than the romantic point of view, Rhoda Gale[24] is the most interesting person in the book. As has been noted, Charles Reade omitted "The Autobiography of a Thief" from *It Is Never Too Late to Mend* because "a story within a story is a frightful flaw in art"; and he rarely included one. However, two exceptions come to mind — the ghost story told by the villain in *Put Yourself in His Place* and Rhoda Gale's story told in five chapters (XIV - XIX) of *A Woman-Hater*. Rhoda, born of an American father and an English mother, studies medicine in Zurich until a rush of women students without serious purpose brings about the deterioration of the college; she then transfers to a famous old school in the south of France (presumably Montpellier). After a year of study there in the congenial company of a brilliant female student a bit older than she, Rhoda receives news of the opening to women of Edinburgh University College of Medicine.

After all sorts of disgraceful subterfuges, plots, votes, and counter-votes, Rhoda finally is accepted as a student. But when word of her trials and the constant insults to which she has been subjected reaches her father in America, he insists that she transfer back to the French school, where she can study in dignity as well as with equality. She graduates, Rhoda Gale, M.D., only to receive word at her graduation exercises of her father's death. Panic-stricken, she awaits word of her mother's death; but the mother survives to struggle long and hard with dishonest trustees of the small estate.

While Rhoda awaits her mother's arrival in England she is found by Harrington Vizard in a London park; she is scarcely able to rise from her bench because she is so weak from hunger. Insisting that she accompany him to an eating place, woman-hater Harrington hears the brave and pathetic story of a fighter for women's rights. Although he quite agrees with the sentiments of her detractors and opponents, he is deeply impressed by her *mannish* intelligence, her *boyish* courage, and the obvious *rightness* of her cause. The susceptible skeptic about women rushes home to shout that he is "saddled with a virago for life!" When Rhoda's mother and his half-sister agree that the young woman doctor ought to earn her living as a governess or by instruction in foreign languages, he is so depressed by their lack of appreciation of all Rhoda has struggled to accomplish that he invites her to become the physician to his Barfordshire staff and tenants.

Sensitive to the possible charge of a gratuitous "story within a story," Reade took pains to point out to his readers and critics that he had woven this story of a woman doctor, so full of intrinsic merit and interest, into the fabric of his plot. For Rhoda, while a medical student in France, discovered that the effeminately handsome young Ned Severne was not dead but only in a cataleptic fit. When they meet as guests on the estate of Squire Vizard, Rhoda recognizes and remembers; but Ned is simply baffled. Thus, quite as he claimed, Reade managed to weave in his story as an important part of the recognition pattern of the villainy of Ned Severne, now a suitor for the hand of Harrington's half-sister, Zoe.

However, Reade spoils his argument for women's rights at two points, one conscious and the other probably unconscious. At no point does the author claim that men and women are equal; he only insists that exceptional women like Rhoda Gale should have an opportunity to exercise their undoubted genius and that women in general should be educated within the range of their peculiar and differing abilities. As the last chapter of the novel eloquently asserts,

"to open the study and practice of medicine to women-folk, under the infallible safeguard of a stiff public examination . . . will . . . import into medical science a new and less theoretical, but cautious, teachable, observant kind of intellect; it will give the larger half of the nation an honourable ambition, and an honourable pursuit, towards which their hearts and instincts are bent by Nature herself; it will tend to elevate this whole sex, and its young children, male as well as female, and so will advance the civilization of the world, which in ages past, in our own day, and in all time, hath, and doth, and will keep step exactly with the progress of women towards mental equality with men.

This argument is clearly conscious and intentional. It is hard to believe, however, that Reade would design the character development of Dr. Gale to prove the very objection of her detractors — that the study of medicine will "unsex women." Yet the qualities woman-hater Vizard admires in Dr. Gale are those of an attractive and deserving boy. When she and Cornelia lived together in France, they had no social connections with young male medical students because it might cause a hoped-for scandal. When Cornelia breaks down and marries a member of the Montpellier faculty, Rhoda considers it a betrayal of her former high purpose in life. When Dr. Gale becomes physician to Ina Klosking, the doctor laments, "I am very unfortunate in my attachments. I always was. If I fall in love with a woman, she is sure to hate me, or else die, or else fly away. I love this one to distraction, so she is sure to desert me because she couldn't misbehave, and I won't *let* her die" (Chapter XXIV). After referring to her patient as "my goddess," the woman doctor hurries off — "to the patient I adore."

When it seems that Madame Klosking must leave Vizard Hall, Rhoda insists that she come to continue her convalescence with her because "I love her better than any man can love her." At the farmhouse where Rhoda resides, the two friends are described as sleeping locked in each other's arms; when they are apart, Rhoda raves to Harrington about Ina's sleeping beauties; when Ina leaves Rhoda's lodging, Rhoda sends her missives she calls "love-letters" twice a week. When Ina's replies arrive, Rhoda exclaims, "There, I must give up loving women. Besides, they throw me over the moment a man comes, if it happens to be the right one." When Ned Severne kisses and cries over Rhoda's hand, she blusters, "Oh, don't do that, or I'm bound to give you a good kick. I hate she-men." Taking into account all the effusiveness permitted between females in Victorian society, it still looks as if Charles Reade ended where the critics of female doctors began — it either unsexes or perverts them!

Along with the specialized interest in the education of women, a number of characteristic Reade touches are found in the novel. Ina and Fanny are blondes; but the great beauty is Zoe Vizard, whose darkness comes from her Greek mother; and the blond and the brunette are once again set in opposition. Ned Severne is another of the weak, effeminate males (usually heroes, but here a villain) in whom no woman with the slightest particle of sense could be interested but to whom every woman in the book is enormously attracted — Fanny Dover, Aunt Maitland, Ina Klosking, and Zoe Vizard — and all ask nothing better than to lie in Severne's lily-white arms. He can have any one or all of them if he chooses; but worthy Lord Uxmoor has a hard time convincing Zoe to marry him even on the second round, and the highly eligible Harrington must pursue Ina clear around the world.

In many ways, *A Woman-Hater* is a unique blend of the two main streams of Reade's novelistic genius: the novel is a complicated and sensational romance; the narrative evinces the author's concern for social justice and the exposure of society's ills. The blue books issued by government investigators do not overwhelm the characters or the plot; the plot does not warp and twist the native character of the persons involved; and the romance is moderated to fit the authorial quip that "the true business of the mind was resumed; and that is love-making, or novelists give us false pictures of life, and that is impossible" (Chapter XXI).

CHAPTER 4

# The Cloister and the Hearth

I  *Forerunner of the Novel*

AFTER the demise in 1859 of Charles Dicken's journal *House-hold Words*, Messrs. Bradbury and Evans began publication of *Once a Week* to take its place. In order to launch the new venture with all possible *éclat*, the first number published a piece by Alfred Tennyson, some illustrations by Sir John Everett Millais, cartoons by artists formerly associated with *Punch*, and the opening chapter of a serial entitled *A Good Fight* by Charles Reade. In spite of all these special preparations, dissatisfaction reigned from the very beginning. The editor, in his anxiety that nothing should be criticized, changed passages of Reade's text without consulting the extremely thin-skinned author. When Reade suggested to the editor that he "distinguish between anonymous contributions and those in which an approved author takes the responsibility by signing his own name," the editor stuffily replied that he had no intention of resigning "his editorial function."[1]

Meanwhile, the serial, *A Good Fight*, had reached a very delicate situation in the narrative. The Dutch artist Gerard Eliasson is seeking his fortune in Italy so that he may return to Holland and marry his betrothed, Margaret Brandt. Margaret is expecting a child, but Gerard, at so great a distance, is not even aware of her pregnancy. The editor, probably mopping his brow in distress at the forthcoming illegitimate birth, requested the author to end the serial as soon as possible. When  Reade acceded by giving the story an unsuitably happy ending in a most abrupt manner, any perceptive reader must have recognized that the tale had been too quickly terminated. Reade, whose personal pride often meant more than his artistic integrity, admitted: "I have — 'Away with melancholy!' — reversed the catastrophe; made Gerard and his sweetheart happy; sent Kate

135

[Gerard's crippled and angelic sister] to Heaven, and they [the editors] and their weekly may go to the other place. Anyway the story is finished, and they are rid of me, and I of them — *for ever!"*[2]

Along with the natural pique of a born story-teller told to end his novel as quickly as possible, one senses Reade's relief — a reaction excused by what was proving an exhausting literary exercise — the historical novel. Angry and relieved though he might have been, the author could not finally leave the result of all his medieval research in so truncated a state. After his recovery from a prolonged and dangerous illness and after the publication of *The Eighth Commandment* in July, 1859, Reade left London for the peaceful quiet of Oxford, which became for the next three years his principal place of residence. There he picked up the broken-off novel, and he produced in 1861 his masterwork, *The Cloister and the Hearth*, which is not only much longer than *A Good Fight* but also much more appropriately concluded.

After writing it [*A Good Fight*] I took wider views of the subject, and also felt uneasy at having deviated *unnecessarily* from the historical outline of a true story. These two sentiments have cost me more than a year's very hard labour . . . to describe it [*The Cloister and the Hearth*] as a reprint, would be unfair to the public and to me. The English language is copious and, in any true man's hands, quite able to convey the truth; namely, that one fifth of the present work is a reprint, and four fifths of it a new composition. (preface, *The Cloister and the Hearth*)

## II  *Sources*

In his long-standing literary feud with Carlyle's worship of heroes, Reade had reached the point of desiring to tell the tale of heroes and martyrs who were scarcely known to fame. In 1856, he had read of James Lambert, who had saved more than forty persons from drowning in the River Clyde. The Glasgow *Times* of October 2, 1856, had a feature article about a little boy who was drowning in the river, and, although a score of people stood on the bank, none had the courage to plunge into the swelling tide. When the great hero James Lambert appeared, now blind from his many immersions in that very river, neither his age nor his blindness restrained him. " 'Let me to him! let me to him!' he cried; 'I'll save him yet' . . . his appeal was unheeded at first. Then he screamed out in generous fury, 'Ye daft fules, a mon disna soom with his een; just fling me in the water, and cry me to him, and ye'll see.' Perhaps some of the bystanders might have done as he demanded, but his granddaughter threw her arms about her grandfather's knees and cried 'Na, na ye wadna — ye wadna!' "

A rather meager subscription for the hero was raised in 1856 by Mr. Hugh M'Donald, a Glasgow citizen renowned for many acts of charity and public interest. Twelve years later, when Reade began his personal investigation, this small income had ceased, and the aged man was entirely without funds. When Reade located Lambert's lodging at 36 Little Street, Calton, he talked with Mrs. Lambert about her husband's exploits, only to receive the dour comment, "Ay, he has been a curious mon in his time — a mony a great faitour he did — and mony a good suit he destroyed that I had to pay for." When asked if she had ever witnessed any of his rescues, she replied disdainfully, "Na, na; I was aye minding my wark at hame. I saw leetle o' his carrying on."

When Reade finally had the opportunity to talk with Lambert himself, the aged man commented sadly, "I hae — obsairved, sirr, that the mair part — of them I hae saved — shuns me." At this point, the splenetic Reade exploded at the baseness of humanity; but Lambert simply chided him, "Na, sirr, I just — think — it is ower great — a debt — to awe to ony man; and they feel it a burrden."[3] In 1874, Reade wrote about the exploits of James Lambert in *A Hero and a Martyr* and attempted to redress belatedly the neglect of a public that should have showed greater gratitude.

In *Christie Johnstone*, Reade had satirized a disciple of Carlyle who was eloquent in his praise of the Middle Ages, and who used Abbot Sampson and Joan of Arc as his special exemplars. Although Lady Barbara Sinclair might have been taken in by such eloquence, Viscount Ipsden wisely pointed out that the Carlylean was judging an age by its heroic exceptions. Reade's character's remark seems to have lain dormant in his mind until his interview with the neglected Scottish commoner-hero James Lambert. Reade's reading of a brief autobiography of Desiderius Erasmus fused Ipsden and Lambert in dual opposition to the hero-worship of Thomas Carlyle, Reade began Chapter I of *The Cloister and the Hearth* with his anti-heroic thesis: "Not a day passes over the earth, but men and women of no note do great deeds, speak great words, and suffer noble sorrows." Reade's thesis of the importance of insignificant lives is supported by the historical fact that, even if their lives were unknown to history, the parents of Erasmus must be considered important in their own right by a kind of historical retrospect. Thus Reade manages to combine the hero-worship of Carlyle with his own rather sentimental egalitarianism.

Heroes are indubitably important; the genealogical studies of Gregor Mendel or Charles Darwin also indubitably prove the importance of the insignificant generations that, in a golden hour, burst into the blossoming of a genius, a hero, a botanical mutation, or a biological sport. So, after devoting ninety-nine chapters of *The Cloister and the Hearth* to the heroism of common folk, the author finally brings his narrative in the hundredth chapter to the birth of Erasmus: "The yellow-haired laddie, Gerard Gerardson, belongs not to Fiction but to History." Then the dramatist-novelist proceeds to explain his interest in Erasmus, the greatest scholar of his era and one of the most important church reformers: " . . . he was also the heaven-born dramatist of his century. Some of the best scenes in this new book are from his medieval pen, and illumine the pages where they come; for the words of a genius so high as his are not born to die."

In 1524, when Erasmus feared that he was fatally ill, he wrote in Latin a compendium of his life and sent it with an accompanying letter to a friend.[4] First printed in Leiden in 1607, along with a copy of the attached personal letter, the work was edited by Paul Merula, professor of history at the University of Leiden, under the title *Vita Des. Erasmi Roterodami ex ipsius manu fideliter repraesentata.* Eight years later it was reprinted at Leiden and edited by Peter Scriverius, a professor of jurisprudence. Contemporary references establish the existence of the original manuscript until about 1649, after which it seems only copies were extant. Reade refers to it as "a musty chronicle, written in tolerable Latin, and in it a chapter where every sentence holds a fact." The facts, "told with harsh brevity," constitute the tangled history of a man and woman who lived and died four hundred years ago without any recognition and who were now almost forgotten. Reade's intent in his historical novel was to reveal the lives hidden beneath the dry chronicle, to correct the imperceptiveness of time, and to "give those two sore-tried souls a place in your heart — for a day" (Chapter I, *The Cloister and the Hearth*).

The section of the compendium from which Reade drew his plot reads in part as follows:

He [Erasmus] was born in Rotterdam on the eve of Simon and Jude. . . . His mother was called Margaret, daughter of a certain doctor named Peter.

She came from Septimontium, in the common tongue Zevenberge. . . . His father was named Gerard. He secretly had an affair with the said Margaret, hoping for marriage. And there are those who say they were betrothed. Both the parents and brothers of Gerard were incensed at this happening. His father was Elias, his mother Catherine; each of them attained extreme old age, Catherine well nigh her ninety-fifth year. There were ten brothers but no sister; all born of the same father and mother; all married. Gerard was the youngest, except one. It seemed best to them all that from so great a number one should be consecrated to God. . . . Gerard, seeing he was shut off, in every way, from matrimony by general agreement, did what desperate men are wont to do; he secretly took flight. . . .

In the meantime, his intended wife was left with child. The boy was brought up in his grandmother's home. Gerard betook himself to Rome. There by writing he did a fair business, for the printer's art had not yet arrived. . . . His parents, when they learned he was in Rome, wrote him that the girl whom he had sought to marry was dead. Believing this, he became a priest for grief and turned his whole mind to religion. Returning home, he discovered the trick. Nevertheless she would never marry afterward, nor did he ever lay hand on her.

He had the boy well educated, however, and put him to study his letters when he was barely four. . . . When he was in his ninth year, Gerard sent him to Deventer; his mother came with him . . a pestilence, raging violently there, carried off his mother, leaving the boy now in his thirteenth year. . . . Gerard, upon receiving the sad news, began to languish and shortly afterward died. Both parents died not much after their fortieth year.[5]

The resemblance between Reade's "musty chronicle" and the *Compendium* is unmistakable; and after the novelist's death in April 11, 1884, his friend Annie Fields wrote an article for the *Century Magazine* entitled "An Acquaintance with Charles Reade," which firmly substantiates the claim. She could "recall his [Reade's] taking down the 'Autobiography of Erasmus' from the shelf in the great library at Oxford, and showing us a brief description (only a line or two) of the father and mother of Erasmus, with a few dates concerning them, saying, 'There is all the foundation for my story, "A Good Fight." ' " In addition to these personal memories, Mrs. Fields published a letter from Reade in which the novelist enumerated a large number of works that had been read in preparation for writing *The Cloister and the Hearth.*

Actually begun by Reade to give verisimilitude to his books about current social and economic abuses, his notebooks were the indispensable technique for the writing of historical fiction; as this entry indicates: "You may well be surprised that I am so long over 'Good Fight,' but the fact is, it is not the writing but the reading

which makes me slow. It may perhaps give you an idea of the system
in which I write fiction, if I get down the list of books I have read,
skimmed, or studied to write this little misery." Reade appended an
impressive but only partial list of seventy-nine works he had con-
sulted, including books by Erasmus, Martin Luther, Victor Hugo,
Robert Southey, Michel de Montaigne, Jean Froissard, and Ben Jonson, as well as many obscure studies of medieval architecture, dress,
convents, inns, and liturgies.[6]

But besides Reade's passion for research, a deeply personal factor
may have aided his imagination as he pored over the monkish
chronicle. In the *Compendium*, the unfortunate Gerard was unable
at first to marry Margaret because he was destined for the priesthood
by his parents; and later, when he discovers she is still alive, he is
once again unable to marry her because, in anguish over her supposed death, he had renounced the world and become a priest.
Reade's plot book for 1876, numbered "59" contains the following
significant entry under the heading "Celibacy of the Clergy": "In
my mediaeval romance *The Cloister and the Hearth* I use this expression celibacy of the clergy, an invention truly devilish. A French
critic is surprized at the violence in me since the rest of my work in
general deals benevolently and benignly with Pope, Priests,
Convents and the unreformed Church in general. . . . The opinion I
uttered in 1860 was even then twenty years old in me: it is now
thirty-six." The strong word "devilish" suggests some emotional
response to the topic; and the careful dating of the opinion, its oral
enunciation, and its later written version also suggest some personal
reference. The writers of the *Memoir* handily identify the reference
and present a theory of interpretation: "Celibacy also with its cruel
claw held Charles Reade prisoner. Had Gerard married, he would
have starved. Two-thirds of his [Reade's] life had passed before he
could dream of dispensing with what he often termed his prop, viz.,
his Fellowship at Magdalen."[7]

John Coleman, in *Charles Reade as I Knew Him* (1903), declares
that Reade fell deeply in love with a girl in Scotland; that some
difference arose between them; and that some years later, when he
returned to find the girl, she had died. Coleman identifies the girl as
the heroine of *Christie Johnstone* (1853). The official *Memoir*
(Chapter XIII) admits, more cautiously, such a possibility: "As a
matter of plain fact, the alliance he may secretly have coveted was,
for pecuniary reasons, an impossibility. . . . His dependence on the
College was perhaps his misfortune, since it interposed a barrier

between him and the one lady whom in the best days of his manhood he idealized, and never forgot, even in his dying moments." The *Memoir* never positively identifies "the one lady," but its authors state categorically that, in depicting Margaret in *The Cloister and the Hearth*, the author did not have in mind Mrs. Seymour, who kept house for him and gave him her comradely friendship for many years. Elwin, although suspicious of Coleman's account, is led by the confession of the usually reticent *Memoir* to guess that Charles Reade probably fell in love about 1840 and desired to marry, but his dependence on the Magdalen fellowship, coupled perhaps with opposition of his family to marriage with a woman of lower social rank, made the match impossible.[8] The celibacy requirement for the Oxford fellowship may well have seemed, therefore, a "devilish invention" that had caused Reade great personal misery and frustration.

### III   The Cloister and the Hearth

The title of the book indicates a central dualism. Holland, as the hearth, with its picture of Elias and Catherine of Tergou with their nine children, offers illusory hope to the lovers, Gerard Eliasson and Margaret Brandt of Sevenbergen, that they too will someday settle down into the bourgeois comfortable happiness of Gerard's parents at Tergou. But Italy, as the cloister, traps the youth in holy orders, thus robbing him of the domestic fulfillment of the hearth.

The plot is advanced by picaresque journeys between the two poles of tension and is complicated by letters fraudulent and valid. Gerard, son of Elias, visits Rotterdam; and, falling in love with Margaret Brandt, is secretly betrothed to her. He must make his fortune to marry her, and he must make it outside Holland because his family, having destined him for the Catholic Church, will oppose marriage. His journey leads through Germany, Burgundy, Lombardy, to Venice and finally to Rome. There, just as he is financially ready to return to Margaret, he receives a forged letter from Holland stating that she is dead.

Declaring that there is no God and turning instead to Satan, Gerard attempts suicide in the Tiber River, is rescued, and is nursed back to health and sanity at a Dominican monastery. With dreams blasted about the hearth in Holland, he embraces the cloister in Italy and becomes Brother Clement, a preaching friar. But in St. Laurens's Church, Rotterdam, he recognizes Margaret. He curses his brothers and his family for their part in the fraudulent letter, and, crawling into a cave, becomes the hermit of Gouda. Margaret wins him back to the world by leaving their little son in his cell. Gerard becomes pastor at Gouda, and their son is later sent to school at Deventer. Hearing of a plague epidemic there, Margaret hastens to the school, finds the pupils have been taken away for safety, but contracts the fatal disease. Soon after her death, Gerard enters the Dominican convent a sick man; and he dies full of sanctity. But their son, Gerard Gerardson, becomes one of the famous of the earth as Erasmus, great writer and theologian of the Protestant Reformation. Thus Reade, consistent with his desire to extol unknown heroes, devotes his novel to the humble parents and ends his tale with the famous son still a youth in school.

Although the bare facts of Erasmus's *Compendium* somewhat restrained Reade's enthusiasm for plot complexity, he nevertheless managed to conduct some characteristic sleights-of-hand. The Eliasson offspring have been pared from ten to nine; and one of them, Kate, is made a saintly cripple. Reade heightens the dramatic contrast by making the girl sickly but of great purity of character, and by portraying seven of her brothers as healthy villains. So large a family presents problems for the novelist; if each is differentiated, the burden of characterization overwhelms the plot. If undifferentiated, the large group simply becomes a chorus in an art form that does not traditionally admit so classical a technique.

Reade solved his problem by the sharp delineation of four sons out of the eight; but, the hero, Gerard, is of course given full-length treatment. The eldest son, Cornelis, and the youngest, Sybrandt, are paired as the lazy, greedy villains whose main concern is lest the family property "should be diminished" by further division with one whose claims had been disposed of by setting him aside for the priesthood. By clear and pejorative characterization of two of the brothers, Reade has not only pulled himself off the horns of the choral dilemma but has made it possible to impute to the two villains all the unpleasantness that otherwise would have had to be shared by the whole family. The *Compendium* clearly indicates that the family treated Gerard shabbily; but, since the shabbiness is now polarized in Cornelis-Sybrandt, the remaining members may be viewed far more sympathetically.

The fourth brother, Giles, is the literary brother to Quasimodo of Victor Hugo's *Notre-Dame de Paris* (1831). Giles is "a dwarf, of the wrong sort . . . all head and claws and voice, run from by dogs and unprejudiced females"; Quasimodo is a hunchback of normal height whose small left eye is overhung by a bushy red eyebrow and whose right eye is completely hidden by a monstrous wart. Giles can swing

by his teeth from the edge of a table; he considers climbing a rope
hanging from a high tower only a pleasant prank. Quasimodo swings
out with the bells of the cathedral and clambers over the west
facade. Both Giles and Quasimodo are presented as mischievous and
malicious. But Quasimodo is pathos and tragedy; Giles is pathos and
comedy. Quasimodo is a Gothic horror; Giles a charming Victorian
gargoyle.[9]

The marvelous exhibition of all the learning Reade could pour into
a character is made pedantically clear in the delineation of the
heretical Fra Colonna. And the portrait of the proud and beautiful
Roman Princess Claelia is alive with all the gentleness necessary to
win love; but, having lost love, she is aroused to such fury as to kill
her rejecter. Like Pietro Vanucci or Fra Jerome, or Margaret van
Eyck, such characters did not have to be included as essential to the
main stream of the story; but the scenery on both banks is im-
measurably enriched and enlivened by their presence. Although
they are often clumsily introduced, they are quickly related to the
major theme of the painting and become supporting figures of great
value and deep chiaroscuro that set off the tragicomedy of the
cloister-crossed lovers. If Robert Louis Stevenson could say of
Samuel Pepys that while paying attention to the most fastidious
details, he pushes all ahead in the rapid flow of his narrative, the
masculine vigor of Reade's narrative might better deserve such an
accolade than the fussy and rather meandering diary of the plague
years in England.

Reade felt quite free to embellish the "musty chronicle" of
Erasmus's *Compendium* with fresh motivation, with historical or
semi-historical characters, and with complication of plot. In a way,
the plot reveals the incredible clutter of his notebooks; but this Victorian failing significantly compares with the Flemish school of
painting, which also exulted in exotic possessions such as maps, rugs,
pitchers, and flamboyant textures of materials. These Dutch interiors
show the owners caught in a particularly complacent moment of inventory, and the importance of the human figure derives from the
ownership of all the things jammed into the painting. A contemporary
journal pointed out the relationship between a Nativity painting by
Hans Memling (one of the historical figures introduced for a moment into the burgeoning cast) and the narrative art of Charles
Reade:

The "Cloister and the Hearth," like that master-piece of the old Fleming,
has one lovely, almost abstract ideal group — not indeed the divine child

and mother — a human mother and child; but the background behind and
around is full of an infinite variety of scenes, the life of man in that masterful
and violent age, drawn with the quaintest realism — and the life of a woman
beset by a woman's trials and difficulties, which are less changeable. On
every little slope of the landscape there comes an independent picture.
There are paths innumerable leading up and down to Rome, to the sea, to
the hills, by walls of towns and walls of convents, across the silent fields and
bewildering woods, and by the brink of great rivers. And in every village and
cabaret, and boat and road, human creatures with all their natural defects
and excellences are swarming.[10]

Reade's pages, like the Memling canvas, bulge with such items of
itinerary as the terrible hostelries of Germany, where no dinner is
prepared until all the guests are in and waiting, and where vermin
and dirt almost overwhelm the human race. When, in the
*Athenaeum* of November 2, 1861, an objection was raised to the
"coarse" description of German inns, Reade wrote on the margin
"Ass." One reads in *The Cloister and the Hearth* about the terrors of
travel — bears, robbers hanging from rural gibbets, gentlemen who
encourage their retainers to plunder inoffensive wayfarers, generals
snatching forced drafts into their dwindling armies, medieval cities
with their pageantry and their filth, and the convents with here and
there those tranquil souls who kept lighted the flickering torch of
Western learning and the spirit of true piety. There is an especially
vivid portrayal of Rome by the Tiber, with more than a trace of the
classical still informing its life; but it is a Rome about to be struck by
the printing press and its movable type and by the subsequent
Protestant Reformation.

Given a crabbed chronicle in monkish Latin, Reade was the very
man to transform that single bone into the full figure of a bygone
age; and his medieval interiors in *The Cloister and the Hearth* are
little Flemish masterpieces. A phrase clothes a character in the
costume of the period, and almost inadvertently Reade assumes a
general knowledge of long-gone customs of the European Middle
Ages on the part of his reading public of the Victorian era. Whereas
all his other novels might be considered to be plays written with un-
usually lengthy stage directions but called "novels," *The Cloister
and the Hearth* may be considered a picture gallery bringing to the
visitor a personal experience of the dangers, discomforts, and glories
of the Middle Ages. For example, the activities of the vermin at one
German inn make one itch along with Gerard and Denys; at another,
one trembles for his life; at a third, one is as bored and annoyed as if

he, too, had been long on the road. Indeed, there are altogether too many of these inns; but Reade had picked up a wonderful *Tractate on the Inns of the Middle Ages,* and how could he be expected to omit anything? Much as one marvels at Gerard's splendid beauty, his fine mind, and his remarkable passion that is aroused by art, at battle, or in love, and much as one is warmed by the healthy assurance of Denys that that longtime enemy of mankind, the Devil, is dead, one finds the novel too lengthy. When two robber bands are outwitted in strikingly similar fashion, one suspects that Reade wrote variant versions, could not decide which to use, and resolved his problem by using both.

Although a modern reader might think there is too much move-ment and action in the novel, the author did not think so; for, in chapter thirty, while Reade and the reader catch their breath after all sorts of hairbreadth escapes and escapades, the writer apologizes that there are periods in life that are bare of stirring adventure; he suggests that such blank moments must be avoided by the sen-sational novelist for an excellent reason: "Now all narrators, whether of history or fiction, are compelled to slur these barren portions of time — or else line trunks."

To return to the similitude of a Memling painting and a Reade manuscript, it is illuminating that amid all the vignettes of the com-mon life of medieval man, Memling's painting is still indubitably a Mother Mary - Child Jesus study. Amid all the picaresque ex-hibitions of Gerard's derring-do, there still resides the central unity of a mother-child relationship — Margaret, human mother of a famous son, little Erasmus. These are the two mother-child energies that compete for the life of the hero. Is Gerard to be the servant of Mary-Jesus ("the cloister") or the husband-father of Margaret-Gerard ("the hearth")? Like so many of Reade's novels that trace the course first of one and then of another stream, and finally celebrate their confluence in a united narrative, the very title of the tale es-tablishes the twin poles of tension that must be reconciled in the story as well as in the hero's life. In Holland, the land of the hearth, Gerard's family attempts to force him to accept, instead, the cloister. In Rome, the land of the cloister, Gerard accepts, in the mood of world-despair, the religious vocation he had repelled when his family had attempted to thrust it upon him. Having accepted the cloister voluntarily — with the double take that was so dear to Reade — he must return, a monk, to the land of the hearth and find that a hearth waited for him, which now, by his own choice and the false testimony of others, he is unable to fill. So the tale falls into three parts: Gerard's journey from Holland to Rome; his return from Rome to Holland; and the parish priest and his wife, the mother of his child, living together as brother and sister in the parsonage of Gouda, thereby bringing the two streams together with a vengeance!

Although Walter Frewen Lord considered *The Cloister and the Hearth* "the song of a century [fifteenth century],"[11] a modern reader, amid all the medieval stage props, is more likely to be aware of the odd ways in which the author's Victorian Protestantism keeps popping from the wings. In chapter fifty-five, Gerard staunchly refuses to pray to saints; he will pray only in the name of Jesus Christ. In chapter seventy-two, Reade records the stirring Evangelical conversions of the hero, of a weak villain, Ludovico, and of the haughty Princess Claelia. When Gerard, now Brother Clement, is forced to hear Princess Claelia's confession of her sins, which came from her love and hatred for Gerard, he counsels the penitent, "Pray much to Christ, and little to his saints." When the Pope, with the aid of the Franciscan order, adds to the Hail Mary: "And blessed by thy Mother Anna, from whom, without blot of sin, proceeded thy virgin flesh," Gerard counsels his parishioners to pay no attention to the new dogma. When Gerard dies, he anticipates Martin Luther by his impassioned use of the very same texts from Romans that insist that a believer is justified not by works but by faith and by faith alone. Even the author's assessment of the mood of the age has a decidedly condescending Victorian cast:"*This* was your true medieval. Proud, amorous, vindictive, generous, foolish, cunning, impulsive, unprincipled: and ignorant as dirt" (Chapter LXIV).

The author's odd interest in androgynism asserts itself in two strange passages. When Gerard is painting a portrait of the beautiful Princess Claelia, who meanwhile has fallen madly in love with the painter, she insists, "You are far fairer than I am. You are more like Apollo than I to Venus. Also you have lovely hair and lovely eyes" (Chapter LXI). When Gerard goes on a buffalo-hauled-boat trip on the Tiber River, he takes with him Andreas, Pietro Vanucci's boy servant, dressed in woman's garb. "Gerard's companion was a peerless beauty . . . her face a perfect oval . . . her cheeks a rich olive with the eloquent blood mantling below; and her glorious eyes fringed with long thick silken eyelashes, that seemed made to sweep up sensitive hearts by the half-dozen. Saucy red lips, and teeth of the whitest ivory" (Chapter LXV).

Although Andreas disguised as Marcia is exquisitely beautiful, he is not tactful; he proceeds to expose the false cosmetic charms of the real women in the boat. When the moody Gerard tells Andreas to be quiet, he replies, " 'It was only to make you laugh; you are distraught, you are sad. . . . Dear Signor Gerard, would I were what they take me for. You should not be so sad.' Gerard sighed deeply, and shook his head. But touched by the earnest young tones, caressed the jet black locks, much as one strokes the head of an affectionate dog." Reade's curious interest in these episodes suggests they were areas the novelist would have explored if the times had permitted.

In *The Cloister and the Hearth,* the author permits himself more personal comments than in his pure fiction; and many of them express a pleasant sarcasm. Speaking of the love that once existed between artists and artisans, he jibes, "even Christians loved one another at first starting" (Chapter I). At the death of Prince Philip of Burgundy, the author ridicules both his physicians and his morals. The duke's complaint is diagnosed as diptheria; and, since it is a weakening malady and the duke is old, "Dr. Remedy" bleeds him. As a consequence, the duke turns very cold; and the author adds, sarcastically, "wonderful!" Then Dr. Remedy turns to the arcana of magic and commands, "Flay me an ape incontinent, and clap him to the duke's breast!" But the duchy happens to be fresh "out of apes" — continent or incontinent! Therefore the doctor substitutes a dog, but stipulates that it must be one all of the same color. "So they flayed a liver-coloured dog, and clapped it, yet palpitating, to their sovereign's breast; and he died. Philip the Good, thus scientifically disposed of, left thirty-one children: of whom one, somehow or another, was legitimate; and reigned in his stead" (Chapter LXXI).

Reade took broadside aim at Thomas Carlyle when he began chapter six with this satiric paragraph:

"Look into your own heart and write!" said Herr Cant [Carlyle]; and earth's cuckoos echoed the cry. Look into the Rhine where it is deepest, and the Thames where it is thickest, and paint the bottom. Lower a bucket into a well of self-deception, and what comes up must be immortal truth, mustn't it? Now, in the first place, no son of Adam ever reads his own heart at all, except by the habit acquired, and the light gained from some years' perusal of other hearts; and even then, with his acquired sagacity and reflected light, he can but spell and decipher his own heart, not read it fluently.

The satire of Thomas Carlyle's Socratism is devastating, but it is ironic that Carlyle, who wrote with such Germanic turgidity, should have assumed the reading of the human heart to be a simple matter,

148                                    CHARLES READE

while Reade, who wrote with melodramatic clarity, should have recognized the turgid difficulty of psychoanalyzing the self.

## IV  Reade's Masterpiece?

*The Cloister and the Hearth* is customarily considered to be Reade's masterpiece, but he himself would have retorted, as he once did, "If that's your opinion, you ought to be in a lunatic asylum."[12] Swinburne,[13] W. L. Courtney,[14] and Hugh Walpole[15] argued convincingly that *Griffith Gaunt* is in many ways the best novel that Charles Reade ever wrote. Swinburne claimed that "there is not another of his books . . . can be set beside or near this masterpiece [*Griffith Gaunt*]," but *Hard Cash* was described by Dickens as "incomparably [Reade's] best production."[16] The mention of Dickens throws light on Reade's savage reaction to those who admired his historical romance, for what would Dickens's reaction have been to critics who thought *A Tale of Two Cities* to be incomparably his best work and who assumed that it and it alone represented his main claim to lasting fame? He might have felt, like Reade, that they had dismissed all his typical novels, chosen his atypical novel as his best, and insisted that only by that one odd work would he be known to posterity.

Indeed, Swinburne raised the issue about whether or not a popular novelist ought to be judged solely on the basis of one work. In so doing, he referred to Trollope's criticism of Charlotte Brontë — could it be right "to judge the work of a novelist from one small portion of one novel . . . and to say of an author that he is to be accounted as strong as he shows himself to be in his strongest morsel of work?"[17] Of course, Trollope's own judgment of Reade was that he had left in all his works not "a character that will remain."[18] Compared with the marvelous gallery of Grantlys, Luftons, and Proudies of Trollope's Barset chronicle, this judgment may seem secure; but, if one abstracts the characters and the settings from Trollope's work, surprisingly little remains — indeed, almost nothing. The comparison makes it clear that Trollope's judgment was that of a superb painter of portraits in realistic settings upon a master of terse, enthralling narrative and of sheer excitement of plot.

A. T. Quiller-Couch tells of buying a new sixpenny edition of *The Cloister and the Hearth*, published hastily by Messrs. Chatto and Windus. In it he found Walter Besant's introduction, which he had not read in a former, more expensive edition, that contains the arresting claim: "I do not say that the whole of life, as it was at the end of the fourteenth century, may be found in the *Cloister and the Hearth;* but I do say that . . . it is a picture of the past more faithful than anything in the works of Scott." When Besant's claim was first published in the *Gentleman's Magazine,* it seemed a very bold one to many critics. To Quiller-Couch, and probably to the modern critic, it seemed quite reasonable; for now criticism largely discounts the phony medievalism of Scott and considers the smaller epics of Scottish life to be his chief forte.[19]

### V   *Charles Reade and George Eliot*

Of course, the comparison most frequently made is not with the novels of Scott or Trollope but with the *Romola* of George Eliot. Professor Elwin has pointed out that, since her romance did not begin as a *Cornhill* serial until June, 1862, she doubtless obtained the idea of writing a medieval story from Reade. When Edmund Gosse confirmed the suspicion that George Eliot had modeled her story on Reade's, he also explained that, when Reade's *Never Too Late to Mend* appeared in 1855, George Eliot considered it to be the "harbinger" of a whole new school of literature.[20] In a contemporary journal, *Once a Week,* the possible derivation of *Romola* was bluntly asserted: "In 1860 Mr. Reade produced a mediaeval novel with an idea-ed title, 'The Cloister and the Hearth.' His faithful imitator soon followed suit with a mediaeval novel, whose title was unidea-ed — 'Romola.' Here the two writers met on an arena that tests the highest quality they both pretend to — Imagination."

When the anonymous journalist of this article compares Reade's work to George Eliot's, he finds hers both narrower in scope and fainter in color. The petty politicians of medieval Florence may be made to sit up in their graves, but they never emerge from the coffins; the gossip of *Romola* is simply modern Florentine gossip about medieval subjects. As for the title character, she is simply "a high-minded delicate-minded, sober-minded lady of the nineteenth century, and no other. . . . One great historical figure, Savonarola, is taken, and turned into a woman by a female writer: sure sign imagination is wanting. There is a dearth of powerful incidents, though the time was full of them." In short, although George Eliot's characters may "talk nineteen to the dozen . . . they are little more than voluble shadows."[21]

The strong bias in favor of sensational plot rather than subtle characterization is quite apparent in this journalistic criticism, but Swinburne recognized that Reade would have been totally incapable of Eliot's delicate psychological study of Tito, in which the reader is offered an exquisite anatomy of every process through which a human soul passes in the course of decomposition. Swinburne felt that the total effect was spoiled to some degree by what he called "something . . . of the preacher's or the lecturer's aim," but the triumph of art nevertheless remained. It is probably true that George Eliot was too refined and thoughtful an artist to make her characters the didactic types and the admonitory moral lessons that Reade customarily made his, but George Eliot also lacked the dramatic touch, the skillful and vivid verve that carries all along to the very brink of the precipice. "A story better conceived or better composed, better constructed or better related, than *The Cloister and the Hearth*," declares Swinburne, "would be difficult to find anywhere; while "the most enthusiastic dévotées of *Romola* must surely admit the well nigh . . . puerile insufficiency of some of the resources by which the story has to be pushed forward or warped round before it can be got into harbour."

Swinburne adduces, as an example of Eliot's ineptness at plot, the "almost infantine audacity of awkwardness in the device of handing your heroine at a pinch into a casually empty boat which drifts her away to a casually plague-stricken village, there to play the part of a casual sister of mercy dropped down from the sky by providential caprice, at the very nick of time when the novelist was helplessly at a loss for some more plausible contrivance." Scott, Dumas, or Reade, he claimed, would not have permitted such obvious awkwardness in the merest adventure story, particularly not when "his genius was still on the whole at its best and brightest; as George Eliot's most indisputably was, when *Romola* was written."[22]

Swinburne somehow seems to have purged from his memory all the casual coincidences of a Reade plot, but he generally agrees with the critic who found George Eliot's study of Savonarola

a laborious, conscientious, absolute failure — as complete as the failure of his own actual attempt to purge and renovate the epoch of the Borgias by what Mr. Carlyle would have called the "Morison's Pill" of Catholic Puritanism. Charles Reade's Dominican is worth a dozen such "wersh," ineffectual, invertebrate studies, taken by marshlight and moonshine, as this spectre of a spectre which flits across the stage of romance . . . but when we come to collation of minor characters and groups the superiority of the male novelist is so obvious and so enormous that any comparison between the full robust proportions of his breathing figures and the stiff thin outlines of George Eliot's phantasmal puppets would be unfair if it were not unavoidable.[23]

## VI . *The Perfect Archetype*

Alfred Lord Tennyson found in the myth of Tithonus, in the lotos-eaters of Homer's *Odyssey*, and in the Arthurian legends the very figures from the past best suited to bear into the Victorian era his freight of melancholy dubiety ("Tithonus," "The Lotos-Eaters," *Idylls of the King*). Robert Browning discovered in an old yellow book the account of a medieval ecclesiastical court trial that precisely suited his nineteenth-century vision of a multitude of viewpoints that must be added to produce the composite truth *(The Ring and the Book)*. In the Erasmus *Compendium* — musty, dry, factual — Charles Reade uncovered the perfect "Reade plot" — four hundred and thirty-five years old! The medieval autobiographic fragment is full of event, and Reade is a master of eventful narrative. The plot hinges on a picaresque journey, and Reade casts his heroes far from home. The catastrophe is the result of a fraudulent letter, and Reade's heroes and heroines might well hesitate before they open a fictitious letter and stagger back before the ill news it bears. A misunderstanding mars all, and this is Reade's own way with the dynamic of evil in his novels. Gerard is a semihistorical figure, but is he not also one of the long line of "Reade's Resourceful Heroes" who can do and be anything required by the entirely dominant situation? And Margaret is another of his frank, honest heroines who could easily don the garb of a farmer's daughter in Victorian England.

Thus to melodrama's own god — Coincidence — must go the final credit for Reade's masterpiece. The authorial hand found the perfect glove, and its grasp of character, setting, and narrative became masterly. And, if the hand trembled a bit under the pressure of imposed celibacy, the grasp simply became tighter as a hero under the same pressure met the imposition of celibacy with high gallantry and unending faithfulness.

CHAPTER 5

# Conclusion

W ILLIAM Dean Howells probably placed his critical finger as accurately as anyone on the pulse of Charles Reade's singular weakness. When Howells was a youth, everyone was reading Reade's jaunty, knowledgeable books; and so great was his effect upon that generation that young men were wondering if they had not discovered someone better than Thackeray, Dickens, or George Eliot. Years later, when Howells was visiting his old home he picked up a copy of *Christie Johnstone*, which he had read and loved thirty years before. But upon rereading it, he was amazed by its prevailing artistic vulgarity, by its many aesthetic errors, and by the sense that something fresh and new was about to be born, but not quite. "He was a man who stood at the parting of the ways between realism and romanticism," wrote Howells, "and if he had been somewhat more of a man he might have been the master of a great school of English realism; but, as it was, he remained content to use the materials of realism and produce the effect of romanticism."[1]

Of course, Howells was using the term "realism" in a favorable sense because he was one of the first great American realistic novelists, whereas he referred to romanticism in a pejorative manner. He called romanticism a "fool's paradise" and spoke of its "inanity and impossibility." Obviously these are judgments with which to argue; for although romanticism may be a "fool's paradise," it still is a kind of paradise, even though a foolish one. On the other hand, realism clearly is no paradise at all; and it often settles down with the merely tedious and banal. By an odd conjunction, Howells's critical position is the same as Swinburne's in his discussion of "the brilliant story of *A Simpleton* [in which] there are passages of almost as superfluous dullness as the dullest superfluities of the self-styled naturalist whose horrors Mr. Reade undertook to adapt for presentation on the English stage: and the dullness is of the same order as M. Zola's: it is deliberate and systematic, based on the French realist's great principle that a study from life should be founded on what he calls 'documents' — nay, that it should be made up of these, were they never so noisome or so wearisome.''[2]

The materials of realism and the effect of romanticism provide the twin poles of the tension that once made Reade seem significant but that now makes him seem insignificant. Nothing could be clearer, biographically or literarily, than Reade's excessive devotion to the materials of realism. In his dramas, he displayed an extraordinary interest in stage business, in ingenious and realistic settings, and in the most explicit stage directions. He publicly thanked the London *Times* for news articles that provided the plots for at least two of his most popular novels. Moreover, Reade's process of artistic creation never got beyond arm's reach of his compendious notebooks, his index files, and his enormous notecards that stood like screens in his study. All of these provided the facts with whch the novelist could pride himself that he was keeping in touch with real life. His readiness to dash to his own defense in cases of literary controversy was certainly related to his conviction that criticism ought not to be primarily devoted to such matters as style, symbolism, and character development, but to basic adherence to fact. Indeed, if any journalistic idiot doubted the credibility of a Reade character or plot, Reade had only to reach out to a notecard and produce the clipping — dates, with names, and places — the indubitable stuff of real life.

Probably Reade's readiness to translate, collaborate, and plagiarize rested upon the twin pillars of his need for a basic outline provided by a newspaper story or by someone else's written work, and of the creative penury that resulted from his deep distrust of the creative imagination. In a way, this distrust was his great strength as a British writer: he might start with a Gallic plot for a drama, or with a newspaper clipping for a novel; but by the time he had immersed it in Victorian morality, had included British coarseness of taste and love of violence, and had studded it with names of places near the country estate where he was reared and with the family names of his parents' neighbors and dependents, he had produced a profoundly British work. Orwell, by way of reparation for temporary forgetfulness, confesses that

in any of Reade's three best books, *Foul Play, Hard Cash* and *It Is Never Too Late to Mend*, it is not fair to say that the sole interest is in the technical detail. His power of descriptive writing, especially of describing violent action, is also very striking, and on a serial-story level he is a wonderful contriver of plots . . . he . . . had the advantage of believing in even the absurdest details of his own stories. He wrote of life as he saw it, and many Victorians saw it in the same way: that is, as a series of tremendous melodramas, with virtue triumphant every time. Of all the nineteenth-century novelists who have remained readable, he is perhaps the only one who is completely in tune with his own age. For all his unconventionality, his "purpose," his eagerness to expose abuses, he never makes a fundamental criticism. Save for a few surface evils he sees nothing wrong in an acquisitive society, with its equation of money with virtue, its pious millionaires and erastian clergymen.[3]

The materials of realism can easily be transliterated into a doctrine of realistic materialism, and Charles Reade successfully made this transformation. His exhaustive research into the techniques of mining gold and diamonds geared perfectly into the period of the full flowering of the industrial revolution. His horror at the mounting abuses of labor unions endeared him to manufacturers unaccustomed to sympathy from writers. Even when he explained the precise details of forgery, Victorians had the solid feeling that they were learning something while they read. When he exposed the prison system and the sanitoriums for the insane, he appealed strongly to that marked Evangelical tendency to rejoice in one's own righteousness while condemning the wickedness of others. When he claimed that the origin of a novel was a *Times'* clipping, latter-day Puritans — who did not believe in the inspiration of the muse but did believe in real life — read and rejoiced. Fiction was suspect; but life was indubitably real.

When he studded his pages with little gems of research into a period or a profession, he satisfied that deep Victorian passion for inventory, that rising middle-class need to be constantly bolstered by the sense of ownership expressed in precise description and number. When his spirit temporarily sank beneath the onslaughts of his critics, he triumphantly produced the sure proof of his literary genius — the investments in land, stocks, and furnishings that he had made as a result of his literary publications. And, in doing so, he well knew that this was the only kind of proof that would be absolutely persuasive to his solid burgher reading audience.

Although Reade's native genius was for the brief, dramatic narrative, he padded his tales so that they might match the overstuffedness of the period. Thus the picaresque journey goes on .

almost interminably, and what does it matter that two battles with thieves in almost identical inns are also almost identical in incident? Pages have been filled, chapters fleshed out, and the demands of the circulating libraries met. The dizzying change of place and the rapid passage of time keep the reader excitedly enthralled; and they need be motivated by nothing but the sheer demands of geography and the calendar. Since a fat novel needs bulky construction, Reade hit upon the simplest pattern of all — two streams that eventually flow into one — as the portentous machinery of his basically rather disjointed collection of sensational incident, false *dénouement*, *fausse sortie*, double take, and anticlimax that bring his tales to a close.

Since a fat novel also needs to be rather extensively populated, he fell back upon a useful but shopworn gallery of stock types: the blond heroine and the brunette rival; the weak and worthless male strenuously beloved by battling heroines; the hero of infinite resourcefulness; the female built upon heroic classic lines and the ladylike clinging vine; the weak villain from the upper class who employs a strong villain, usually from the lower classes; the comic blacks, Yankees, and doctors who are patently cut from the same design and the same cloth. All of these represented for Charles Reade the materials of realism, which he used with self-congratulation and upon which he depended for artistic immortality. This was novelistic creation — nineteenth-century style — linked with the new scientific outlook and with the flood of raw materials pouring in from the colonies and pouring out in torrents of ready-made goods stamped Manchester, Birmingham, or Sheffield.

But Reade's absorbed interest in the facts of life — the statistics, data, and techniques of the modern world — was made to serve essentially old-fashioned ideals. After all the years Reade had haunted stage doors, consorted with actors and managers of theaters, dined with journalists, and explored the dark spots of England, he might have been expected to exhibit in his writing the knowing leer and the cynically raised eyebrow of the thorough man of the world. In actual fact, the interior of the man remained the boy from Ipsden, naive, simple in his understanding of human personality, and entirely traditional in his philosophical and ethical outlook. Thus all the spate of facts, and clippings from newspapers, the written testimony of seamen, the research of hacks, and the musty monkish compendia had to be fitted into a very simple ethical pattern. Good had to triumph: evil had to be defeated; men had to prove their masculinity under the same forms of danger as the Greek compatriots of

Odysseus whom Homer had described; women had to be simple farm girls or silly, tender ladies. The essence of the sensational melodrama, both in his plays and in his novels, always resided in the same situation: evil may appear to triumph and good to fail, but one need not fear. Although the plot winds its convuluted way and turns back upon itself, at the moment when all hope is lost, the kaleidoscope is shaken by a Celestial Hand, and all the pieces fall at last into their rightful places and relationships.

Yet Reade had his moments of aberrant curiosity: transvestism obviously titillated some hidden emotional nerve; he evidently liked to play with the idea of women who would be the sexual aggressors rather than the tepidly passive recipients of *amour*. He obviously noted strengths in women and weaknesses in men that jolted but never destroyed his pleasant old formula of masculine-feminine characteristics. In a modern divinity school, students of preaching are warned never to set up, in a sermon, a straw man of evil that they are unable to knock down in the peroration. No one ever gave this sage advice to Reade, the novelistic preacher in the good Victorian didactic tradition; therefore, he constantly sets up evils, villainies, and incredible thickets of cross-purposes, which he could never knock down with evidence, logic, or strength of narrative. He only invokes a kind of moralistic *tour de force* that must once have seemed effective but that now seems simply improbable. He so handled the materials of realism that they conveyed, therefore, the effect of a starry-eyed and idealistic romanticism, which more properly, in Reade's case, ought to be judged as sentimentalism.

William Dean Howells was fingering the pulse of this failure when he described Reade as a man who stood at the parting of the ways between realism and romanticism. This stance was Reade's challenge and his opportunity, but it became his failure when he publicly espoused a realism that he had privately decided to bend to romantic ends. To the question of why Reade made this particular form of the Victorian compromise, Howells had only the rather mawkish judgment to offer that "if he had been somewhat more of a man he might have been the master of a great school of English realism." Anthony Trollope, who found it equally awkward to delineate the problem of Charles Reade, literally threw up his hands by setting up the traditional dichotomy between emotion and intellect — "so good a heart and so wrong a head."[4] But, by an interesting coincidence, both Howells and Trollope actually put their fingers on the same diagnosis: Reade's failure was in some manner intellectual. He could sense the demand of his age for factuality; he could produce a faint counterfeit; but he had then flown as high as he could mount, and, unimaginatively and somewhat ignorantly, the Oxford don fell back upon trite solutions and banal moralities.

In his youth, Howells had wondered if "we ought not to set him above Thackeray and Dickens and George Eliot."[5] W. L. Courtney attempted a comparison with exactly the same triad — "literary giants such as Thackeray, and Dickens, and George Eliot" — but he ended by rejecting the comparison: Reade could not compare with the artistry of Thackeray, with the prodigality of gifts of Dickens, nor with the keen analysis and profound thoughtfulness of George Eliot. The rejection was quite proper. Reade was not really a literary artist; he could not people the squares and inns of Dickens's London; he lacked the intellectual depth of George Eliot.

So Courtney, having failed in a comparison of Reade to the literary giants of the day, tried a comparison with a different and less luminous triad — "he has more points of comparison with writers for whom he had a great admiration, though they were in many respects his inferiors, such as Wilkie Collins, Bulwer Lytton, and Miss Braddon."[5] Thus, perhaps as aptly as possible, Charles Reade is placed just below the giants and just above the second rank of merely popular writers of the day. He remains in a distinguished but perhaps lonely limbo of his own.

# Notes and References

## Chapter One

1. John Coleman, *Charles Reade as I Knew Him*, p. 417.
2. Charles L. Reade and Compton Reade, *Charles Reade, D.C.L., Dramatist, Novelist, Journalist: A Memoir Compiled Chiefly from His Literary Remains*, p. 315. Hereafter referred to as *Memoir*.
3. *The Wandering Heir*, appendix.
4. Michael Sadleir, *Excursions in Victorian Bibliography* (London: Chaundy & Cox 1922), title motto.
5. Jerome Hamilton Buckley, *The Victorian Temper: A Study in Literary Culture* (Cambridge, Mass.: Harvard University Press, 1951), Chapter V.
6. James Joyce, *A Portrait of the Artist as a Young Man*, (New York: Viking Press, 1958). Chapter V, pp. 480 - 82.
7. Coventry Patmore, *The Angel in the House*, (London, 1898); Alfred Tennyson, *The Princess* (London, 1847), Part VII.
8. Thirty-two volumes of Reade's notebooks are in the London Library, St. James's Square (see E. G. Sutcliffe, "Charles Reade's Notebooks," *Studies in Philology*, XXVII, 64 - 109). Another group of Reade notebooks were in the possession of Mr. Michael Sadleir as of 1961. A third group of notebooks and other papers are in the Morris L. Parrish Collection of the Princeton University Library.
9. E. W. Hornung, "Charles Reade," *London Mercury*, IV (June, 1921), 150.
10. "Cremona Fiddles," *Pall Mall Gazette*; first letter, August 19, 1872; second, August 24, 1872; third, August 27, 1872; fourth, August 31, 1872.
11. *The Ladies' Battle* (London, 1851), introduction.
12. COUNTESS: What do you expect, milord? In order to win, it is not enough to play well.
   MONTRICHARD: It is necessary to have the aces and the kings.
   COUNTESS: (aside, glancing at Henry). Especially the king! . . . in the ladies' battle.
13. *The Courier of Lyons*, introduction.

CHARLES READE

14. Malcolm Elwin, *Charles Reade: A Biography*, p. 192.

15. *Ibid.*

16. Coleman, p. 236.

17. William Archer, *English Dramatists of Today*, pp. 36 - 38.

18. Coleman, pp. 97 - 101.

19. Professor William H. Scheuerle (see Preface) suggests that the duality of light-dark heroines seems to have been a favorite device in nineteenth-century fiction: Sir Walter Scott, *Ivanhoe*; George Eliot, *Middlemarch*, *Adam Bede*; Wilkie Collins, *The Woman in White*; Emily Brontë, *Wuthering Heights*; Henry Kingsley, *Mademoiselle Mathilde*; Charles Dickens, *David Copperfield*.

20. Professor Scheuerle notes that the odd Victorian fictional device was to couple strong women with weaker men: Scott's *Heart of Midlothian* and *Waverley*.

21. *Memoir*, p. 117.

22. Elwin, p. 44.

23. Coleman, p. 49.

24. *Ibid.*, pp. 59 - 60.

25. *Memoir*, p. 228ff.

26. Large folio called "Red Digest," p. 167. London Library.

27. Elwin, p. 90; Coleman, p. 421.

28. Walter Frewen Lord, *The Mirror of the Century*, p. 252.

29. Justin McCarthy, "Charles Reade," *Galaxy*, XIV, no. 4 (April, 1872), 441 - 42.

30. *Memoir*, p. 198.

31. Archer, p. 31ff.

32. The Defoe-like turn of Reade's mind appears ("Journalium 1," p. 71) in his praise of the diaries of a beggar and a swindler, which he had read in *Household Chronicle*. London Library.

33. "Androgynism; or, Woman Playing at Man; from the Unpublished MSS. of the late Charles Reade," *English Review*, IX (August, 1911), 10 - 29; IX (September, 1911), 191 - 212.

34. Elwin, p. 355.

35. *Ibid.*, p. 92.

36. *Ibid.*, p. 196.

37. Sir Johnston Forbes-Robertson, *A Player under Three Reigns* (Boston: Little, Brown and Company, 1925).

38. Coleman, p. 309.

39. Elwin, p. 194.

40. Bradford A. Booth, "Trollope, Reade and 'Shilly-Shally' " (Part One), *The Trollopian: A Journal of Victorian Fiction*, I, no. 4 (March, 1947), 46.

41. Anthony Trollope, *Autobiography* (London, 1883), Chapter XIII p. 233.

42. Booth, pp. 48 - 49.

43. "Shilly-Shally," drama review in the *Spectator*, February 15, 1873.
44. Booth, p. 48.
45. *Memoir*, pp. 322 - 25.

## Chapter Two

1. *Memoir*, p. 181.
2. *Peg Woffington: A Novel* (London, 1853; actually published December 17, 1852).
3. Thomas Seccombe, introduction to George Herbert Gissing, *House of Cobwebs* (Freeport, New York: Books for Libraries Press, 1971), *viii*.
4. Professor William H. Scheuerle lists as examples of the superiority of the female sex: George Meredith, *The Egoist;* Sir Walter Scott, *Heart of Midlothian;* William Thackeray, *Vanity Fair;* Thomas Hardy, *Tess of the D'Urbervilles;* also Mario Praz, *The Hero in Eclipse in Victorian Fiction.*
5. *Memoir*, p. 228.
6. Malcolm Elwin, *Charles Reade*, p. 130.
7. Reade notebooks, "*Excerpta Miscellanea*," p. 71. Two articles on Mrs. Bloomer in the London *Times*, May 13, 1851; May 27, 1851. Parrish collection.
8. Algernon Charles Swinburne, *Miscellanies*, p. 291.
9. William Leonard Courtney, "Charles Reade's Novels," *Studies, New and Old*, p. 157.
10. Reade notebooks. "*Index variorum et manuscriptorum*," p. 15, "Curialia": "Bigamy — the 2 injured wives make friends. Xtra 1 letter to pseudo husband, do. to wife affecting scene in court. Xtra 10 curious party used in Griffith Gaunt. Wives making friends Griffith Gaunt XLII; curious party Griffith Gaunt XXXIII - XXXIV." Lond. Lib., St. James' Sq.
11. "Charles Reade's Novels," *Blackwood's Edinburgh Magazine*, CVI, no. 648 (October, 1869), 498.
12. Swinburne, p. 286.
13. Justin McCarthy, "Charles Reade," p. 443.
14. Elwin, p. 188.
15. *Ibid.*, p. 216.
16. *A Terrible Temptation*, closing note, p. 475.
17. See Wilkie Collins, *The Woman In White.*
18. John Coleman in *Charles Reade as I Knew Him* identifies the Magdalen College acquaintance as Goldwin Smith and tells an amusing anecdote to explain the early beginning of Smith's animosity (p. 67).
19. S. M. Ellis, *Henry Kingsley 1830 - 1876: Towards a Vindication* (London: Grant Richards, 1931), p. 187.
20. Swinburne, pp. 284 - 85.
21. Reade's notebooks, "No. 9 Folio." An unnumbered red and green notebook of the period contains a pasted-in copy of an article from the New

York *Sun*, August 16, 1871: "... new worlds of vice ... opened up to thousands of young and innocent minds." Parrish Collection.

22. Elwin, p. 242.

23. *A Simpleton*, preface, pp. 4, 5.

24. Reade's Notebooks, "*Mareria novae fabulae*, 26." A memorandum in Reade's handwriting: "For the second woman use Boucicault's second character in Hunted Down; and perhaps the little actress in Caste with particulars of class." London Library.

25. Professor Scheuerle remarks that Henry Kingsley has a comparable "corny Yankee" in *The Hillyars and the Burtons* and suggests that this literary stereotype was popularized to a large extent in England by Mrs. Trollope's *Domestic Manners of the Americans* (1832) and by Dickens's *Martin Chuzzlewit* (1844).

26. Charles Reade and Henry Pettitt, *Love and Money: An Original Drama in a Prologue and Four Acts*.

27. Emerson Grant Sutcliffe, "Plotting in Reade's Novels," *Publications of the Modern Language Association*, XLVII, no. 3 (September, 1932), 841.

## Chapter Three

1. Professor William H. Scheuerle considers that "particular peccadillo" may describe the earlier Dickens novels but that his later works, especially *Our Mutual Friend*, often make a strong "general indictment."

2. George Orwell, *New Statesman and Nation* (August 17, 1940) and *The Collected Essays, Journalism and Letters of George Orwell*, eds. Sonia Orwell and Ian Angus (London: Secker & Warburg, 1968), II, pp. 34, 35.

3. In Reade's notebooks, an untitled folio dated 1867 - 70 is mostly in the handwriting of William Barrington Reade, Charles's nautical brother. London Library, St. James' Square.

4. Reade's notebooks, "Digest" — "*memoranda agenda*": "13. Having wasted too many years to be learned I must use cunning. Think of some way to make young active fellows run and collect materials for me. Think of a Machinery. Government though not very brainful produces books Briareus like; why might not I, and lick the rough cub into shape. Thus start the conception. Learn the sources by Watts Bibliotheca, Mr. Donne, Bandinel etc. Then put my hacks on, *leaving gaps;* so that they may not see the whole design, and steal the capital idea. German hacks good for this. University hacks ditto. Pay them well and keep them dark."

5. Walter Frewen Lord, *The Mirror of the Century;* pp. 252 - 54.

6. Malcolm Elwin, *Charles Reade*, p. 114.

7. E. W. Hornung, "Charles Reade," pp. 151 - 52.

8. "It is two o'clock: All is well: sleep, masters, sleep!"

9. Professor Scheuerle, in defense of Henry Kingsley, points out that although the youthful Henry James was ostensibly reviewing Henry Kingsley's *The Hillyars and the Burtons*, he was actually launching an attack

on Charles Kingsley and the whole "Noble School of Fiction." Thus James was almost committed to find things wrong with the Kingsleys, and by contrast, things right with writers who were not part of the "Noble" circle.

10. Algernon Charles Swinburne, *Miscellanies*, p. 294.

11. *Ibid.*, p. 274.

12. "Charles Reade's Novels," *Blackwood's Edinburgh Magazine*, CVI, no. 648 (October, 1869), 506.

13. "Very Hard Cash: A Novel," *Brownson's Quarterly Review*, I (April, 1864), 236.

14. William Leonard Courtney, "Charles Reade's Novels," p. 151.

15. A passage in Reade's notebooks, "No. 9 Folio," seems to suggest that the character of Jane Hardie, a religious enthusiast, was taken from Horatio Bonar's popular study *A Stranger Here*. Parrish Coll.

16. Reade's notebooks. "Folio 2 Plot Book," 1871 - 76. Pamphlet inserted at end called "Curialia J. G. S. 1876." From p. 61b ff. there are references to insurance plots in J. G. Saunders's (Reade's secretary) handwriting with Reade's marginal comments: "Used in A Simpleton," "Used in Foul Play," "Not used at all," "Not yet used at all." Parrish Coll.

17. Orwell, pp. 35 - 36.

18. "Charles Reade's Novels," *Blackwood's*, 513.

19. "Charles Reade," *Once a Week*, XXVI, no. 212 (January 20, 1872), 86.

20. P. Brantlinger, "The Case Against Trade Unions in Early Victorian Fiction," *Victorian Studies*, XIII, no. 1 (September, 1969), 37 - 52.

21. P. J. Keating, *The Working Classes in Victorian Fiction* (New York: Routledge & Kegan Paul, 1971), p. 310ff.

22. Reade's notebooks. "Notebook #60, Comments on *Opera Readei Theatrum*": A clipping from the *Weekly Dispatch*, May 29, 1870, states that Henry Neville, an actor in the dramatic version of *Put Yourself in His Place*, had been taken by Mr. Reade to Sheffield to learn the art of forging a knife. The notebook also identifies Grotait with Mr. Broadhead, a leading labor organizer in Sheffield. London Library.

23. Courtney, pp. 166 - 67.

24. Reade's notebooks. Letter from feminist Millicent Garrett Fawcett refers to the success in medical examinations of a Miss Ogle, evidently known to Reade, and almost an anagram of (Rhoda) Gale. London Library.

*Chapter Four*

1. E. W. Hornung, "Charles Reade," p. 153.

2. Albert M. Turner, *The Making of "The Cloister and the Hearth,"* p. 1.

3. *A Hero and a Martyr: A True Narrative*, pp. 5 - 30. Also in *Readiana*, pp. 29 - 35.

4. In Reade's notebooks, a clipping of a *Spectator* (October 12, 1861) article refers to the medieval document: "It will be seen at once that we have

here the outline of a noble romance." Reade wrote in the margin: "That outline was 300 years in print, and nobody did anything with it." Parrish Collection.

5. Turner, pp. 16 - 17.
6. Annie Fields, "An Acquaintance with Charles Reade," *Century Magazine*, XXIX (November, 1884), 73. See Turner, *The Making of "The Cloister and the Hearth*," for literary sources of the novel.
7. *Memoir*, pp. 181 - 83.
8. Malcolm Elwin, *Charles Reade*, p. 43.
9. Nathaniel Wanley, *Wonders of the Little World* (London, 1678), p. 37.
10. "Charles Reade's Novels," *Blackwood's Edinburgh Magazine*, CVI, no. 648 (October, 1869), 510 - 11.
11. Walter Frewen Lord, *The Mirror of the Century*, p. 267.
12. Hornung, p. 154.
13. Algernon Charles Swinburne, "Charles Reade," *Nineteenth Century*, XCII (October, 1884), 553 - 57.
14. W. L. Courtney, "Charles Reade's Novels," *Fortnightly Review*, n.s. CCXIV (October, 1885), 463 - 64.
15. Hugh Walpole, "Novelists of the Seventies," *The Eighteen Seventies*, ed. Harley Granville-Barker (Cambridge University Press, 1929), pp. 34 - 35.
16. Wayne Burns, "*The Cloister and the Hearth*, A Classic Reconsidered," *The Trollopian: A Journal of Victorian Fiction*, II, no. 2 (September, 1947), 72.
17. Algernon Charles Swinburne, *Miscellanies*, p. 299.
18. *Ibid.*, p. 296.
19. A. T. Quiller-Couch, "Charles Reade," *Adventures in Criticism*, p. 129ff.
20. Elwin, p. 157.
21. Anonymous review in *Once a Week*, XXVI (n.s. IX), no. 212 (January 20, 1872), 80.
22. Swinburne, *Miscellanies*, pp. 281 - 82.
23. *Ibid.*, p. 282.

## Chapter Five

1. William Dean Howells, *My Literary Passions*, pp. 193 - 97.
2. Algernon Charles Swinburne, *Miscellanies*, p. 275.
3. George Orwell, *Collected Essays, Journalism and Letters of George Orwell*, eds. Sonia Orwell and Ian Angus (London, 1968), II, pp. 36 - 37.
4. Anthony Trollope, *Autobiography* (London, 1883).
5. Howells, *My Literary Passions* p. 193.
6. W. L. Courtney, "Charles Reade's Novels," *Studies Old and New*, p. 152.

# Selected Bibliography

PRIMARY SOURCES

1. Notebooks and Notecards

Michael Sadleir's chapter on Charles Reade in *Excursions in Victorian Bibliography* (London: Chauncy and Cox, 1922), p. 159ff., contains no judgment on his place in literature because at times he was "so fine, so resilient, so impressive; at others, the dullest of pamphleteers, a cramped Meredith in style, a very waxwork among sensationalists." Although a number of Reade notebooks were in his possession and a large collection available at the London Library, Sadleir was interested only in bibliographic references to Reade's novels and plays.

E. G. Sutcliffe, in "Charles Reade's Notebooks," *Studies in Philology*, XXVII (January, 1930), 64 - 109, made the pioneer attempt to classify and analyze the contents of the thirty-two notebooks in the London Library, St. James's Square. Eight years later, Albert M. Turner, in *The Making of "The Cloister and the Hearth"* (Chicago: University of Chicago Press, 1938), produced a thorough study, but he seems to have assumed that no notebooks were available as source material for the writing of Reade's most famous work.

Morris L. Parrish, who followed the precedent of Mr. Sadleir, listed only the first editions of novels, plays, and pamphlets, without any analysis of the notebooks or notecards, in *Wilkie Collins and Charles Reade* (London: Constable and Company, 1940). This omission was to some degree rectified by Wayne Burns's study of the four Reade notebooks then in the Parrish Collection, "More Reade Notebooks," *Studies in Philology*, XLII (1945), 824 - 42. Two years later, Bradford A. Booth drew heavily upon the Reade correspondence in the Parrish Collection for his articles "Trollope, Reade, and 'Shilly-Shally,'" *Trollopian* (March, 1947; June, 1947).

Robert B. Martin published brief appreciations of the new accessions to the Parrish Collection in two articles in the *Princeton University Library Chronicle* in 1956 and 1958. Since these articles are now more than a decade old and did not then aspire to be a complete catalogue of contents, there may be some usefulness in a brief reference to the notebook and notecard holdings as of 1969.

166

CHARLES READE

"Miscellanea, 1861 - 2" (also dated July 1861 - 1862, 3) with a notation inside "Kept at Oxford," has an ownership ascription indicating that Reade was living at the time at 6 Bolton Row, Mayfair. Among the topics, indexed alphabetically at the beginning, are: biographies of Sir Astley Cooper, surgeon; other doctors, and the Abbé Prévost; biblical studies; executions at Cambridge in its early years; the "Dreadful Suffering of a Ship's Crew"; "Negri loci"; and a section entitled "Homo in Curia," with newspaper articles on two murders and on rape, infanticide, and filicide.

"Notes for Hard Cash" contains material on such topics as: Bazalgette (*Love Me Little, Love Me Long*), Lunaticum, Dickson, doctors, Julia, shipwreck, *vivi feminaque*, financial panic, milliners, Dickeybird, plagiabilia. After quoting the adage of Corneille: "Il est facile aux speculatifs d'être sévère" (It is easy for the uninvolved to be severe in their judgments), Reade makes the following memoranda: "This book will be a success if I fight against Nature & inclination, and hunt up men and women and talk to them. Otherwise it will be a failure, and the worst of failures, a *fine subject spoiled*." Probably in reference to the earlier Corneille quotation, there is Reade's resolution: "Be more judicial and two sided than in Sera nunquam / *It Is Never Too Late to Mend*."

Reade's Picture Book and Dictionary ("Caroli Pict & D—— Lib —— ium"): biographical tour, epistolae, Abe Lincoln, statues for the living, photography, good citizens, heroes and martyrs, subjects for illustration, vicaria.

"Duodecimo Digest 2". Among topics considered are: life assurance, America, bonae fabulae, bibliographia, archeology, anonymuncules, copyrights, duarum pueri artium, dramatizanda, Sap. Gent., strikes (*Times*, October 2, 1859), and the memorandum that a blue book on organized labor was to come out in 1861.

"Octavus Lex": apothegms, inventors and patent laws, blunders by English judges, wit, new terms (such as "cephalomancy"), subtle frauds, pith, evidence, the wrongs of authors.

"Old Notes Cloister & the Hearth" is the notebook Professor Turner assumed to be lost or otherwise unavailable. It considers such relevant topics as: the contemporaries of Gerard son of Eli, medieval details, Dominicans, Italian costume, characteristics, the pros and cons of the monastic life, Van Eyck, Libri, plot, Margaret.

"Miscell. Faemina nat. Vera": Libri, female traits (with the notation "Try and know a Doctress. See whether it unsexed her"), female bigamists, transvestism, and a newspaper item from the September 15, 1860, issue of the *New York Illustrated News*, which was evidently the basis of one narrative strand in *The Wandering Heir*.

A small black leather notebook with the title destroyed: colleges ("negro blood. Not admitted to them. Why?"), Negrocide, incidents from slavery, distinguished Negroes, miscellanea ("Describe the virtues of Southerners warmly").

"The Practical Advertiser": advertisements Charles Reade thought interesting or well written clipped from newspapers.

Nine packages of notecards: (1) nineteen notecards for *Hard Cash;* (2) "Nova Scientia," containing references to *Hard Cash, A Terrible Temptation, The Cloister and the Hearth* (five cards marked "Used"), *Joan,* insanity, bonae fabulae, claris ad Sera nunquam, libri clasificati, Oxoniensia, banking and nautical, judicialia, "Dark Places of the Land," bloodletting, Dickeybirdiana, and trade unions; (3) cards and fragments: *Foul Play, A Simpleton, The Wandering Heir,* loci Sauliani paginati (medical), marina et insularia, obscure diseases of the brain and mind, curiosities of insanity, the character of patients, and Seymour vs. Curling; (4) *Put Yourself in His Place, Foul Play,* bonae fabulae, Rus, Nanciana es Capell., Defoe, banking; (5) statistics of labor, wages, drink, taxation; key to *It's Never Too Late to Mend,* vita eremetica et monastica; (6) *Put Yourself in His Place* and *The Wandering Heir;* (7) twelve half-size cards on *Put Yourself in His Place;* (8) *Put Yourself in His Place* and *A Simpleton;* (9) a miscellaneous, unnumbered, untitled folio.

Holdings of the Pierpont Morgan Library (as of September, 1969) include original manuscripts of *Hard Cash,* dated "begun June 1862 ended March 1863," 3 volumes, 823 manuscript pages (along with original drafts of various passages later suppressed or rewritten); *Love Me Little, Love Me Long,* dated 1857, 619 manuscript pages, with original (?) title "Maid, Wife, and Widow," frequently inscribed in English and French: and *A Simpleton,* untitled, unsigned, page 2 only. In addition there is a presentation copy with autograph of *It Is Never Too Late to Mend: A Matter of Fact Romance* (London: R. Bentley, 1857). Among the letters, there is the original draft by Charles Reade to the editor of the *Daily News* replying to an attack by Dr. Bushman, and an autographed letter from Wilkie Collins dated March 31, 1863. Also of interest is the original agreement of Charles Reade and Charles Dickens for the publication of *Hard Cash* in *All the Year Round,* dated 1862.

2. Novels and Tales

*Christie Johnstone: A Novel.* London: Richard Bentley, 1853.

*Peg Woffington: A Novel.* London: Richard Bentley, 1853.

*Clouds and Sunshine and Art: A Dramatic Tale.* Boston: Ticknor and Fields, 1855.

*It Is Never Too Late to Mend: A Matter of Fact Romance.* 3 vols. London: Richard Bentley, 1856. (Reade wrote a pamphlet defending this novel under the title *"It Is Never Too Late to Mend: Proofs of Its Prison Revelations,"* 1859.)

*The Box Tunnel.* Boston: Ticknor and Fields, 1857. (This short story was published in *Bentley's Miscellany,* November, 1853.)

*The Course of True Love Never Did Run Smooth.* London: Richard Bentley, 1857. (First published in *Bentley's Miscellany.*)

*Propria Quae Maribus: A jeu d'esprit; and The Box Tunnel: A Fact.* Boston: Ticknor and Fields, 1857.

*White Lies: A Story.* 3 vols. London: Trübner and Company, 1857. (First published in *London Journal.*)

*Cream.* London: Trübner and Company, 1858. (Contains *Jack of All Trades: A Matter of Fact Romance* [first published in *Illustrated London News,* 1856], and *The Autobiography of a Thief.*)

*Love Me Little, Love Me Long.* 2 vols. London: Trübner and Company, 1859.

*The Cloister and the Hearth: A Tale of the Middle Ages.* 4 vols. London: Trübner and Company, 1861.

*Hard Cash: A Matter of Fact Romance.* 3 vols. London: Sampson Low, Son, and Marston, 1863. (First published in *All the Year Round* as *Very Hard Cash.*)

*Griffith Gaunt: or Jealousy.* 3 vols. London: Chapman and Hall, 1866. (First published in *Argosy.*)

*Foul Play* (with Dion Boucicault). 3 vols. London: Bradbury Evans and Company, 1868. (First published in *Once a Week,* 1868.)

*Put Yourself in His Place.* 3 vols. London: Smith Elder and Company, 1870. (First published in *Cornhill Magazine.*)

*A Terrible Temptation.* 3 vols. London: Chapman and Hall, 1871. (First published in *Cassell's Magazine.* Reade's pamphlet "To the Editor of *The Daily Globe,* Toronto: A Reply to Criticism," 1871, deals with this book.)

*A Simpleton: A Story of the Day.* 3 vols. London: Chapman and Hall, 1873. (First published in *London Society.*)

*The Wandering Heir: A Matter of Fact Romance.* London: Samuel French, 1875. (First published in the *Graphic,* 1872; repeated 1905, 1924.)

*The Jilt: A Novel.* New York: Harper and Brothers, 1877.

*A Woman-Hater.* 3 vols. Edinburgh and London: William Blackwood and Sons, 1877.

*Good Stories of Man and Other Animals.* London: Chatto and Windus, 1884.

*A Perilous Secret.* 2 vols. London: Richard Bentley and Son, 1884. (First published in *Temple Bar Magazine.*)

*Singleheart and Doubleface:* A Matter of Fact Romance. London: Chatto and Windus, 1884. (First published in *Harper's Magazine.*)

*A Good Fight.* Ed. Andrew Lang. London: Henry Frowde, 1910. (First published in *Once a Week,* 1859; was the earliest version of *The Cloister and the Hearth.*)

3. Plays

*Angelo: A Tragedy in Four Acts.* London: Lacy's Acting Editions, no. 57, 1851.

*Peregrine Pickle.* Oxford: privately printed, 1851.

*The Ladies' Battle: or Un Duel en Amour. A Comedy*. London: Thomas Hailes Lacy, 1851

*The Lost Husband: A Drama in Four Acts* (Written and Adapted from the French, *Les Dames de la Halle*). London: Lacy's Acting Editions, no. 86, 1852.

*Gold: A Drama*. London: Lacy's Acting Edition of Plays, v. 11, 1853.

*The Courier of Lyons: or The Attack Upon the Mail; A Drama in Four Acts* (Translated from the French of MM. Moreau, Siraudin and Delacourt). London: Lacy's Acting Editions, no. 220, 1854.

*The King's Rival: A Drama in Five Acts* (with Tom Taylor). London: Richard Bentley, 1854.

*Masks and Faces: or Before and Behind the Curtain; A Comedy in Two Acts* (with Tom Taylor). London: Richard Bentley, 1854.

*Two Loves and a Life: A Drama in Four Acts* (with Tom Taylor). London: Richard Bentley, 1854.

*Poverty and Pride: A Drama in Five Acts* (Being the Authorised English Version of *Les Pauvres de Paris*, a Drama by Edward Brisebarre and Eugene Nus). London: Richard Bentley, 1856.

*The Hypochondriac* (Adapted to the English Stage from the *Malade Imaginaire* of Molière). London: William Clowes and Sons, 1857.

*Le Faubourg Saint-Germain*. Paris: Moris et Comp., 1859.

*Dora: A Pastoral Poem in Three Acts. Founded on Mr. Tennyson's Poem*. London: W. Clowes and Sons, 1867. (Reade's pamphlet "*Dora:* or The History of a Play" appeared in 1877.)

*The Double Marriage: A Drama in Five Acts* (Based on August Maquet's *Le Chateau Grantier*). London: W. Clowes and Sons, 1867.

*It's Never Too Late to Mend: A Drama in Five Acts*. London: Williams and Strahan, 1872.

*The Well-Born Workman: or A Man of the Day*. London: Williams and Strahan, 1878.

*The Scuttled Ship*  Stepney: original promptbooks, 1880.

*Joan: A Drama in Six Acts*. Original promptbooks "Joan Lowrie," 1881.

*The Countess and the Dancer: or High Life in Vienna; A Comedy Drama in Four Acts* (Altered from a Comedy Masterpiece of Victorien Sardou). London: n.p., 1883.

*Foul Play: A Drama* (with Dion Boucicault). London: J. C. Durant, 1883.

*Kate Peyton: or Jealousy*. London: J. C. Durant, 1883.

*Love and Money: An Original Drama in a Prologue and Four Acts* (with Henry Pettitt). London: J. C. Durant, 1883.

## 4. Other Writings

*The Eighth Commandment*. London: Trübner and Company, 1860.

*A Hero and a Martyr: A True and Accurate Account of the Heroic Feats and Sad Calamity of James Lambert*. New York: Harper and Brothers, 1875.

*Readiana: Comments on Current Events.* London: Chatto and Windus, 1883.

SECONDARY SOURCES

ARCHER, WILLIAM. *English Dramatists of Today.* London: Sampson Low, Marston, Searle, and Rivington, 1882. Contains a droll report of attendance at a performance of *It's Never Too Late to Mend.*

BANKSON, DOUGLAS HENNECK. "Charles Reade: Manuscript Notecards for *Hard Cash.*" *Dissertation Abstracts,* XIV (1954), 2341. Useful to show hard facts producing a "solid fiction."

BESANT, SIR WALTER. "Charles Reade's Novels." *Gentleman's Magazine,* n.s. XXIX (1882), 198. Places Reade in the front rank of English novelists after the deaths of Thackeray and Dickens.

BOND, WILLIAM H. "*Nance Oldfield:* An Unrecorded Printed Play by Charles Reade." *Harvard Library Bulletin,* I (1947), 386 - 87. Describes play once in Lord Esher's collection and recently acquired by Harvard College.

BOOTH, BRADFORD A. "Trollope, Reade, and 'Shilly-Shally.' " *Trollopian* (March, 1947), 45. Well-documented, lively account of the Reade-Trollope correspondence regarding Reade's dramatization of Trollope's *Ralph the Heir.*

BOWERS, R. H. "The Cancelled 'Song of Solomon' Passage in Reade's *Hard Cash.*" *Nineteenth Century Fiction,* VI (1952), 225. Uses original manuscripts in Pierpont Morgan Library in New York to show that the subject matter of a suppressed passage is still clear to the careful reader.

BRANTLINGER, PATRICK. "The Case Against Trade Unions in Early Victorian Fiction." *Victorian Studies,* XIII, no. 1 (September, 1969), 37 - 52. Shows humanitarian concern for working classes, but is not in sympathy with trade unions or strikes.

BUCHANAN, ROBERT. "Charles Reade, A Souvenir." *A Look Round Literature: Flotsam and Jetsam.* London: Ward and Downey, 1887. Presents Reade as a Homeric storyteller and creator of the "True Woman."

BURNS, WAYNE. *Charles Reade: A Study in Victorian Authorship.* New York: Bookman Associates, 1961. A Freudian biographical approach to Reade's work; based on considerable research, but lacking notes or bibliography.

———. "*The Cloister and the Hearth:* A Classic Reconsidered." *Trollopian,* II (1947), 71. Suggests that, rather than being a unique masterpiece, *The Cloister and the Hearth* falls into the pattern of Reade's less highly regarded romances.

————. "*Hard Cash:* 'Uncomparably My Best Production.' " *Literature and Psychology*, VIII (1958), 34. Discusses why Reade considered *Hard Cash* to be his best work.

————. "Pre-Raphaelitism in Charles Reade's Early Fiction." *Publications of the Modern Language Association*, LX (1945), 1149. Considers Reade's fledgling attempt at art criticism in *Christie Johnstone*.

"Charles Reade, D.C.L." (Contemporary Portraits). *University Magazine*, XCI (June, 1878), 673. Suggests that it would be best for Reade to adhere to his strong sense of dramatic verity.

"Charles Reade as a Novelist." *Every Saturday*, X (1870), 235. Discusses Reade's adoption of the methods of sensation novelists, and his surpassing them in plot complication, poetry, and passion.

"Charles Reade's Novels." *Blackwood's Edinburgh Magazine*, CVI, no. 648 (October, 1869), 488 - 514. Considers Reade's need for self-restraint and self-denial; suggests that *Griffith Gaunt* is marred by flaws of judgment and taste.

"Charles Reade's Opinion of Himself and of George Eliot." *Bookman*, XVIII (November, 1903), 252. Reprint of a letter possibly by Charles Reade to the editor of *Galaxy*, extolling the virtues of his novels over those of George Eliot. Also contains a reprint of the anonymous review in *Once a Week*, XXVI (n.s. IX), no. 212 (January 20, 1872), 80, and assumes that it was written by Reade himself.

COLEMAN, JOHN. *Charles Reade as I Knew Him*. London: Treherne and Company, 1903. Derived from the *Memoir* and a pyrotechnic memory. Coleman often writes as if Reade were writing in the first person singular.

COURTNEY, WILLIAM LEONARD. "Charles Reade's Novels." *Studies, New and Old*. London: Chapman and Hall, 1889. Delineates Reade as below Dickens and Eliot but as above Collins, Lytton, and Braddon. Classifies his stock characters.

CUMPSTEN, ELLEN. "Why Is Charles Dickens a More Powerful Novelist than Charles Reade?" *Four Years at Novel Reading: An Account of an Experiment in Popularizing the Study of Fiction*. Ed. Richard G. Moulton. Boston: D. C. Heath and Company, 1895. Considers Reade's aim to expose and correct social abuses; calls his style a "Teutonic sledge-hammer."

ELWIN, MALCOLM. *Charles Reade: A Biography*. London: J. Cape, 1931. Important biographical study based upon considerable research with critical commentary on Reade's works.

FIELDS, ANNIE. "An Acquaintance with Charles Reade." *Century*, VII (1855), 67. Contains good list of source books ("Libri") used in preparation of *The Cloister and the Hearth*.

FRIERSON, WILLIAM C., "Some Remarks on Representative Late Victorians." *The English Novel in Transition: 1885 - 1940*. New York: Cooper

# 172

Square Publishers, 1965. Sees Reade's permanent place in literary history as a forerunner of Zola in documentary realism.

"Griffith Gaunt," *Every Saturday*, II, no. 48 (December 1, 1866), 649. Regrets Reade's waste of power as a creative artist in devoting himself to pamphleteering; therefore considers *Griffith Gaunt* a good novel because it has no polemic purpose.

HORNUNG E. W. "Charles Reade." *London Mercury*, IV (1921), 150. States that all Reade's novels were written by the research technique usually reserved for historical fiction; by a coincidence the plot structure of *The Cloister and the Hearth* exactly matches those of the majority of Reade's sensational fiction.

HOWELLS, WILLIAM DEAN. *My Literary Passions*. New York: Harper and Brothers, 1895. Sees Reade as potential founder of English realism, had he not used realistic materials to produce romantic effects.

JAMES, HENRY, "The Noble School of Fiction" (a review of Henry Kingsley's *The Hillyars and the Burtons: A Story of Two Families*). *Notes and Reviews by Henry James*. Ed. Pierre de Chaignon la Rose. Cambridge, Massachusetts: Dunster House, 1921. States that Henry Kingsley's eyewitness view of Australia is not so vivid as Reade's *in absentium*.

LORD, WALTER FREWEN. *Mirror of the Century*. London: John Lane, 1906. Discusses Reade's two good acting plays and one great novel — the rest — "Panorama."

McCARTHY, JUSTIN. "Charles Reade." *Galaxy*, XIV, no. 4 (April, 1872), 437. Sees Reade as powerful storyteller with social conscience and journalistic special correspondent, but not in front rank of English novelists.

PHILLIPS, WALTER C. *Dickens, Reade, and Collins: Sensation Novelists: A Study in the Conditions and Theories of Novel Writing in Victorian England*. New York: Columbia University Press, 1917. Sees Reade as a minor novelist who borrowed enough from the theories of Dickens to reduce them to absurdity.

QUILLER-COUCH, SIR ARTHUR T. *Adventures in Criticism*. London: Cassell and Company, 1892. Considers that Reade's finest novel, *The Cloister and the Hearth*, is better than anything Sir Walter Scott wrote, although Scott was the better author.

de la RAMÉE, L. ("Ouida"). "Charles Reade." *Gentleman's Magazine*, n.s. XXIX (1882), 494. Discusses Reade's excellent sense of humor, and his inability to depict true women.

READE, CHARLES L., and COMPTON READE. *Charles Reade, D.C.L., Dramatist, Novelist, Journalist: A Memoir, Compiled Chiefly from His Literary Remains*. London: Chapman and Hall, 1887. Written by Reade's relatives, this is the usual attempt to glorify the family and restore the subject to popularity; nevertheless, the work is important as a firsthand account of Reade's life, and it records many of his unpublished statements and opinions.

SPOFFORD, H. P. "Charles Reade." *Atlantic Monthly,* XIV, no. 82 (August, 1864), 137. Sees *Very Hard Cash* as Reade's best work to date; suggests that all the preceding novels sound like studies for it.

SUTCLIFFE, EMERSON GRANT. "Charles Reade's Notebooks." *Studies in Philology,* XXVII, no. 1 (January, 1930), 64. Pioneer attempt to classify and describe the thirty-two notebooks and notecards in the London Library, donated in 1916. by Herbert V. Reade.

―――. "Plotting in Reade's Novels." *Publications of the Modern Language Associaton,* XLVII, no. 3 (September, 1932), 832. Thorough study of the patterns of Reade's plots, characters, social issues, and the genesis of individual novels.

SWINBURNE, ALGERNON CHARLES. "Charles Reade." *Miscellanies.* London: Chatto and Windus, 1886. Perhaps the most searching and thorough critical analysis by an eminent contemporary who runs the full gamut of praise and blame.

TOWLE, GEORGE M. "Charles Reade." *Appleton's Journal,* IX, no. 216 (May, 1873), 620. This brief study treats Charles Reade as a disciple of the topics and techinques of Charles Dickens.

TURNER, ALBERT MORTON. "Another Source for *The Cloister and the Hearth.*" *Publications of the Modern Language Associaton,* XL (1925), 898. Establishes Reade's use of Francisque Michel's and Edouard Fournier's *Histoire des Hôtelleries.*

―――. "*Charles Reade and Montaigne.*" *Modern Philology,* XXX (1933), 297. Discusses Reade's use of Michel de Montaigne's travel diary for certain passages in *The Cloister and the Hearth.*

―――. *The Making of "The Cloister and the Hearth."* Chicago: University of Chicago Press, 1938. Exhaustive analysis of sources now sounds more impressive than the novel itself.

"Very Hard Cash." *Brownson's Quarterly Review,* XXI (April, 1864), 223. Predicts that the works of sensation novelists, Dickens, and George Eliot will all be forgotten; that Thackeray's and Reade's works will live.

# Index

175